Opening New Horizons

"Rarely has the 'lion's roar' of interfaith dialogue been so keenly grasped as in this beautifully realized study. Joseph Raab approaches the Merton-Suzuki dialogue with the sensitivity of a poet and sophistication of a practiced theologian. Charting the idol-shattering friendship between Merton and Suzuki, *Opening New Horizons* unfolds like a Zen koan that invites deepening encounter with the mystery of God. Like the dialogue itself, Raab lays down lucid 'stepping stones' for others to follow."

—**CHRISTOPHER PRAMUK**
Author of *Sophia: The Hidden Christ of Thomas Merton*

"This thoughtfully written volume explores Thomas Merton's contemplative path in the light of his dialogue with notable religious figures such as the Dalai Lama, Thich Nhat Hanh, D. T. Suzuki, and others. Laying out the trinitarian features and theological underpinnings of Merton's contemplative path, the author suggests ways toward 'opening new horizons' in Christian theology of religions."

—**RUBEN L. F. HABITO**
Author of *Zen and the Spiritual Exercises*

"In this challenging yet accessible volume, Joseph Raab convincingly shows how Thomas Merton's 'dialogue of religious experience,' exemplified in his fruitful engagement with Zen scholar D. T. Suzuki, led not only to a recognition and appreciation of the wisdom and goodness present in other spiritual traditions, but to a deeper reflection on and insight into essential Christian beliefs on the nature of God, the centrality of Christ, authentic personhood, and the scope of salvation within and beyond the boundaries of the church. This is the most substantial and stimulating discussion of the explicitly theological dimension of Merton's thought since Christopher Pramuk's *Sophia*."

—**PATRICK F. O'CONNELL**
Gannon University

"Especially impressive in this work is the way Joseph Raab traces the ongoing expansion of Thomas Merton's own horizons during his twenty-seven years as a monk. Crucial for this broadening was not only Merton's own reading but also his interchange with persons like Daisetz Suzuki. Readers of this book will certainly find new horizons opening for themselves."

—**JAMES A. WISEMAN**
OSB, The Catholic University of America

"A profound and knowledgeable exploration of Thomas Merton's encounter with Zen Buddhism, beginning with his relationship with D. T. Suzuki, through Merton's writings on Zen, to his final journey to the East. In Joseph Raab the reader has a dependable guide, one who has deeply mined Merton's unique position as an exemplary initiator of monastic interfaith dialogue and who skillfully guides the reader through its lessons for today."

—PAUL M. PEARSON
Thomas Merton Center

"The author's careful study is timely in light of Pope Francis's vindication of Merton in an address to the US Congress. Raab reminds us that Merton was a pioneer of interreligious dialogue and comparative theology. He beckons us to revisit Merton's achievements in order to help us beyond current methodological impasses."

—JOHN D. DADOSKY
Regis College/University of Toronto

"Perhaps the chief insight of Joseph Raab's *Opening New Horizons* is his focus. Avoiding both thick postmodern approaches that focus on subsets of the traditions as well as any detached comparisons of 'Buddhism' vis-à-vis 'Christianity,' Raab offers a Merton horizon familiar to many, a horizon opening into insights beyond either the opacity of localized expressions or the overarching examinations of themes and doctrines that would first choose the fundamentals and then focus on their relationship, whether convergent or disparate. The very first sentence rejects dichotomous thinking, citing Pope Francis. Especially to be prized is Raab's fulsome treatment of the interchanges between Merton and D. T. Suzuki, the most thorough and best account I have read."

—JOHN P. KEENAN
Middlebury College

Opening New Horizons

*Seeds of a Theology of Religious Pluralism
in Thomas Merton's Dialogue with D. T. Suzuki*

Joseph Quinn Raab

PICKWICK *Publications* · Eugene, Oregon

OPENING NEW HORIZONS
Seeds of a Theology of Religious Pluralism in Thomas Merton's Dialogue with D. T. Suzuki

Copyright © 2021 Joseph Quinn Raab. All rights reserved. Except for brief quotations in critical publications or reviews, no part of this book may be reproduced in any manner without prior written permission from the publisher. Write: Permissions, Wipf and Stock Publishers, 199 W. 8th Ave., Suite 3, Eugene, OR 97401.

Pickwick Publications
An Imprint of Wipf and Stock Publishers
199 W. 8th Ave., Suite 3
Eugene, OR 97401

www.wipfandstock.com

PAPERBACK ISBN: 978-1-7252-7936-0
HARDCOVER ISBN: 978-1-7252-7937-7
EBOOK ISBN: 978-1-7252-7938-4

Cataloguing-in-Publication data:

Names: Raab, Joseph Quinn, author.

Title: Opening new horizons : seeds of a theology of religious pluralism in Thomas Merton's dialogue with D. T. Suzuki / Joseph Quinn Raab.

Description: Eugene, OR: Pickwick Publications, 2021. | Includes bibliographical references and index.

Identifiers: ISBN 978-1-7252-7936-0 (paperback). | ISBN 978-1-7252-7937-7 (hardcover). | ISBN 978-1-7252-7938-4 (ebook).

Subjects: LCSH: Merton, Thomas 1915-1968. | Suzuki, Daisetz Teitaro, 1870-1966. | Religious pluralism. | Zen Buddhism. | Religion—Philosophy. | Theology of religions (Christian theology).

Classification: BL410 R33 2020 (print). | BL410 (ebook).

01/21/21

"Lent (A Fragment)," by Thomas Merton, from *The Collected Poems of Thomas Merton*, copyright ©1977 by the Trustees of the Merton Legacy Trust. Reprinted by permission of New Directions Publishing Corp.

"Sacred Heart 2 (A Fragment)," by Thomas Merton, from *The Collected Poems of Thomas Merton*, copyright ©1977 by the Trustees of the Merton Legacy Trust. Reprinted by permission of New Directions Publishing Corp.

"When in the Soul of the Serene Disciple," by Thomas Merton, from *The Collected Poems of Thomas Merton*, copyright ©1957 by The Abbey of Gethsemani. Reprinted by permission of New Directions Publishing Corp.

"In Silence," by Thomas Merton, from *The Collected Poems of Thomas Merton*, copyright ©1957 by The Abbey of Gethsemani. Reprinted by permission of New Directions Publishing Corp.

"Stranger," by Thomas Merton, from *The Collected Poems of Thomas Merton*, copyright ©1957 by The Abbey of Gesthemani, Inc. Reprinted by permission of New Directions Publishing Corp.

"O Sweet Irrational Worship," by Thomas Merton, from *The Collected Poems of Thomas Merton*, copyright ©1963 by The Abbey of Gethsemani. Reprinted by permission of New Directions Publishing Corp.

Excerpts from "Mystics and Zen Masters" and "Contemplation and Dialogue" from *Mystics and Zen Masters* by Thomas Merton. Copyright © 1967 by the Abbey of Gethsemani. Copyright renewed 1995 by Robert Giroux, James Laughlin, and Tommie O'Callaghan as trustees of the Merton Legacy Trust. Reprinted by permission of Farrar, Straus and Giroux. All Rights Reserved.

Excerpts from *The Hidden Ground of Love: Letters of Thomas Merton on Religious Experience and Social Concerns* by Thomas Merton, edited by William H. Shannon. Copyright © 1985 by the Merton Legacy Trust. Reprinted by permission of Farrar, Straus and Giroux. All Rights Reserved.

Scripture texts in this work are taken from the *New American Bible, Revised Edition* © 2010, 1991, 1986, 1970, Confraternity of Christian Doctrine, Washington, DC, and are used by permission of the copyright owner. All Rights Reserved. No part of the New American Bible may be reproduced in any form without permission in writing from the copyright owner.

In loving memory of two men
who lived lives of great faith, hope, and love:
my father, C. Edward Raab Jr. (1940–2019),
and my father-in-law, Robert F. Ziolkowski (1933–2017).

Contents

List of Figures | ix
Acknowledgments | xi
List of Abbreviations | xiii

Introduction | 1
1. Cracking Idols with the Lion's Roar: Snapshots of an Iconoclastic Spirit | 13
2. Dogma, Dialogue, and Dialectics | 37
3. The Dialogue with Dr. D. T. Suzuki | 51
4. From Communication to Communion | 75
5. Interiority and the Meanings of "God" | 91
6. *Anatman* and the Reality of *Persons* | 109
7. Seeds in the Garden of New Growth | 124

Bibliography | 151
Index | 161

Figures

Figure 1: Photograph of D. T. Suzuki and Thomas Merton | 51
Used with permission of the photographer, Mihoko Okamura.

Figure 2: John Heidbrink, Thomas Merton, and Thich Nhat Hanh | 120
Used with permission of the Merton Legacy Trust and Thomas Merton Center at Bellarmine University.

Figure 3: Thomas Merton and Chatral Rinpoche | 127
Used with permission of the Merton Legacy Trust and Thomas Merton Center at Bellarmine University.

Figure 4: Thomas Merton and His Holiness Dalai Lama XIV | 131
Used with permission of the Merton Legacy Trust and Thomas Merton Center at Bellarmine University.

Figure 5: Reclining Buddha, Polonnaruwa | 134
Photograph by Thomas Merton. Used with permission of the Merton Legacy Trust and the Thomas Merton Center at Bellarmine University.

Acknowledgments

MANY FRIENDS, TEACHERS, MENTORS, and family members have had a hand in bringing this project to completion. In 2011 Dr. Paul M. Pearson and Dr. Patrick F. O'Connell graciously invited me to serve as co-editor of *The Merton Annual: Studies in Culture, Spirituality, and Social Concerns*, a position I have shared first with Dr. David Belcastro and now with Dr. Deborah Pope Kehoe. These people and this role put me at the center of the most current Merton-related research, and without them I could not have tackled this project. I am especially indebted to Patrick F. O'Connell who read drafts of this manuscript and provided valuable feedback. I am also indebted to Dr. Roger Lipsey who answered my questions and provided guidance regarding book publications. Finally, I am grateful for the gentle and reliable encouragement of Dr. Michael W. Higgins, who more than two decades ago served on my dissertation examining committee and has patiently encouraged me over the years to write this book on Merton's theology of religious pluralism.

I especially wish to thank Mihoko Okamura-Bekku for permitting me to use the photograph of Thomas Merton and D. T. Suzuki that she had taken more than fifty years ago. In the letter she wrote granting her permission, she described the pair as "two enlightened beings who had transcended borderlines, geographical and spiritual." She described the moment she captured on film writing: "Their free burst of joyous laughter is an ultimate human achievement."

Many colleagues at Siena Heights University (SHU) where I teach, including Cindy Anderson, Dr. Eric Kos, Dr. Ian Bell, and Dr. Wendy Crosby, have supported my scholarship and teaching in many ways—the latter two by shouldering extra work so that I could have the sabbatical I needed in order to finish this book. Prof. Melissa Sissen, Research Librarian at SHU, helped me countless times by securing obscure and rare materials. I am

Acknowledgments

also grateful to the Adrian Dominican Sisters who founded and continue to sponsor SHU, especially Professor emerita Dr. Patricia Walter, OP, and Vice President for Academic Affairs, Dr. Sharon Weber, OP, who have supported and encouraged my work over the years.

I am most grateful to my amazing wife Mary Jane (Ziolkowski) Raab who has been a rock and a north star, and for our children, Kate, Charlie, and Maggie. Thanks to the Raab, Ziolkowski, McDonnell, and Dunhill families, and countless friends who continue to enrich our lives with joy and laughter.

Abbreviations

Works by and about Thomas Merton

AJ	*The Asian Journal of Thomas Merton*
AT	*The Ascent to Truth*
AHTW	*At Home in the World*
CF	*Cassian and the Fathers*
CFF	*Cistercian Fathers and Forefathers*
CFMT	*The Cistercian Fathers and Their Monastic Theology*
CGB	*Conjectures of a Guilty Bystander*
CP	*Contemplative Prayer*
CPTM	*The Collected Poems of Thomas Merton*
CT	*The Courage for Truth*
CWA	*Contemplation in a World of Action*
Encounter	*Encounter: Thomas Merton and D. T. Suzuki*
ES	*Entering the Silence*
HGL	*The Hidden Ground of Love*
ICM	*An Introduction to Christian Mysticism*
IE	*The Inner Experience*
L&L	*Love and Living*
LL	*Learning to Love*
MISS	*A Monastic Introduction to Sacred Scripture*

Abbreviations

MZM	Mystics and Zen Masters
NMI	No Man Is an Island
NSC	New Seeds of Contemplation
OB	Opening the Bible
OSM	The Other Side of the Mountain
PBM	Pre-Benedictine Monasticism
RJ	The Road to Joy
RM	Run to the Mountain
RU	Raids on the Unspeakable
SC	Seeds of Contemplation
SE	Selected Essays
SJ	The Sign of Jonas
SS	A Search for Solitude
SSM	The Seven Storey Mountain
TME	Thomas Merton Encyclopedia
TMR	A Thomas Merton Reader
TSC	The School of Charity
TTW	Turning Toward the World
WCT	The Way of Chuang Tzu
WD	The Wisdom of the Desert
WF	Witness to Freedom
ZBA	Zen and the Birds of Appetite
ZR	"The Zen Revival"

Vatican Documents

AG	Ad gentes
CCC	The Catechism of the Catholic Church
DI	Dominus Iesus

Abbreviations

DP	*Dialogue and Proclamation*
DM	*Dialogue and Mission*
DV	*Dei verbum*
FR	*Fides et ratio*
GS	*Gaudium et spes*
LG	*Lumen gentium*
NA	*Nostra aetate*
UR	*Unitatis redintigratio*

Introduction

An Unconventional Contemplative

IN HIS 2015 ADDRESS to the United States Congress, Pope Francis warned against the kind of dichotomous thinking that leads to scapegoating and violence. He noted that in our attempts to be freed from the "enemy without" we may inadvertently "feed the enemy within." Instead of fomenting the forces of fear, division, and demonization he called for peacebuilding through dialogue, service, and the work for justice. He spoke about Abraham Lincoln, Martin Luther King Jr., Dorothy Day, and Thomas Merton as models to follow in our tumultuous times. He described Merton as "a promoter of peace between peoples and religions" and "above all a man of prayer, a thinker who challenged the certitudes of his time and opened new horizons for souls and for the Church."[1]

Michael W. Higgins, a Vatican affairs analyst and a Merton scholar,[2] noted the significance of the Pope's decision to valorize Day and Merton, writing: "He could have chosen any number of tiresomely conventional candidates for canonization. He could have played it safe. . . . Instead he opted for the redoubtable journalist/activist and . . . the Trappist sentinel on the world's frontier."[3] Dorothy Day's anti-capitalist Christian anarchism leaves many Catholics uncomfortable, so too her sordid pre-conversion past. Merton's polemical political writings, his awkward affair, and his

---

1. Francis, "Address of the Holy Father to Congress."

2. Higgins is an analyst for Toronto's *Globe and Mail* and for the CTV Network. He is also author of the critically acclaimed *Heretic Blood: The Spiritual Geography of Thomas Merton* (cited hereafter as *Heretic Blood*) and co-author (with Kevin Burns) of *Genius Born of Anguish: The Life and Legacy of Henri Nouwen*.

3. From Correspondence with the author, December 8, 2015. For the full text of Higgins's comment, see Raab, "Celebrating the Questions," 9–10.

incessant spiritual searching make him no less an unconventional candidate for ecclesiastical approval. The Pope's decision to laud these publicly flawed pilgrims, however, likely shows that he is onto something. They are the kind of wounded healers who might prove to be relatable enough to similarly flawed pilgrims today searching for the same God.

Merton's monastic vocation was equally contemplative and prophetic. Steeped in the rhythms of a silent life punctuated by the canonical hours of daily prayer, he was ever mindful that his ancient way was simultaneously a retreat from and a relevant rebuke of the so-called modern world driven by consumerism, materialism, and unending political power struggles. He relished the role of the gadfly, the outsider who could stimulate his readers and irritate the authorities with the arrows of his finely crafted pensées. He was a kind of iconoclast, ever criticizing a placid acceptance of prevailing norms, destroying the idols of wealth and power, and the false images that truncate and pigeonhole the reality of God. He was drawn to people on the margins, to those involuntarily marginalized by poverty and injustice,[4] and to the voluntarily marginalized contemplatives, poets, and peacemakers. His attraction was non-sectarian. He was just as enamored with Chuang Tzu (Zhuangzi) as he was with St. John of the Cross, with Mahatma Gandhi as with Dorothy Day. He found this iconoclastic spirit in the poetry of William Blake, in the philosophy of Camus, and in the unsettling and sometimes alarming declarations of desert hermits, ancient Sufi mystics, and Zen masters.

The pioneering theologian Anne E. Carr[5] claimed that Merton produced a kind of "autobiographical theology" and that his "own texted life story has become an important symbol" that is ever open to fresh interpretation.[6] That is to say, he has become a classic. David Tracy argued that if any human being "produces some classical expression of the human spirit on a particular journey in a particular tradition, that person discloses permanent possibilities for human existence."[7] Merton disclosed enduring

---

4. During his early discernment, Merton seriously considered devoting himself to the corporal works of mercy and volunteered for a time at the Friendship House in Harlem. For a pithy presentation and insightful analysis of this period see Coady, "Fire That Burns." See also McGregor, "Persistence of Harlem."

5. Anne E. Carr (1934–2008) was an influential American theologian and the first woman to hold a permanent faculty appointment at the University of Chicago's Divinity School.

6. Carr, *Search for Wisdom and Spirit*, 5.

7. Tracy, *Analogical Imagination*, 14.

Introduction

possibilities for seekers with or without religious affiliation, and for his own Catholic Church. Through his journals, letters, books, and lectures, he left a record of the work that opened new horizons and helped to lead the Church toward a more robust assertion of a normative ethic of non-violence, and toward a more capacious embrace of religious pluralism.[8]

There is no doubt that Merton remains a pivotal figure in the history of interreligious dialogue[9] and that his legacy continues to shape the Church's efforts in that arena.[10] Though he left abundant clues and discernable patterns in his writings, Merton's own theology of religious pluralism is largely allusive, fragmentary, in need of framing and light. His untimely death at the age of fifty-three[11] meant he would never abstract and synthesize from the wealth of his own experience an integrated view of the new horizon attained through dialogue. Then again, he may never have been interested in systematically working out such a view. He possessed the intelligence of a keen and capable logician but he preferred the freedom of a poetic lyrical voice over the methodical restrictions of theoretical discourse. His contemplative vocation and the prophetic stance of his monastic commitment were inexorably tied to his being a poet, a Blake for a new era.[12] Rather than erecting elaborate systems Merton preferred creating images and symbols, and subverting them in service of the inexhaustible mystery. As Carr noted, Merton's contemplative theology "functions through image and symbol rather than through logic and argument in suggesting more than it literally says, in connoting both the familiar and the unknown, both

---

8. For substantive recent accounts of Merton's contributions in the area of peacebuilding and non-violent resistance see Oyer, *Pursuing the Spiritual Roots of Protest*; and Forest, *Root of War Is Fear*. For a substantive treatment of Merton's Christology, which opens a way toward affirming religious plurality not only *de facto* but in some mysterious way *de jure*, see Pramuk, *Sophia*, esp. 163–74. See also Raab, "Insights from the Intercontemplative Dialogue," 90–105. Much of the material from Raab's article is reproduced here in chapter 5, "Interiority and the Meanings of God."

9. Merton was not alone in opening the horizons of dialogue. He was pioneering along with others such as Hugo Enomiya-LaSalle, William Johnston, Raimon Panikkar, Bede Griffiths, and Dom Aelred Graham.

10. See Park, *Thomas Merton's Encounter with Buddhism and Beyond*.

11. Since the recent publication of Martin and Turley *Martyrdom of Thomas Merton*, it is no longer plausible to *conclude* that Merton's death was the result of an accidental electrocution. Martin and Turley, emboldened by the discovery of inaccuracies and inconsistencies in the traditional narrative, conjecture that Merton was the victim of foul play and likely murdered by the CIA. The evidence, however, that Merton was murdered still remains inconclusive.

12. See Higgins, *Heretic Blood*.

present experience and future possibility."[13] Nonetheless, when he encountered vexing issues in his dialogues he did not shy away from insightfully engaging highly technical and theoretical discourse in an effort to find greater clarity.[14]

Engaging the Third Question

Elizabeth Johnson has explained that Catholic theological reflection on the issue of religious pluralism has evolved through a series of three distinctive questions.[15] They can be expressed as (1) can individual persons who are not explicitly Christian, be saved? If yes, (2) are they saved in spite of their own religious beliefs and practices or are they in some sense assisted by them? And finally (3), if "assisted by them" then how are Christians to understand the positive meaning of the role played by these other religions in God's one plan for creation? Merton himself can be seen evolving through the same series of questions: first as he basks in the afterglow of his conversion to Catholicism, then as he begins to conjecture about the possibility of "supernatural" mysticism in non-Christian contexts, and finally in his last years where he affirms genuine knowledge of God in those contexts and seeks to understand that in relation to his own faith.

Since Vatican II, Catholic theologians have been employing a tripartite schema, i.e., *exclusivism, inclusivism,* and *pluralism,* for discussing Christian perspectives on the issue of religious plurality.[16] An *exclusivist* responds negatively to the first question above and holds that explicit Christian faith is necessary for salvation, affirming the uniqueness and normativity of Jesus Christ at the expense of the spiritual legitimacy of other religious traditions. A *pluralist*, on the other hand, believes that God has gifted humanity with many equally valid and efficacious paths to human liberation/salvation, affirming the legitimacy of other religions at the expense of the uniqueness of Christian revelation. The *inclusivist* position

---

13. Carr, *Search for Wisdom and Spirit*, 6.

14. His dialogue with Suzuki, the focus of chapter 3, provides numerous examples. Also, when Merton taught novices he often exhibited an expertise and facility with hermeneutics and historical theology that equals and often surpasses that of officially credentialed philosophers and theologians. See, for example, Merton, *Cistercian Fathers and their Monastic Theology* (cited hereafter as *CFMT* within the text).

15. Johnson, *Quest for the Living God*, 153–60.

16. See Johnson, *Consider Jesus*, 129–44.

Introduction

responds affirmatively to the first question, and moves into the second and third, while maintaining fidelity to Christ crucified and risen as the *fullness of divine revelation.*

It took almost two thousand years for a strong consensus in Catholic theology and doctrine to emerge in favor of the affirmative position regarding the first question.[17] The Second Vatican Council clarified that explicit Christian faith was not necessarily a pre-requisite for salvation, and it sowed the seeds for the possibility of a positive assessment of the value of non-Christian religions as such. Vatican II formally endorsed inclusivism, affirming *both* the uniqueness of Christ *and* the potential value of other religions in a creative and mysterious tension without attempting to explain their compatibility. Within the new horizon of the third millennium Catholic theologians continue to grapple with the third question, trying to better understand and more deeply appreciate the positive meaning of other religions in God's universal plan.

Since Vatican II some theologians have proposed answers to the third question that appear to relativize the uniqueness and normativity of Jesus Christ,[18] or that seemingly sever Christology from ecclesiology, leaving the Spirit of Christ to work independently of the church which is his body.[19] Enthusiasm has sometimes outpaced prudence. Jacques Dupuis, on the other hand, made reasonable and responsible advancements *toward* a Catholic theology of religious pluralism.[20] Still, his work drew the attention of what Merton liked to call the "theological watchdogs," who worried about its ambiguities and difficulties that might lead readers into heresy.[21]

---

17. See Galvin, "Salvation Outside the Church."

18. See, for example, essays by Samartha and Knitter in Hick, *Myth of Christian Uniqueness.*

19. See Panikkar, *Unknown Christ of Hinduism.*

20. Dupuis, *Toward a Christian Theology of Religious Pluralism.*

21. The Congregation for the Doctrine of the faith (CDF) launched a formal examination of the text, concerned that the author, in his entertaining of questions "hitherto largely unexplored" might have failed to remain within the boundaries of orthodoxy. Dupuis's work proposed that religious pluralism was not just a fact of the world, a problem to be solved, but in accord (*de jure*) with God's plan for humanity. The investigation did not result in a formal condemnation of the book, but the CDF did find that the book "contained notable ambiguities and difficulties on important points, which could lead a reader to erroneous or harmful opinions." Hence the CDF required that further editions contain a "notification" reminding readers of what must be firmly and faithfully held in the deposit of faith. Originally published in 1997, the 2001 edition contains three appendices: (1) the CDF's notification, (2) a statement by the then Superior of the

Merton did not live to see the theological ferment inspired by the council, especially in the struggle to answer the second and third questions referenced by Johnson. But his own contemplative theology, which "suggests more than it literally says" engages the third question in ways that reveal future possibilities.

Furthermore, throughout his journey Merton exhibited various ways of thinking about the diversity of religions, similar to what Paul Knitter would later call "models of religious pluralism."[22] Early in the wake of his conversion to Catholicism Merton often seemed to have favored "the replacement model" (only one religion can be true), and late in his life "the mutuality model" (many true religions called to dialogue), but it turns out that he is impossible to pin down with labels at any point in his life. Invariably, however, he remained committed to the belief that Christ is, in the words of *Dei verbum*, "the mediator and the fullness of all revelation" (*DV* 2).[23] Merton's unwavering focus on Christ would seem to preclude him from going beyond "the fulfillment model" (one religion fulfills the many), but this is not quite the case either. While he remained committed to the belief that persons find their fulfillment "in Christ," he did not appear to anticipate a future without religious pluralism, nor did he imagine that joining the Christian *religion* (as he had), marked the fulfillment of anyone's spiritual journey.[24] Indeed, in his later years he became quite an admirer of Karl Barth and although he did not go all in with Barth's dismissal of *religion* as "unbelief" he celebrated Barth's Christocentricity.[25]

Society of Jesus, Peter-Hans Kolvenbach, and (3) the foreword to the Indian edition by Henry D'Souza. It was Dupuis's book, along with Haight's *Jesus Symbol of God* (1999) that prompted the CDF's Declaration *Dominus Iesus* to be issued on August 6, 2000. I attempt to show that the theology of religious pluralism developed here from the seeds of Merton's example, avoids the pitfalls and prohibitions set forth in *Dominus Iesus*.

22. Knitter, *Introducing Theologies of Religions*.

23. *The Dogmatic Constitution on Divine Revelation*, or *Dei verbum*, is one of the sixteen documents produced by the Second Vatican Council. It was promulgated by Pope Paul VI on November 18, 1965.

24. As Merton wrote in "Openness and Cloister": "We must learn to distinguish between 'religiosity' and 'discipleship of Christ.' 'Religion' was an essential part of medieval culture. 'Irreligion' is an essential part of modern culture. What is of importance today is not to get modern man to accept *religion* as a human or cultural value (he may do so or he may not) but to let him see that we are witnesses of Christ, of the new creation, of the Resurrection" (*CWA*, 133).

25. See *TME* on "Religion" (385–86), which summarizes Merton's ambivalence regarding religion by stating: "When religion is recognized and practiced as an orientation toward the sacred that leads to inner-transformation and to an attitude and acts of

Introduction

Though Merton does not easily fit into typologies, he was undeniably Christocentric. As Christopher Pramuk wrote:

> Many pluralist theologians today argue, not without merit, that no matter how well-intentioned or creative new articulations of christocentric inclusivism may be, to put Jesus Christ (or his body, the church) at the center of truth is to perpetuate a worldview that, at best, is no longer credible and, at worst, justifies a thousand forms of prejudice and imperialism.[26]

Pramuk goes on to say, however, that "for Christians who have been formed . . . by the Gospel, it is not ourselves whom we see at the center, but Christ." *How* one sees Christ, and *who* one sees *as* Christ, makes all the difference. Seeing Christ as the one who casts down the mighty from their thrones and lifts up the lowly (Luke 1:52), who identifies the hungry, the homeless, the sick, and the prisoner *as himself* (Matt 25), in fact subverts human pretentions to empire and erodes prejudice and discrimination. In this way, Merton's focus on Christ evinces the opposite of a prideful triumphalism that gloats over having found Christ in one particular cultural form or institution, and exemplifies instead a humble appreciation for the Christ who is to be found in the other, especially the stranger and the outsider.

Merton's contemplative theology of religious pluralism grows out of the seeds he had found sown in the world's contemplative traditions. Theology is not reducible to doctrine; it is a process rather than a product, and Merton's life reveals a hermeneutical process that evinces both a fidelity to Christ and an affirmative openness to the other religions as valuable in their own right, from the vista of a new horizon afforded by dialogue.[27] The new horizon creates the possibility of a theological reading of religious pluralism that appreciates and celebrates the diversity of religious expression. To see other contemplative traditions as complementary to his own Catholic tradition is not for him to admit an insufficiency in Christ and what Christ

---

compassion, it is seen as crucially important for authentic human existence. When it is adherence to a formalized system of cult and dogma that domesticates the divine and is directed toward a comfortable acceptance of a current social or economic system, it must be challenged" (385).

26. *Sophia*, 50.

27. Throughout the book I distinguish between religions, on the one hand, and contemplative or *sapiential* traditions, on the other. The former is much broader and inclusive of complex histories, belief systems, moral precepts, and cultic rituals associated with a particular cultural phenomenon, while the latter identifies what Merton considered the *core* of religions, their emphasis on personal and social transformation.

reveals, but for him to recognize and affirm that he, *as a Christian*, can and did learn from Buddhists, Jews, Muslims, Hindus, and others in ways that enhanced his own understanding, not only of the other's tradition, but also of his own, and even of the God with whom he was in love. His example suggests that the Christian may even stand in need of what others can offer in order to reach a deeper understanding and a more committed faith. "I will be a better Catholic," Merton wrote, "if I can affirm the truth" in the world's great religious traditions, "and still go further" (*CGB*, 129).

This Book

The present work explores Merton's contemplative theology of religious pluralism, which grows out of his experience with interreligious dialogue.[28] I attempt to frame and elucidate this theology and consider its heuristic possibilities. The first chapter, "Cracking Idols with the Lion's Roar," highlights Merton's iconoclastic spirit, revealed in his fascination with transcendent mystery and his determination to realize an authentic subjectivity. It offers a frame for thinking about his dual dedication to both dogma and dialogue. The second chapter, "Dogma, Dialogue and Dialectics," elucidates the commitments guiding Merton's approach to interreligious dialogue, and his method for dealing with differences and difficulties that emerge from it.

The landscape of Merton's interreligious encounters is vast and varied, however, and this book avoids the attempt to engage it *en masse*.[29] The third chapter, "The Dialogue with D. T. Suzuki," provides a representative locus of material for subsequent interpretation and analysis. Suzuki was the most influential expositor of Zen Buddhism to the West during

---

28. I consider a theology of religious pluralism to be a Christian *interpretation* of religious plurality that affirms the value of other religions as playing a positive role in God's universal plan for humanity—without claiming to fully understand that role. This interpretation does not render a judgment regarding the "*equal* validity" of all religions and in fact resists it. This is different from a *pluralistic* theology of religions that begins with a quasi-Kantian premise that no particular religious tradition can claim universal validity, or perhaps even relevance, and thus affirms each to be true in analogously limited ways and reinterprets religions from that pluralistic position. Jacques Dupuis exemplifies the former approach while John Hick (and to a lesser degree Paul Knitter), exemplify the second.

29. Merton conversed on religious and spiritual matters with a broad range of interlocutors such as Thich Nhat Hanh, the Dalai Lama, Abraham Joshua Heschel, Dr. John Wu, and Abdul Aziz, to name a few. For a representative display of this landscape see Apel, *Signs of Peace*.

Introduction

Merton's lifetime.[30] Over his long career, Suzuki published more than thirty books in English, mostly on Zen, and Merton read many of them. Merton's understanding of Buddhist wisdom was not singularly determined by Suzuki, nor by Zen, but was informed by other authors, interlocutors, and cultural strands. Still, his friendship with Suzuki is profoundly influential in shaping his appreciation for Buddhism as a wisdom tradition complementary to his own Catholic faith, an appreciation that is key to teasing out his theology of religious pluralism.

The fourth chapter, "Communication to Communion," analyzes the terms of their dialogue, primarily Wisdom and Emptiness, and considers developments in Merton's own understanding of Suzuki's positions.[31] The fifth chapter, "Interiority and the Meanings of 'God,'" illustrates how Merton, by adverting to his own interior life, was able to affirm common meanings of ultimate terms across religious boundaries. It also explores his developing understanding of the relationship between his Catholic faith and the truth he discovered in other religious traditions, and reveals the Trinitarian features of his contemplative theology of religious pluralism. Thomas Merton is the central figure of this book, and his dialogue with Suzuki provides the material for analysis, but the work of Bernard Lonergan plays an essential role in this chapter by providing the tools for the analysis and for explicating Merton's theology of religious pluralism. Lonergan's discovery of a generalized empirical method (GEM) operative in human consciousness offers a way of grounding and critically assessing the terms of the dialogue, points of convergence and divergence that emerge from it, and of heuristically elucidating the theology of religious pluralism that Merton's efforts offer.

The sixth chapter, "Anatman and the Reality of Persons," examines Merton's ontology of the human person that prioritizes *relation* over *substance* as the primary category for understanding human beings—a position

---

30. Though Suzuki was primarily a scholar (he never officially functioned as a Roshi representing a lineage of Zen Masters), he studied Zen under Soyen Shaku (1860–919), a renowned master of the Rinzai tradition. Paul Carus (1852–1919), a scholar of comparative religion, asked Shaku to help him with some translations of important Eastern religious texts. Shaku recommended his pupil for the job. Suzuki collaborated with Carus on a translation of the *Tao te Ching*, which was published as *The Canon of Reason and Virtue (Lao tze's Tao teh King)*, translated by D. T. Suzuki and Paul Carus (1913). This project launched Suzuki's career as a voice from and for the East to the Western world.

31. For an examination of the Merton–Suzuki dialogue that gives more attention to what Suzuki thought about Christianity and to what he may or may not have learned from Merton, see Corless, "In Search of a Context for the Merton–Suzuki Dialogue."

that clarifies the positive meaning of "person" from both a Christian and a Buddhist perspective. The final chapter, "Seeds in the Garden of New Growth," returns to Merton's last days in Asia and considers some characteristic features of his contemplative (read Trinitarian) model of religious pluralism. It situates Merton's theology in relation to the developments of Vatican II and considers its compatibility with post-conciliar parameters set by the Congregation for the Doctrine of the Faith.[32]

A Note on Dialogue

The Pontifical Council for Inter-Religious Dialogue (PCID) and the Congregation for the Evangelization of Peoples outlined four distinct forms of dialogue, emphasizing their interrelation and refraining from claiming an order of priority among them.[33] The forms are:

> (a) *The dialogue of life*, where people strive to live in an open and neighborly spirit; (b) *The dialogue of action*, in which Christians and others collaborate for the integral development and liberation of people; (c) *The dialogue of theological exchange*, where specialists seek to deepen their understandings of their respective religious heritages, and to appreciate each other's spiritual values; (d) *The dialogue of religious experience*, where persons, rooted in their own religious traditions, share their spiritual riches, for instance with regard to prayer and contemplation, faith and ways of searching for God or the absolute.[34]

Though this fourfold schema post-dates Merton's dialogue with Suzuki, he clearly and consistently situated his dialogue within what this framework

---

32. *Dominus Iesus* (*DI*) explicitly rejects theologies of religious pluralism that propose or presuppose an incompleteness with respect to Christian Revelation whereby what has been revealed in Christ would stand in need of complementary revelations found in other religions (See *DI* 6, 9). However, Merton's position that Buddhism and Christianity "well complement each other" does not assume a lack or insufficiency in Christian Revelation, or in the sacramental ministries of the Catholic Church as ordinary means of grace, but views their complementarity in terms of their being "mutually supportive" and "mutually enriching" for persons seeking union with God.

33. PSNC, "Reflection and Directives on Dialogue and Mission" (cited hereafter as *DM* parenthetically in the text). The forms are also discussed in "Dialogue and Proclamation" (cited hereafter as *DP* parenthetically in the text). See Burrows, *Redemption and Dialogue*.

34. From *Dialogue and Proclamation*, printed in Burrows, *Redemption and Dialogue*, 104.

Introduction

calls *the dialogue of religious experience*. The universal phenomenon of religious experience provides the proper foundation for dialogue and the diversity of religious expressions presents the invitation and the challenge. According to Bernard Lonergan, religious experience is universal at its core and "does not occur with labels attached; of itself it is not formulated."[35] Dialogue, on the other hand, necessarily involves formulation in the effort to meaningfully mediate religious experience and conversion through languages, lifestyles, and "styles of religious thinking." It is only in affirming the interrelation between the infrastructure of experience and the suprastructure of languages,[36] cultures, and contexts that one can appreciate the value of dialogue and the opportunities for genuine bridge-building it affords.

If suprastructure is emphasized to the neglect of the inner experience, it is difficult to find grounds for dialogue; if infrastructure is emphasized to the neglect of traditions and historical contexts, it is difficult to see any value in it. Thinkers who emphasize infrastructure over suprastructure often wind up concluding that religious differences are merely nominal and therefore inconsequential.[37] They see a one-way relation from experience to formulation. All the arguing merely results from the absence of the inner experience, or the poor quality of the expression.[38] Others who invert the one-way relation tend to doubt genuine dialogue is even possible. Any religious experience is so uniquely determined by contextual parameters and cultural antecedents that people from vastly

---

35. Lonergan, "Prolegomena," 70. Here Lonergan refers to Pannikar's diacritical theology and to several works of William Johnston (also Wilhelm Stekel and Robley Edward Whitson) to support his claim regarding the universality of religious experience.

36. Merton's own language reflects the standards of his time and is not, for the most part, gender-inclusive. I change his own words to make them more inclusive only when doing so causes negligible disruption. I do try in my own writing to avoid applying androcentric pronouns universally and to avoid gender exclusive language.

37. Works by Eckhart Tolle and Fritjof Schuon come to mind in this regard.

38. John P. Keenan, in his article "The Limits of Thomas Merton's Understanding of Buddhism," argues that Suzuki emphasizes infrastructure to the neglect of suprastructure. Quoting Robert Sharf, Keenan faults Suzuki for presenting Zen as "a way of experiencing the world, rather than a complex form of monastic practice" and as "some sort of nonsectarian spiritual gnosis." He faults Suzuki for privileging experience to the extent that all other cognitive operations seem superfluous, or at least subordinate. See Thurston, *Merton & Buddhism*, 124–25.

different traditions cannot successfully understand each other, and cannot be speaking of a shared experience.[39]

Merton, however, believed there were sufficient grounds for dialogue and good reason for it. While the differences between and among doctrinal traditions were important to him, worth discussing, and in some cases resolvable, he believed that persons from different traditions could benefit spiritually from one another through the encounter.[40] I regard Lonergan's work as indispensable in terms of offering an explanation of the interdependent relationship between the infrastructure of religious experience and the suprastructure of religious traditions, which is an issue at the heart of *the dialogue of religious experience* and essential to the successful explication of Merton's anticipatory theology of religious pluralism. In short, Bernard Lonergan's work helps me to explain on the level of theory what Thomas Merton and D. T. Suzuki achieved on the level of practice.

---

39. See Katz, *Mysticism and Philosophical Analysis*, 22–75.

40. Lonergan would call this process "mutual self-mediation." See Dadosky, "Church and the Other."

1

Cracking Idols with the Lion's Roar

Snapshots of an Iconoclastic Spirit

As a thinker who "challenged the certitudes of his time," Thomas Merton exhibited an iconoclastic spirit. His friend Thich Nhat Hanh called this spirit "the roar of the lion" and "the spirit of Buddhism" and described it as a determination "not to be idolatrous of theories and ideologies," or of one's own ideas and opinions, even religious ones.[1] When this spirit turned Merton toward the world he roared prophetically against racism, colonialism, militarism, and dehumanizing technological forces.[2] When it turned him inward he roared as a mystic against inadequate conceptions of God and illusory images of the self.[3] He needed no special training, having been born in wartime and witnessed the rise of fascism, to see how the seeds of fanaticism and intolerance yield a harvest of violence and destruction. Discovering how those seeds initially emerge and take root in minds, however, required contemplative practice. His contemplative practice sensitized him further to the lion's roar, enabling him to hear it in the silence.[4]

    1. Nhat Hanh, *Being Peace*, 89.

    2. See Merton, *Seeds of Destruction*; *Raids on the Unspeakable*; *Faith and Violence*; and *Ishi Means Man*. More recently, Monica Weis elucidated Merton's encounter with Rachel Carson and his evolving concern over environmental destruction in her work *The Environmental Vision of Thomas Merton*.

    3. See especially Merton, *No Man Is an Island*; *Thoughts in Solitude*; and *New Seeds of Contemplation*.

    4. See Nhat Hanh, *Thundering Silence*.

Opening New Horizons

What follows in this chapter is a series of snapshots and interpretive reflections. They highlight particular events and encounters in his life, some very familiar, some maybe less so, that reveal the interior dimension of the iconoclastic spirit that shaped him as a theologian, compelled him to explore other wisdom traditions, and to incessantly reexamine, reinterpret, and reappropriate his enduring religious commitments.[5] In each instance the lion's roar cracks or shatters some idol, be it an inadequate conception of God or an exaggerated image of himself. Whether it was reading Étienne Gilson or conversing with Gregory Zilboorg he invariably came through the event and encounter feeling "relief" and "gratitude" as if a great burden had been lifted by a graceful intervention.

In the context of the larger work of this book, these vignettes help to elucidate not only what attracted Merton to Zen Buddhism, and many other contemplative traditions, but also why he would refuse, as a Christian, to dismiss or discard those traditions as unworthy of his attention, or as being opposed to his own faith tradition. Most of the events recounted in this chapter occurred in his life prior to writing his first letter to Suzuki, so they also predate his Asian excursion and epiphany at Polonnaruwa, which will be visited later. This first chapter ends with a snapshot of Merton framed as a Zen poet and explores the voice that most clearly conveys the interior dimension of his iconoclastic spirit, the thundering silence of the lion's roar.

Cracking the Idol of a Too-Small God—Reading Gilson

In one of the more popular vignettes from his life story, Merton encountered the lion's roar when he read Etienne Gilson's *The Spirit of Medieval Philosophy*.[6] He had left his studies at Cambridge under a cloud of scandal[7] and

---

5. The fact that Merton rendered an "autobiographical theology" means revisiting familiar stories is unavoidable, but the interpretation rendered here is intended to be original in its focusing, framing, and elucidating a particular aspect of his autobiographical theology.

6. Numerous biographers have commented on this, but Bishop Robert Barron's inclusion of the story in his bestselling *Catholicism*, 228–31, has more recently brought it to the attention of a twenty-first-century audience.

7. The fact that Merton had irresponsibly impregnated a woman when he was at Cambridge, then ended up leaving for the United States, was a source of guilt and affliction for him. It meant that he would come to know himself as a sinner in need of mercy. Though he accepted and celebrated God's mercy, the knowledge of this sin never left him and remained for him a source of compunction and humility. Harold Talbott called this event "the key to [Merton's] life," (see Talbott, *Tendrel*, 269–86).

arrived at Columbia University in 1935 as an atheist; having lost his mother as a young boy, his father when he was a teenager, and whatever religious beliefs he may have had along the way. Outwardly he was playful and popular, but inwardly he was dealing with dread, frightened by "the abyss that walked around in front of [his] feet everywhere [he] went" (*SSM*, 181).

In February of 1937, as he was walking down Fifth Avenue in New York City with "five or ten loose dollars burning a hole in [his] pocket," he peered in the window of Scribner's Book Store and saw Gilson's book displayed in the window (*SSM*, 187). He was immediately interested since he was already signed up for a course in French medieval literature, so he went in and bought it. Beginning to "gloat over [his] acquisition" on his way home on the train, he opened the cover and was struck with disgust, "like a knife in the pit of the stomach," by the "*nihil obstat*" and "*imprimatur*" that appeared in the front matter. "Such is the terror that is aroused in the enlightened modern mind by a little innocent Latin and the signature of a priest." He confessed with still fresh and honest surprise, "I consider that it was surely a real grace that, instead of getting rid of the book, I actually read it" (*SSM*, 188).

Through his reading he discovered a God he had never considered before. Gilson's God was not "a being" existing as one of the many beings that exist, but characterized by *aseitas*, unconditional existence or absolute being, upon which all contingent being depends. Gilson's God was *actus purus*, or "pure actuality, the pure act of existing." This God denied the insufficient notion of God as a "something" existing "somewhere out there." Gilson went even further and reminded Merton that a general and vague conception, *ens in genere*, still needed to be distinguished from the true God, *ens ipse*, who transcended all human understanding, all conceptions, and was beyond human comprehension. As Gilson wrote, and Merton recorded in his autobiography:

> Beyond all sensible images, and all conceptual determinations, God affirms Himself as the absolute act of being, in its pure actuality. Our concept of God, a mere analogue of a reality which overflows in every direction . . . and lying beyond every object, contains in itself the sufficient reason of objects. (*SSM*, 190)

Merton said this meaning of "God" and this apophatic approach to God "was to revolutionize my whole life." Paradoxically, there seemed to be here an affirmation of his atheistic leanings, but also a challenging invitation to discover the true and living God, set free from the prison of selfish "desires and strivings and subjective ideals" (*SSM*, 190). His enduring fascination with the non-dual mystical traditions, whether Christian, Buddhist, or any other, may well trace back to this revolutionizing discovery; the discovery that God is no-thing. Instead, God *is* the transcendent source and ground of all things that depend upon and somehow participate in the God who *is*. As he would write much later, "God is pure Being, that is to say He is the pure and infinite Act of total Reality. All other realities are simply reflections of His pure Act of Being, and participations in it granted by His free gift" (*CGB*, 221).

The German theologian Karl Rahner later expressed in different terms the same revolutionizing insight. He wrote:

> *That* God really does not exist, who operates and functions as an individual existent, alongside of other existents, and who would thus as it were be a member of the larger household of all reality. Anyone in search of such a God is searching for a false God. Both atheism and a naïve theism suffer under the same false notion of God.[8]

As an atheist Merton had been suffering under a false notion of God and he had inferred that all people of faith were naïve theists. He wrote: "I had simply taken it for granted that the God in Whom religious people believed, and to Whom they attributed the creation and government of all things, was a noisy and dramatic and passionate character, a vague, jealous, hidden being" (*SSM*, 190). Merton did not believe in this idol, but he did assume that he had had the right idea about God. Gilson helped Merton encounter the true God by destroying that idol. Although he could not at the time fully appreciate all the implications this shattering revelation would have for him, Merton learned a lesson from *the roar of the lion* to be on guard against idolatry, even of his own ideas. He wrote: "What a relief it was for me, now, to discover not only that no idea of ours, let alone any image, could adequately represent God, but also that we *should not* allow ourselves to be satisfied with any such knowledge of Him" (*SSM*, 191).

Heading East with Huxley, Then Back with Brahmachari

In the early months of 1937 he had only "taken the dead letter of Scripture at its very deadest." He had never been to mass, knew almost nothing of the sacraments, but he was being opened to them by the intellectual purification

---

8. Rahner, *Foundations of Christian Faith*, 63.

afforded by *The Spirit of Medieval Philosophy*. It was now a very quick path, albeit a circuitous one, from Gilson's explication of *aseitas* to believing that the center of human history was a first-century Jewish prophet, and the *axis mundi* a cross on a hill in Jerusalem. The route to Christ was surprisingly circuitous because, in the eyes of the converted monk, providence had deemed that he be led to Christ through his interest in Eastern religions and through his friendship with a Hindu monk.

Near the end of 1937, his friend Robert Lax[9] advised him to read Aldous Huxley's *Ends and Means*, a book about spiritual experience and personal transformation as a ground for social development, and one heavily influenced by Eastern religious wisdom. The effect compelled him to go "ransacking the library" for more to read, which brought him to "the Jesuit Father Weiger's French translations of hundreds of strange Oriental texts" (*SSM*, 205), in a fervor that was nearly all consuming. As Michael Mott put it, "he was interested in Eastern religion. He wasn't the least bit interested in the Church Fathers. He wasn't interested in the teachings of the Catholic Church. No, he wasn't."[10]

About the same time, the Hindu monk and scholar Mahanambrata Brahmachari appeared and started to steer Merton back toward the West. Brahmachari, already acquainted with Merton's friends Seymour and Helen Freedgood, came to live at Columbia after finishing his doctoral studies at the University of Chicago.[11] He practiced meditation daily, and begged for his sustenance. He almost never spoke of his own religious beliefs but "would simply make statements of fact, and then burst out laughing" (*SSM*, 214). Merton recalled, "we got along very well together, especially since he sensed that I was trying to feel my way into a settled religious conviction, and into some kind of a life that was centered, as his was, on God" (*SSM*, 214).

Knowing Merton's attraction to Eastern religions and thinking it a bit misguided, Brahmachari told him, "You should read St. Augustine's *Confessions* and *The Imitation of Christ*" (*SSM*, 216). "Yes," he said, "you must read those books" (*SSM*, 217). Following the monk's advice, Merton read much more than those and "ended up being turned on like a pinball machine by . . . Thomas Aquinas, Augustine, Eckhart, Traherne, Hopkins, Maritain,

---

9. Lax, a celebrated poet in his own right, is the subject of Michael N. McGregor's recent biography *Pure Act*.

10. Mott, *Seven Mountains*, 115.

11. Brahmachari's doctoral thesis was "The Philosophy of Sri Jiva Goswami (Vaisnava Vedanta of the Bengal School)." An excerpt from it appears in Hartshorne and Reese, *Philosophers Speak of God*.

and the sacraments of the Catholic Church" (*L&L*, 11–12). His reading of Gilson and Huxley generated "more an intellectual realization than anything else" but his further reading evoked a yearning for an encounter with divine love, and to become "one with God" (*SSM*, 209). He started to pray more regularly, then he attended mass for the first time.

Dogmas and Koans

Merton remembered the sermon given by the young priest on that Sunday in August of 1938. It was all about Christ, the Second Person of the Trinity, the Incarnate Word, and the hypostatic union of two natures in one Person. Other people in the pews may have been drifting off, but Merton was intrigued by the denials implied by the affirmations made in the Christological doctrines (*SSM*, 228–29). He recalled "Jesus Christ was not simply a man, a good man, a great man. . . . He was something that made all such trivial words pale into irrelevance. . . . He was not simply a spirit without a true body, God hidden under a visionary body" (*SSM*, 229).

This recollection reveals his sensitivity to the decidedly apophatic and iconoclastic function of dogmatic formulas. The claim that Christ is "consubstantial with the Father" originally emerged as a *denial* of Arianism, adoptionism, and any kind of subordinationism that would reduce or deny the divinity of Jesus. The claim that Christ is "consubstantial with us with respect to his humanity" emerged as a *denial* of docetism, monophysitism, and any position that would deny or reduce the humanity of Jesus.[12]

The heretical positions were regarded by the orthodox as attempts to diminish the shock of the Incarnation and make Jesus more amenable to human expectations, or have him conform to existing religious and philosophical frameworks. The doctrinal formulas do not solve the problem of the paradoxical Christ but merely point to Him. They are then, simultaneously, kataphatic affirmations about a subject, this Jesus who "suffered under Pontus Pilate," was "crucified, died, and was buried"—a person whose historical and human existence cannot reasonably be denied.

Resisting the impulse to domesticate Jesus was perfectly commensurate with the orthodox faith regarding who Jesus was/is and what Jesus taught/teaches. For in Jesus there is no duplicity, no fissure between who he is, what he does, and what he teaches. As a teacher, Jesus used the form of

---

12. On the dialectical development of the Christological doctrines, see Lonergan, *Way to Nicea*. This originally appeared as part one of Lonergan's two-part *De Deo Trino*.

parables to compel an encounter with mystery. His stories frustrate the ordinary and judgmental mind so that the superabundant mystery of love and mercy might be existentially encountered and more generously affirmed and embraced. His parables challenge his listeners to see their enemies as love-worthy neighbors (Luke 10:25–37), to renounce their limited sense of retributive justice (Luke 15:11–32) and distributive justice (Matt 20:1–16), and moves them in the direction of a widening compassion.

Just as Jesus' parables puzzle and challenge listeners to a change of mind and heart (*metanoia*), so too the Christological dogmas. Merton appreciated that the Christological doctrines, like roaring lions, simply stifled any answer to Jesus' question "Who do you say that I am?" (Matt 16:15) that reduced him to being just a great man or dismissed him as not really human at all. They forced the question to stand like a koan that might compel an encounter with the mystery of Divine Mercy.

Poetic metaphors are normally intended to establish a figurative identification between similar or unlike terms. Doctrinal metaphors, on the other hand, are intended in a strong sense in which there is an ontological identification of opposed and unlike terms. I suspect that reading Gilson prepared Merton to approach doctrines as metaphorical paradoxes that prevent the ordinary mind from foisting its own limitations upon the illimitable. As a poet he was already sensitive to metaphor's capacity to evoke wonder and awe by joining terms of *unlikeness*; now through the process of religious conversion he was beginning to respond with wonder and awe to doctrines. As Northrop Frye observed:

> The sense in Christianity of a faith beyond reason, which must continue to affirm even after reason gives up, is closely connected with the linguistic fact that . . . its doctrines . . . can only be expressed in the form of metaphor. Thus Christ *is* God and man; in the Trinity three persons *are* one; in the Real Presence the body and blood *are* the bread and the wine . . . the use of concrete paradox . . . enlightens the mind by paralyzing the discursive reason, like the Koan of Zen Buddhism.[13]

Doctrinal metaphors, or dogmatic formulas, do not just *compare* in terms of likeness the goodness of a man Jesus to the goodness of the God of Israel. They *contrast* and intentionally identify unlike terms in a mind-blowing paradox.[14] Such paradoxes, as Michael Sells convincingly argued, are not

---

13. Frye, *Great Code*, 55.
14. See Sevant, "Follow That Metaphor."

just "apparent" contradictions. In order for the language to be taken seriously, not dismissed as meaningless or absurd, one must appreciate that the subject of discourse is "not an object" in the usual sense. "The logical rule of non-contradiction" Sells writes "functions for object-entities" but when the subject of discourse "is a non-object and no-thing, it is not irrational that such a logic be superseded."[15] This is, as Sallie McFague argued, the "deeper level to the semantics of metaphor" in which the *tension of duality* between the affirmed terms compels an extended and new interpretation, since a conventional one self-destructs.[16] Traditionally the dogmas were called "symbols" which more accurately suggests their metaphorical function, which is to free the imagination, whereby, as Paul Ricoeur said, "the word takes up the world and turns it in to a hierophany."[17]

John Hick, the philosopher of religion, completely missed the point of such formulas when he argued that "the orthodox task is to spell out in an intelligible way the idea of someone having both a fully divine nature . . . [and] a fully human nature . . . merely to assert both . . . is to utter a form of words which as yet has no specified meaning."[18] Hick argued that the conciliar dogmatic formulas intentionally obfuscate Biblical titles such as "Son of God" and "Incarnate word of God" which, he contends, were intended to accentuate the belief "that Jesus' earthly goodness and love were a limited reflection of the infinite divine goodness and love."[19] His interpretation of metaphor places the emphasis on figurative identification, comparison and likeness, and diminishes the tension of duality. Ironically, this approach allows for interpretations of the dogmatic formulas that the formulas were intentionally designed to deny.

St. Paul, however, used the bridge of metaphor to join terms of unlikeness in a strong sense when he commanded: "Let this mind be in you, the

---

15. Sells, *Mystical Languages of Unsaying*, 3–4. Sells calls the language "performative" rather than descriptive or declarative, saying it is a "propositionally unstable and dynamic discourse in which no single statement can rest on its own as true or false, or even meaningful."

16. McFague, *Metaphorical Theology*, 39.

17. Ricoeur, *Freud and Philosophy*, 16.

18. Hick, *Metaphor of God Incarnate*, 47–49. Hick erects a simplistic and false dichotomy between a "literal" and a "metaphorical" reading of high Christological titles, whereby he judges the former to be meaningless and the latter to be meaningful, but only insofar as they can be interpreted in ways that the dogmatic formulations were explicitly designed to deny. In other words, Hick's approach leads directly to the conclusion that Jesus was a good man, a great man, like God, but not God.

19. Hick, *Metaphor of God Incarnate*, 45–46.

mind of Jesus Christ, Who though he was in the form of God, did not deem equality with God something to be grasped. Rather he emptied himself, taking the form of a slave, coming in human likeness" and concluded the hymn with the confession "Jesus Christ is Lord" (Phil 2:6–11). *Christos* (the Greek translation of the Hebrew word *Messiah* or "the anointed") does not of itself include an affirmation of divinity, but *Kyrios* (the Greek term used for the Hebrew *Adonai* for Lord or God) does. In this regard the expression "Jesus Christ is Lord" functions as a joining of unlike terms.[20] The human and the divine are contrasted here and united, and there is no sense in which Paul seems intent on accentuating positive human attributes by comparing them to a divine superlative.

If Gilson, the mass, and his own poetic imagination opened the Catholic door for Merton to the mystery of God, then Suzuki opened the Zen door to transcendent reality by introducing him to the koan. Merton first came to appreciate Buddhist spirituality through the mondo and the koan of the Japanese Rinzai tradition. The extended periods of sitting meditation popular in the Soto school and in the Raja marga of Hindu tradition did not immediately appeal to him. But the exchange (mondo) between disciple and master over the meaning of an enigmatic expression (koan) that culminates for the disciple in *satori*, an enlightening breakthrough, appealed to him tremendously.

While Merton was gravitating toward Catholicism, his interest in Zen stayed with him, though his serious study of Zen was still on a distant horizon. On a Thursday night in August of 1938, he wrote a letter to Lax that he closed with the words: "I think to go and read pieces of Aquinas, and I think to read about Zen Buddhism" (*RJ*, 144).

We have to fast-forward a bit to see how Merton connects the effect of a koan to the Christian act of faith. Nearly twenty years after his conversion he was reflecting on his conflicted relationship with American culture and wrote in his journal:

> All this has to boil up from time to time. The boiling is part of my life. Thank God for it. There is no solution in withdrawal. No solution in conforming. A Koan! What sound is made by one hand clapping . . . ? That is where I think Zen is smart: in its absolutely fundamental psychological honesty. This honesty is inseparable from the interior poverty and sincerity which Christ asked of us when he said: "Can you believe? All things are possible to one who can believe." (*SS*, 138–39)

20. See Brown, *New Testament Christology*, 71–89.

Opening New Horizons

In his posthumously published *Opening the Bible* Merton again connected the Christian act of faith to what he often called "the Zen insight" generated through the struggle with a koan. The Bible, he argued, did not so much provide information *about* God, but facilitated an encounter *with* God by generating questions regarding ultimate identity and offered liberation from illusion, sin, and alienation. He suggested that "God" is a kind of "non-word" in the Bible, a sort of placeholder standing for the mysterious reality that permeates the text and confronts the reader. The Bible both conceals and reveals God.[21] Following Karl Barth and Dietrich Bonhoeffer, he noted how God turns the tables of interrogation on the Biblical reader who then comes to the question, "who is it that reads?" While he does not mention the specific koan, one thinks of that iconic question: "what is your original face which you had before your parents were born?" He wrote: "In many ways Zen does come close to the existentiality and spontaneity of the personal act of Biblical faith, though here we must distinguish carefully between faith in dogmatic propositions *about* God and faith as a personal, inscrutable *event and encounter* which revolutionizes one's entire sense of being and identity" (OB, 61–62).

The distinction here between faith in propositions (*fides quae*), and faith as personal event and encounter (*fides qua*), is important for illustrating that he understood the latter as necessary for rendering the former personally meaningful in a potentially transformative way.[22] In no way does he set these two in contradictory opposition to one another. The *event and encounter* underpins the objective expressions (propositions), and they in turn, provide access to an encounter and a realization—similar to the function of a koan. In fact, Merton saw reading the Bible (which as a text is part of the *fides quae*) as an iconoclastic event, by which the word "breaks through" our ordinary view of ourselves and the world "and shatters" our intransigent ego-centricity "and challenges us to risk a higher and more

---

21. As the Catechism claims, with reference to St. Augustine, "Even when He reveals himself God remains a mystery beyond words: 'If you understood him, it would not be God'" (*Catechism of the Catholic Church*, para. 230 [cited hereafter as CCC parenthetically in the text]).

22. For a helpful discussion concerning the relationship between *fides qua* and *fides quae* see Nichols, *Shape of Catholic Theology*, 15–17. He defines *fides quae* as the objective content of belief, the faith as articulated by the church which believers affirm. *Fides qua* is the subjective experience which "enables us to share here and now in the knowledge which the saints enjoy in heaven and which, more fundamentally, God has of himself. St. Thomas refers to it as the *semen gloriae*, the seed of glory, or the *inchoatio gloriae*, the first shadowy sketch of the vision of God."

fundamental freedom" (*OB*, 83). But this event and encounter does not happen for everyone who reads the same words. Some only follow the narrative.

Lecturing to the novices in the 1960s he commented on how St. Augustine, St. Gregory, and St. Bernard saw theology as a practice that cultivates wisdom (*sapientia*), which is *knowing* God, as distinct from knowing *about* God. Theology, Merton wrote, "culminates in experience of the reality of the dogmas revealed by God. The . . . theologian is one who . . . has an experiential realization of the mysteries of faith rather than just a book knowledge *about* God and the mysteries of faith" (*CFMT*, 238).

Creedal formulas (*fides quae*) can remain remote and appear obscurantist, but humble and open meditation upon them can mediate a return to an experience of the mysterious reality they intend to express. Their value lies in this function, not in providing *information* that somehow clears up the mystery of God, or by magically modifying the countenance of God through repetitious recitation or reading, but by effecting a turning toward and intimacy with the Divine *mystery*.[23] Early monks and hermits, Merton said, "clung to" the dogmatic formulas in ways that allowed them to seek God without maps and charts within the "arid horizons of the desert" where they refused "to be content with arguments, concepts, and technical verbiage" (*WD*, 6). Flannery O'Connor put it this way: "Dogma can in no way limit a limitless God. . . . For me a dogma is only a gateway to contemplation and is an instrument of freedom and not of restriction. It preserves mystery for the human mind."[24]

In other words, the task of orthodoxy is not, as Hick thinks, "to spell out in an intelligible way" the meaning of dogmatic formulas. Rather, the formulas intentionally prevent us from judging our finite acts of human understanding as valid in a way that would erroneously reduce God's inexhaustible mystery, God's infinite intelligibility.[25] They should prevent our

---

23. Merton notes, "But those forms of religious and liturgical worship which have lost their initial impulse of fervor tend more and more to forget their contemplative purpose, and to attach exclusive importance to rites and forms for their own sake, or for that sake of the effect which they are believed to exercise on the One Who is worshipped" (*IE*, 20).

24. O'Connor, *Collected Works*, 943.

25. As an undergraduate student at the University of Dayton in a course called "Doctrines and Dogmas," I remember finally getting this. After my professor, James L. Heft, SM, had already taken us through the notion of God's transcendence *a la* Gilson and Rahner, he then taught us the doctrine of the Incarnation. I remember telling him, "If God by definition is illimitable and transcendent, then Jesus, who was fully human could not possibly be God." Heft said nothing. Then I began to wonder, and I asked, "How could a human being also be God?" Fr. Heft replied, "Exactly! Now you are getting it!

confusing and mistaking our own images and understandings of God for the unbounded totality of God. They remind us, as Merton said, "that we *should not* allow ourselves to be satisfied with any such knowledge of Him" (*SSM*, 191). The *raison d'etre* of dogmatic formulas is the prevention of idolatry. They are inscribed instances of the lion's roar.

While Catholicism would dominate his early spiritual formation, the iconoclastic and purifying spirit that also attracted him to Zen would remain with him his whole life. His interest in Buddhism as a tradition, however, would temporarily be brushed aside by the overwhelming power of the Christian conversion that began to sweep him up in the midst of writing his master's thesis. Less than four months after he wrote the aforementioned letter to Lax, he was baptized at the Catholic Church of Corpus Christi in Manhattan.

Cracking the Idol of the Social Self

After completing his MA, Merton moved to Perry Street, where he became consumed with the desire to publish his writing and establish his name in the literary world. He wrote: "My chief concern was now to see myself in print. It was as if I could not be quite satisfied that I was real until I could feed my ambition with these trivial glories, and my ancient selfishness was now matured and concentrated in this desire to see myself externalized in a public and printed and official self which I could admire at my ease" (*SSM*, 258–59).

Lax, however, rebuked Merton for his egocentric motivations. He encouraged Merton's writing but he yearned for a voice in print that could speak to the deepest needs of people, a voice "capable of telling [people] of the love of God in language that will no longer sound hackneyed or crazy, but with authority and conviction: the conviction born of sanctity" (*SSM*, 259). In the now famous exchange that followed, Lax raised Merton's consciousness with a question: "What do you want to be, anyway?"

The question immediately made Merton uncomfortable; he began searching for an adequate response, one that transcended the obvious

---

Your question is *the point* of the Dogma! It's not an explanation but an affirmation *and a question*. The question is can you believe it?" He was so excited and nearly laughing as he said this, and his countenance, as much as his words, generated my insight. Heft later edited two significant contributions to interreligious dialogue, *Beyond Violence: Religious Sources of Social Transformation* and *Catholicism and Interreligious Dialogue*.

superficiality of his literary ambitions, so he replied, "I guess what I want to be is a good Catholic." But Lax thought this response unworthy and challenged him further: "'What you should say'—he told me—'what you should say is that you want to be a saint.' A saint! the thought struck me as a little weird. I said: 'How do you expect me to become a saint?' 'By wanting to,' said Lax, simply" (*SSM*, 260).

With this exchange Lax had quite possibly articulated for Merton a question that generated for him "an almost single-minded effort to reach a decision," as Walter Conn put it, "a decision constitutive of his very life, of the kind of person he would be."[26] It accelerated his conversion, turning him away from an obsession with establishing a "public and printed and official self" and toward the pursuit of holiness, where Christ would increase and he would decrease, to the point of becoming a "nobody."

On October 23, 1939, eleven months after his baptism, he was writing in his journal and considering how St. Francis was so much like Christ, and that if he were to aspire to be like Christ, he too "would need to set no store on pride in knowledge, or possessions, or ambitions" but set himself on "being, first, *nobody*: [like] this peasant, obscure and dark and silent, and not knowing much how to talk" (*RM*, 70). Ironically, his pursuit of holiness would involve the production of a "public self" that he would have to deal with. The allure, however, of becoming nobody, or in Brahmachari's terms, of transcending all the *purusarthas* save *moksha*,[27] slowly started to draw him like an undertow. It led him first to the Franciscans, who rejected him,[28] and then to the Trappists, who accepted him.

Just before he left for Gethsemani he wrote to Lax, confident that God would teach him the "language of love" and "to use that language like a

---

26. Conn, *Desiring Self*, 118.

27. Many Hindus recognize four aims or goals of life, in Sanskrit "*purusarthas*." They are (1) *kama*, the pursuit of sensual and aesthetic pleasure; (2) *artha*, the acquisition of material goods, wealth, fame, and worldly power; (3) *dharma*, living according to one's caste and the moral obligations established by birth, age, sex, etc.; and (4) *moksha*, liberation from all illusion, and all constraints. When a person embraces moksha as the chief aim of life, she begins the ascetic practices that culminate in the *sannyasa* stage of life, the renunciation of all possessions and attachments, including name and family ties. On September 24, 1961 Merton wrote in his journal "I am determined now to embrace the long task of unweaving the garment of *artha*, my writer-self, my official business of being, so as at last to step out of it" (*TTW*, 164).

28. For a thorough exploration of Merton's life through a Franciscan lens that accentuates the Franciscan character of Merton's intellectual and spiritual formation and development, see Horan, *Franciscan Heart of Thomas Merton*.

child and a saint. Until which, I cannot talk about Him, Who is all I want to talk about." He concluded his letter assured that "in Him will be also: Lax . . . and Brahmachari and the whole mystical body of Christ, everybody . . . All days, all times, all ages, all worlds, all mysteries, all miracles" (*RJ*, 164).

Cracking the Idol of a "Sacred Self"

In 1915, the year Merton was born, the First World War was in full ferment and ravaged the French landscape not far from the little town of Prades, where he had come into the world. In 1941 the Second World War was underway, when he left the world for the monastery. Japan had bombed Pearl Harbor on December 7 and the United States declared war the following day. On December 10, Merton walked into the cloistered space of Gethsemani, in Kentucky, under the doorway inscribed *Pax Intrantibus* ("Peace to those who enter"), looking to devote his life to "God Alone" and to be freed from the frustrations and false promises of a world once again in the welter of decline.

Being out of the world came with a kind of euphoria that carried him through the first years at Gethsemani. He celebrated instead of lamented the hardships normally associated with Cistercian life in the 1940s. In winter the monks slept on their straw beds and breathed plumes of gray fog through the dark nights. When spring came and the thawing earth brought forth flowers to dot the greening fields and forests, so too came the bugs and the brutal Kentucky heat. All through summer, the monks worked in the hot fields, donning the long hooded cowls and hefty leather belts that drank up the sweat running over their ribs. In the years between making his simple vows in 1944 and his final vows in 1947 he lived the structured life of work and prayer, and performed the tasks assigned by the Father Abbot, one of which was writing.[29]

The Cistercian solemn vows are *obedience*, *stability* and *conversatio morum*. The vow of obedience commits the monk to living the Rule of St. Benedict, and places him under the authority of an abbot. Stability requires an expressed willingness to live out the rest of one's days rooted in one specific community. The vow is meant to plant the monk like a seed

---

29. For example, the Abbot had Merton translating devotional books for the monks to use in prayer, e.g., Jean-Baptiste Chautard's *Soul of the Apostolate* and St. John Eudes's *Life and Kingdom of Jesus in Christian Souls*, and writing lives of Cistercian saints, e.g., *Exile Ends in Glory* and *What Are These Wounds?*

for his growth and fertility, not to lock him into spiritual intransigence. Although he would later struggle with a profound restlessness that would have him looking beyond the monastery walls toward the Carthusians and the Camoldolese, he managed to keep this vow, and remained a Cistercian until his death.[30] The vow of *conversatio morum* is an explicit commitment to seek holiness, to persevere in the continual turning away from sin toward greater communion in love. This vow includes the familiar vows of *poverty* and *chastity*. The vows make the monk's earthly life a sacrifice as he commits to a process of conversion that goes on as long as he is still breathing (and even after in a post-mortem purgative process). For Merton this meant that he had to remain open to the possibility that whatever self-image he might adopt, even the image of the solitary monk, could become a dangerous illusion, an idol that would have to be destroyed.

By the end of 1947 he had begun to lose his monastic anonymity and acquire the fame he had so desperately desired in his pre-monastic years. James Laughlin at New Directions had published Merton's little book, *Thirty Poems*, in 1944, and though it was not a commercial success it attracted the attention and respect of some prominent literary figures.[31] In 1946 he published a second collection of poetry, *A Man in the Divided Sea*, and followed that with an essay entitled "Poetry and the Contemplative Life" in the July 4, 1947, issue of *The Commonweal*.

The fact that he had been born a writer seemed to him to be an impediment to the solitary life of prayer. He did not initially like the fact that for a silent monk he was prolific, making a name for himself in the world. Compounding his own anguish he concluded, in this early period, that good discernment could mean that he needed to be a monk and relinquish the writing of poetry. In his essay "Poetry and the Contemplative Life" he suggested that "the ruthless and complete sacrifice of his art" could well be the safest way to true contemplation. He recognized that such a view would "only appall someone who does not understand the infinite distance between the gifts of nature and those of grace, between the natural and supernatural order, time and eternity, man and God"[32]

---

30. For an in depth study of this struggle, see Grayston, *Thomas Merton and the Noonday Demon*.

31. Most notably, Mark Van Doren, who selected the poems that comprise the book. See the entry "Thirty Poems" in *TME*, 471–74.

32. *Commonweal*, July 4, 1947, 285.

Nonetheless, he went on to produce over a thousand pages of poetry and a massive body of other work; a body still growing over a half century since his death.[33] He eventually came to appreciate, however, that his call to holiness had to be followed through his natural gifts as a poet and a writer.[34] He later wrote:

> I have tried to learn in my writing a monastic lesson I could probably not have learned otherwise: to let go of my idea of myself, to take myself with more than one grain of salt.... This is simply a matter of accepting life, and everything in life as a gift, and clinging to none of it, as far as you are able.... All life tends to grow like this, in mystery inscaped with paradox and contradiction, yet centered in its very heart, on the divine mercy.... Such is my philosophy... [which] consists not in statements about a truth which cannot be adequately stated, but in grace and mercy and in the realization of a new life that is in us by the gift of the Holy Spirit.[35]

Three Trips Outside the Cloister

August 12, 1948

The Seven Storey Mountain was published in 1948. Merton had been writing it as early as 1945, and by the time the book had made him famous, he was already beginning to grow out of the identity he celebrated so enthusiastically in that autobiography. On August 12, 1948, not long after he had received a copy of his soon-to-be-famous book, he left the monastery for the first time in seven years in order to accompany the vicar general of his order, Dom Gabriel Sortais, on a trip to Louisville. Although Merton admitted in his private journal that he was feeling alienated from the world on that day, he also wrote that the people in Louisville "seemed more real than they ever had before and more worth sympathizing with" (*ES*, 223). When recalling the same episode in his public and polished journal, *The*

---

33. For example, Patrick F. O'Connell recently edited and published nine volumes of Merton's lectures in a series subtitled *Initiation into Monastic Tradition* with Cistercian Publications. O'Connell is now in the process of producing three more volumes of Merton's "Novitiate Conferences on Scripture and Liturgy" with Cascade (Wipf & Stock).

34. The novelist Mary Gordon explores Merton's struggle with his dual vocation as a monk and a writer in her recent book, *On Thomas Merton*.

35. "First and Last Thoughts," in Merton, *Thomas Merton Reader*, 17 (cited hereafter as *TMR* parenthetically in the text).

Sign of Jonas, he goes a bit further, saying "I met the world and found it no longer so wicked after all. Perhaps the things I had resented about the world when I left it were defects of my own that I had projected upon it. Now, on the contrary, I found that everything stirred me with a deep and mute sense of compassion" (*SJ*, 91–92).

William Shannon cited *Seeds of Contemplation* (1949), *The Sign of Jonas* (1953), and *No Man Is an Island* (1955), as indicative of a new perspective in Merton's writing. In these works, Merton began to speak more directly of his experience of God in his own voice, unmasked by the "official" languages of a systematic or dogmatic theology.[36] Although *The Seven Storey Mountain* does not strictly follow the rigid theology of the manuals it communicates "the narrowness of Merton's early Catholicism" which shows itself in the "sharp cleavage between the supernatural and the natural" that Merton draws therein.[37] Years later, in *Conjectures of a Guilty Bystander* he would indict his own earlier view, writing: "We have got ourselves into a position where, because of our misunderstanding of theoretical distinctions between the 'natural and the supernatural,' we tend to think that nothing in [our] ordinary life is supernatural" (*CGB*, 81). In the latter years of his monastic life he continually challenged that misunderstanding. Though he never discarded this distinction as meaningless, it becomes subtler, more elusive, as his sacramental vision matured and he began "accepting everything in life as a gift" (*TMR*, 17).

July 22–August 4, 1956

July of 1956 presented the occasion for another significant trip outside the monastery. He was headed to St. John's Abbey, near St. Cloud, Minnesota for a conference on psychoanalysis and religion. The famous psychiatrist and convert to Catholicism, Gregory Zilboorg, was the scheduled keynote and Merton was excited to meet him. Before the plane rides from Kentucky to Minnesota he was reading D. T. Suzuki, and wondering in his journal what the "profane instruments" of psychoanalysis and Zen could possibly have to do with the "formation of Christ in souls for the Kingdom of God" (*SS*, 48).

---

36. Shannon, *Silent Lamp*, 167–68, 178.

37. Shannon, *Silent Lamp*, 163. "The sharp cleavage" suggests that Merton, in the wake of his early monastic formation, tends not only to distinguish the natural and the supernatural but to divorce them.

Opening New Horizons

On July 23, Merton heard Zilboorg speak, and early in the morning of July 29 he had the chance to meet with him for an hour and a half. His notes on what Zilboorg said to him are nakedly honest:

> "you are a gadfly to your superiors ... very stubborn ... afraid to be an ordinary monk in the community ... you want to be famous, a big shot ... your hermit trend is pathological ... it is not intelligence you lack but affectivity ... Megalomania and narcissism are your big trends."
>
> Things which I know and did not know. And I suppose that is the trouble. I am quite capable of saying, "I am a narcissist" and yet it changes nothing and it has not helped me to understand.
>
> While he said all this I thought "How much he looks like Stalin" but in reality I am tremendously relieved and grateful—and when I sung mass with the monks I was praying hard to know what to do about it. (SS, 59–60)

Merton's meeting with Zilboorg was humiliating. He had gotten used to "a river of compliments" from adoring fans, so the comeuppance from Dr. Zilboorg was, as Shannon described, "an unexpectedly shattering experience" (WF, 139). The following day, he wrote his friend and literary agent Naomi Burton Stone, "[Zilboorg] has told me, more directly and forcefully than I ever thought possible, the exact home truths that need to be told" (WF, 139).[38]

Thomas Keating wrote that the spiritual journey "is a series of humiliations of the false self that become more and more profound. These make room inside us for the Holy Spirit to come in and heal."[39] Merton's meeting with Zilboorg was in some ways devastating, but oddly enough he was grateful for it and closed his letter to Stone writing "and I am very glad I was able to get up here. It was a wonderful session and I have got a great deal out of it. Zilboorg is going to keep in touch with me and will give me whatever advice he can" (WF, 140). Instead of fostering a lingering resentment, he was able to hear the lion's roar in Zilboorg's confrontational bluntness.

---

38. He also conveyed to her that Zilboorg intended to meet with his abbot, Dom James Fox. The impression Zilboorg left upon Dom James, according to Merton, would explain not only the abbot's strong resistance to any of Merton's ideas about transferring to another order, or going off on his own as a hermit, but also why, as he wrote to Ernesto Cardenal, "the Congregation swung in favor of Dom James" in "a decision so final that I am not at liberty to take any further steps on my own behalf, but can only accept and obey" (CT, 121).

39. Keating, *Human Condition*, 38.

If this "shattering experience" was a spiritually necessary humiliation, the experience in Louisville on the corner of Fourth and Walnut was too; but this time the healing it brought was more immediate and profound.

March 18, 1958

On this auspicious day in Louisville, Merton was standing on a populated street corner and suddenly realized that he "loved all of those people"—and was one in being with them. He wrote:

> It was like waking from a dream of total separateness, of spurious self-isolation in a special world, the world of renunciation and supposed holiness. . . . This sense of liberation from an illusory difference was such a relief and such a joy to me that I almost laughed out loud. . . . As if the sorrows and stupidities of the human condition could overwhelm me, now I realize what we all are. And if only everybody could realize this! But it cannot be explained. There is no way of telling people that they are all walking around shining like the sun. (*CGB*, 156–57)

It is difficult to square his narcissism with the universal compassion he exhibits here, and there is no need to do so. The point of recalling these vignettes is to illustrate his honesty, his ability to let go of self-images and to take himself less seriously. In amazement at his own stupidity and spiritual hubris he bemusedly observed: "To think that for sixteen or seventeen years I have been taking seriously this pure illusion" (*CGB*, 157). Where the young man had felt his "isolation crowding in" on him from all sides when he was "living in death," the monk now recognized another kind of isolation in a fantasy world of "supposed holiness."

This experience would later seem to Merton's interpreters so pivotal that Basil Pennington could write: "It is necessary to see all that Thomas Merton wrote before and after this experience in light of the presence or absence of it."[40] This experience, however, along with the others merely confirmed his long standing belief that "the discovery of ourselves is always a losing of ourselves, a death and a resurrection" (*NMI*, xv); and that "we must forget ourselves in order to be truly conscious of who we are" (*NMI*, xvi–xvii). Importantly, he described both the difficult encounter with Zilboorg, and this consoling realization in Louisville with self-deprecating humor, gratitude and relief.

40. Pennington, *Thomas Merton*, 13.

"Shattering the Mirror": A Snapshot of a Zen Poet[41]

Michael Higgins has argued that Merton found in William Blake, and later in his studies of Zen, approaches to recovering paradise by "shattering the mirror" of Cartesian consciousness, the "I" that takes itself to be self-subsisting and substantial and stands over and against the natural world.[42] Some of Thomas Merton's early poems from 1942 bear the marks of a poetic style that Merton would not fully develop for another fifteen years, a style that Sr. Therese Lentfoehr called his "metaphysical-mystical lyric" which carried his "Zen-mystical voice."[43] Recognizing the iconoclastic function of Merton's poetry, whether earlier or later, is essential for understanding the works themselves. These poems often express insight into the illusory nature of individual identity and serve as functional approaches that facilitate the self-transcendence that liberates the mind from idolatry and from the fetters of an entrenched dualism.

In the early poem "Lent (A Fragment)" the poet yearns for a radical self-emptying because of his faith in the promise of an as-yet unknown fulfillment. The desire is akin to that yearning to be "nobody" he wrote about in his journal almost a year after his baptism. The poem is deliberately disorienting as the speaker's identity is ambiguous. In the first line God seems to address the poet beckoning him to "come home" to the desert. But quickly the omniscient voice speaks to the reader about the poet (him). In the middle of the third stanza the voice becomes one with the poet's and speaks of "our ear's small shell" and petitions skill to "forsake these fingers."

> Close, eyes, and soul, come home!
> Senses will seem to perish, in the desert:
> Thought will pretend to live on punishment, among the empty tombs.
>
> 'Til pride, amid the rocks and sepulchers of Thebes, lies quiet,
> The thoughts that foraged for him, kept him fed,
> Find in the stones no sustenance,
> And scatter to another country, and a milder weather.

---

41. Some of the poems I discuss in this section have also been explored by Patrick F. O'Connell. See O'Connell, "Mending Walls"; "Nurture by Nature"; "Islands in the Stream."

42. Higgins, *Heretic Blood*, 252. For lucid commentary on Merton's critique of Cartesian consciousness, see Scruggs, "Contemplation and the *Cogito*."

43. Lentfoehr, *Words and Silence*, 52–63. See also Thurston, "Light Strikes Home."

> Sight will, it seems, dwell idle in her gates:
> Not watch the shafts of the sharp sun
> Nor feel the little thorn light of the moon.
> Sound will sit lifeless in our ear's small shell,
> (Once crowded, and amazed with the din of vendors,
> The clamors of the dead man's funeral bell.)
> And skill, forsake these fingers if you will. (CFTM, 23–24)

Is it one speaker? Is it one voice? The fact that it is difficult to identify just who is speaking when and to whom the voice is speaking, frees the imagination to consider the subtleties of the divine-human relationship, where the human ends and God begins, if anywhere at all.

In "Sacred Heart 2 (A Fragment)," Merton speaks of a "geography" beyond direction and horizon where "(c)ompass has lost all earthly north." This initial evocation of a strange and disorienting land is dismal and without "hope for any special borealis/ To rouse my darkness with a brief 'Hurray'!" But the second stanza, evoking Ezekiel 37:4–6, expresses an awakening, within in an "unseen and unimagined" heart that brings confident hope, and inchoate joy:

> You, You alone are real, and here I've found You.
> Here will I love and praise You in a tongueless death
> Until my white devoted bones,
> Long bleached and polished by the winds of this Sahara
> Relive at Your command,
> Rise and unfold the flowers of their everlasting spring. (CPTM, 24)

This second stanza brings to light the second important feature that characterizes Merton's Zen-mystical voice. The first is the iconoclastic element that facilitates and expresses the self-emptying and the second is the paradoxical counterpart to that of discovering new life, fullness of being, and compassion in the emptiness.

Lentfoehr asserts that in Merton's fifth collection, *The Strange Islands* (1957), the "metaphysical-mystical lyric" fully appears and it is in this "that Merton is most truly himself" and "singularly original."[44] His "Zen-mystical voice" comes through here, and even more clearly in poems that appear in *Emblems of a Season of Fury* (1963). These collections were composed at the time of Merton's serious study of Zen and the second one during his dialogue with Suzuki.

---

44. Lentfoehr, *Words and Silence*, 52.

Opening New Horizons

In "Part Three" of *The Strange Islands* several poems express a radical detachment, and realize, or merely anticipate "the inner experience." This is the focus of the poems "When in the Soul of the Serene Disciple..."; "In Silence"; and "Stranger." Each of these poems expresses an utter humility that amounts to a loss of "self" which corresponds cognitively to a loss of image, thought and speech. In "When in the Soul of the Serene Disciple..." Merton focuses on the kenosis that leads to immediacy, silence, the emptiness. After grace takes away everything, even his reputation and his halo, the serene disciple accepts a poverty that is no achievement, and with words allusive of Simone Weil, "His God lives in his emptiness like an affliction."[45]

In his poems "In Silence" and "Stranger" Merton ends with a stronger emphasis on new life or rebirth. "In Silence" begins with a movement into utter stillness, into the silence of the stones, and God seems to be addressing the poet with the koan like question "Who/Are you? Whose/ Silence are you?" Or perhaps it is the poet addressing his God. The last stanza expresses a discovery when the poet proclaims:

> "I will try, like them
> To be my own silence:
> And this is difficult. The whole
> World is secretly on fire. The stones
> Burn, even the stones
> They burn me. How can a man be still or
> Listen to all things burning? How can he dare
> To sit with them when
> All their silence
> Is on fire?" (*CPTM*, 280–81)

Interestingly, the first version of "In Silence" was written on July 27, 1956, when Merton was at St. John's Abbey in Minnesota, reading Suzuki and just two days before Zilboorg would call him a narcissist (*SS*, 56).

The poem "Stranger" reads almost like a chapter of the *Tao Te Ching*, but in it Merton personifies the silence as an "inward Stranger" whom we never see and who is "closer and clearer/ Than any wordy master." He wrote:

> Now act is waste
> And suffering undone
> Laws become prodigals

---

45. Simone Weil wrote, "Affliction makes God appear to be absent.... The soul has to go on loving in the emptiness, or at least go on wanting to love" (*Waiting for God*, 120–21).

Limits are torn down
For envy has no property
And passion is none.

Look, the vast Light stands still
Our cleanest Light is One! (*CPTM*, 289-90)

The Zen poems in Merton's collection *Emblems of a Season of Fury* are in some ways more iconoclastic than those in *The Strange Islands* while at the same time managing to be more natural, playful, and joyful. Interestingly the poems in that collection that provide social commentary are quite sardonic and severe[46] but "Song For Nobody" is a gentle persuasion to trust in the emptiness and "Song If You Seek . . ." is a celebration of the fecund emptiness of pure being. The poem "O Sweet Irrational Worship" captures the flow of the dynamism of a personal emptiness that blooms into a consciousness that is a simple worship of pure being:

A tall, spare pine
Stands like the initial of my first
Name when I had one.

When I had a spirit,
When I was on fire
When this valley was
Made out of fresh air
You spoke my name
In naming Your silence:
O sweet, irrational worship!

I am earth, earth
My heart's love
Bursts with hay and flowers.
I am a lake of blue air
In which my own appointed place
Field and valley
Stand reflected.

I am earth, earth

Out of my grass heart
Rises the bobwhite.

---

46. See "And the Children of Birmingham" (*CPTM*, 335-37); "Chant to Be Used in Processions around a Site with Furnaces" (*CPTM*, 345-47).

> Out of my nameless weeds
> His foolish worship. (*CPTM*, 344–45)

In sum, Merton's Zen-mystical voice is iconoclastic and exhibits the self-transcendence that frees the poet from the attachments to images that can turn them into idols and prisons. The poetry dislocates and displaces both self-image and God-image in ways that preserve a subtle and elusive distinction between creature and Creator but dissolve illusory separations. Words, like stepping stones, provide a path for the imagination to move well beyond what the stones themselves encompass. This dynamism between wisdom and emptiness, between the expression of an inner insight and the experience that generates it, is precisely the focus of Merton's dialogue with Suzuki. Since they are engaged in dialogue, they are using words, but they are discussing a font of meaning that is not apart from but prior to and more than what human language can exhaust. Before we examine the dialogue, however, the following intervening chapter provides a brief excursus on Merton's own appreciation of divinely revealed truth and how that impacts his approach to dialogue and his strategy for dealing with differences that emerge from it.

2

Dogma, Dialogue, and Dialectics

The (Re)formation of a Contemplative Theologian

BY THE TIME MERTON had entered formal seminary training, the creative and constructive boldness that characterized patristic and medieval theology had given way to a stifling and cautious defensiveness. The Reformation, the subsequent rise of the enlightenment, and the scientific revolution combined to precipitate an enclosed atmosphere in Catholic theological circles that lasted in much of the Catholic world well into the twentieth century. William Shannon wrote that "Merton was received into the Catholic Church at a time when the Church was in the grips of a . . . theological rigidity" and questioning of any kind was suspect.[1]

The theological training Merton received soon after entering the Trappists was typical of the training prevalent in American seminaries prior to Vatican II. In the 1940s theology was, as Lawrence Cunningham described, "a subject taught by priests to future priests" and mainly consisted of "glosses on scholastic manuals written in Latin" and "massively innocent of any historical context or hermeneutical rigor."[2] Bernard Lonergan described that theology as dogmatic and reactionary, writing that it had "replaced the inquiry of the *quaestio* by the pedagogy of the thesis. It demoted the quest of faith for understanding to a desirable, but secondary, and indeed optional goal. It gave basic and central significance to the certitudes of faith."[3]

---

1. Shannon, *Silent Lamp*, 161.
2. Cunningham, *Spiritual Master*, 27–28.
3. Lonergan, "Theology in Its New Context."

In short, the more ancient tradition of theology as "faith *seeking* understanding" (*fides quaerens intellectum*)[4] had been temporarily sidelined by a defensive dogmatism.

As early as the mid-nineteenth century, however, some theologians in Europe were beginning to evince an emergent historical consciousness, awakening to the realization that theology must remain alive to its own uncertainties. John Henry Newman in England, and later Joseph Maréchal at Leuven, were outliers in their own day but their work would underpin later advances in the discipline of theology that would roll out in the massive wake of the Second World War and culminate in the Second Vatican Council.[5]

Within the purview of pre-conciliar dogmatic theology, Scripture itself was often regarded as a series of propositional truths, though sometimes difficult to decipher, mediated through human scribes who had little to no impact on the shape and specific content of biblical texts. Doctrines and dogmas found their validation in particular passages of scripture and theologians deduced their implications for more specific areas of theological inquiry and pastoral guidance. In short, propositions served as the starting point, and the goal of dogmatic theology seemed to be little more than the didactic reinforcement of those axiomatic truths.

Although Merton's seminary training was rather didactic and formulaic, his own extra-curricular reading of ancient monastic sources and mystical literature, what Lawrence Cunningham called his "second education," put him in touch with an older, deeper and livelier theological tradition, one that relished the mystery of the God who is irreducible to the limits of human understanding and rational certainty.[6] This second education

---

4. See Anselm, *Proslogion* c.1 [*PL* 158, col. 227C]. Anselm captures the searching quality of theology also with *Credo ut intelligam*, "I believe that I might understand." See *RM*, 292, for Merton's initial encounter with this text (January 16, 1941); for later reflections, see *CFF*, 55–56, 107–8.

5. St. John Henry Newman (1801–1890), through his own historical studies, came to appreciate the way church teaching develops. His *Essay on the Development of Christian Doctrine* (originally published in 1845), would exercise enormous influence over the later theologians of the *nouvelle théologie*. Prompted by Pope Leo's call in *Aeterni Patris* (1879) to revitalize the study of Thomas Aquinas, Joseph Maréchal (1878–1944) explicated the dynamic role of consciousness and cognitional process in its arriving at truth. Newman's "illative sense" and Maréchal's work in cognitional theory influenced both Karl Rahner and Bernard Lonergan.

6. Cunningham, *Spiritual Master*, 27–28.

Dogma, Dialogue, and Dialectics

prepared him to receive more readily the advances of the more modern theology he would soon encounter.

Roughly eight years after he entered religious life, Merton was called upon to teach and this compelled him to wade into the turbulent waters of theological renewal that were flowing in the postwar era and that would lead to the reforms of the Second Vatican Council. Merton began teaching in November of 1949 (*ES*, 372). From 1951 to 1955 Merton served as master of students, and from 1955 to 1965 as master of novices. For roughly fifteen years he was involved in intensive theological studies that challenged the theological training he himself had received as a novice and seminarian, and that validated his own interest in the more ancient sources of theology he explored in his second education.

Pope Pius XII's *Divino afflante Spiritu* (1943) initiated a renewal of Catholic biblical scholarship with its encouragement of the use of historical-critical methods, or modern exegesis, to help determine the literal sense of scripture.[7] Additionally, Pius XII's statements on religious life encouraged ongoing renewal, one that would be advanced by a return to the sources and Merton adopted this method in his own approach to initiating monks into the monastic tradition (*CF*, 5–6). Merton wrote that besides the "renewal of our own tradition we must of course obviously *adapt* ourselves to the needs of our time" solving the problems of the twentieth century with the spirit that earlier Christians met the problems of their own day (*CF*, 6). This renewal, an *aggiornamento* by *ressourcement,* accompanied the wider *nouvelle théologie*[8] which brought to focus the fact that tradition lived like an organism with its own consequential history and not yet fully known future.[9] It was becoming clear, and suddenly seemed important,

---

7. The "literal sense" refers to the sense intended by the inspired authors. It does not mean the straightforward, or non-metaphorical, or non-symbolic sense, since the author may well have intended symbolic or metaphorical meaning. It focuses on the original intended meaning in the earliest extent copies or fragments of Biblical texts.

8. Theologians associated with this movement include Merton's contemporaries Yves Congar, Henri de Lubac, Hans Urs von Balthasar, MarieDominique Chenu, Karl Rahner, and Joseph Ratzinger, among others.

9. As an educator, Merton was doing similar work through his intensive study of early monastic sources, which included the role of the Cappadocians in the development of Trinitarian doctrine through the Eunomian controversy (see chapter 6). Merton's own *ressourcement* took him into the world of Eastern Orthodoxy and its theological tradition, much of which Pramuk's *Sophia* explores. This "return to the sources" laid the foundations for Vatican II's recovery of an organic, more humble and communal ecclesiology, and a greater optimism regarding God's salvific work in the world beyond the "visible"

that the Biblical canon, the shape of the Church's liturgy, and the terms of its doctrines had not just appeared from the ether but had emerged through dialectical processes in order to protect the kerygmatic proclamation from misrepresentations and misunderstandings.

In the academic years of 1951–1952 and 1955–1956 Merton provided a monastic introduction to scripture to his students and novices at Gethsemani.[10] The task required him to become familiar with the then current state of Catholic scripture scholarship. His preparative reading, under the tutelage of the renowned scholar Barnabas Ahern, CP,[11] sensitized him to the importance and difficulty of accessing the literal sense of Scripture through the tools of historical-critical methods.[12] Through Ahern, Merton was beginning to appreciate that the literal sense of scripture is the indispensable entrée to its spiritual sense, and that understanding the literal sense required study of original languages, of cultural contexts, and of ancient literary forms current when biblical texts were composed. If, for example, the Book of Jonah turned out to reflect the form of an ancient extended parable, "its truth would be spiritual and ethical, not factual and descriptive."[13] Such an observation, of course, begged the question of "Biblical inerrancy" and Merton was sensitive to it.

He accepted Biblical inerrancy as a given, but the question of *how* the Bible was inerrant, given the variety of literary forms, and "the state of scientific, historical, even ethical knowledge at the time of its composition" became for him a question, as O'Connell puts it, of "how inspiration is operating in a particular passage" (*MISS*, xxv). He had been content to accept a general Catholic premise, dating back to Augustine, that the "Bible never intended to teach scientific truths in a scientific way" (*MISS*, 38), but he was also coming to understand that the historical consciousness behind

---

boundaries of the Catholic Church, a topic explored later in chapter 7.

10. Merton, *Monastic Introduction to Sacred Scripture* (cited hereafter as *MIIS* parenthetically in the text).

11. Fr. Barnabas Mary Ahern, CP, was a biblical scholar who studied at *L'École Biblique* in Jerusalem (1947) and obtained a doctorate from the Pontifical Biblical Institute in Rome (1958). He taught Scripture at the Passionist seminary in Louisville, Kentucky in the 1950s and served as peritus at Vatican II. His official biography for the Passionist order is available online. See "Ahern, Barnabas Mary"; Collins "Passionist Friendship."

12. O'Connell notes in his introduction that Merton's lectures were given before "the massive shift" away from a propositional view to a more historical one had "occurred in mainstream theological discourse" (*MISS*, xxi). Still, Ahern's influence helped Merton make that transition for himself and share it with his pupils.

13. Nichols, *Shape of Catholic Theology*, 136.

contemporary exegesis had implications for how the Church would understand the doctrines of revelation, inspiration, and inerrancy.

The Organic Process of Divine Revelation and Human Appropriation

Joseph Ratzinger was a contributor to and an early interpreter of Vatican II's *Dogmatic Constitution on Divine Revelation* (*DV*) and writes with authority regarding the insights integrated into Catholic Biblical scholarship since *Divino afflante Spiritu* had encouraged "modern exegesis."[14] Concerning the composition of the New Testament and the establishment of the Biblical canon, Ratzinger claimed:

> Modern exegesis has brought to light a process of constant rereading that forged the words transmitted in the Bible into Scripture: Older texts are reappropriated, reinterpreted, and read with new eyes in new contexts. They become Scripture by being read anew, evolving in continuity with their original sense, tacitly corrected and given added depth and breadth of meaning. This is a process in which the word gradually unfolds its inner potentialities, already somehow present like seeds, but needing the challenge of new situations, new experiences and new sufferings, in order to open up.[15]

Ratzinger regards revelation as a progressive, organic process of divine self-communication, culminating no doubt in the Christ-event, but one that also unfolds through the composition, redaction, selection, and canonization of biblical texts under the ongoing inspiration of the Holy Spirit.

---

14. As a peritus at Vatican II, Ratzinger was a contributor to *Dei Verbum*. Following the council, he wrote an influential commentary on *DV* for Herbert Vorgrimler's *Commentary on the Documents of Vatican II*. Ratzinger notes *DV*'s development in terms of its emphasis on a single source of revelation, i.e., God's Word, in contrast to an earlier preference for a two-source theory, i.e., Scripture and Tradition. According to *DV* the one source speaks *through* scripture and tradition, and while the former has been set with the establishment of the canon, the latter (tradition) continues to progress, guided by the spirit, and judged by the Magisterium which serves the Word. *Dei Verbum* treats revelation in terms of its threefold manifestation in Scripture, Tradition and the adjudicating role of the Magisterium. Under Pope John Paul II Ratzinger served as Prefect of the Sacred Congregation for the Doctrine of the faith (1981–2005). From 2005 to 2013 Ratzinger served as Pope Benedict XVI. Since his resignation, he has gone by the title "Pope Emeritus."

15. Ratzinger, *Jesus of Nazareth*, xviii–xix.

Furthermore, the Spirit continues to guide the church in its ongoing efforts to authentically interpret scripture and appropriate its redemptive and transformative meaning as the pilgrim church continues to progress along the way "until the words of God reach their complete fulfillment in her" (*DV* 8.2). Recognizing the complexity of a dynamic process by which God continues to communicate through inspired writers, redactors, and interpreters who live(d) in different and evolving contexts, makes contemporary Biblical hermeneutics a challenge in need of some guiding principles.

Ratzinger identified two interdependent principles that happen to mirror Merton's own approach. First, Ratzinger calls for "canonical exegesis" or "reading the individual texts of the Bible in the context of the whole" which "does not contradict historical critical interpretation but carries it forward in an organic way toward becoming theology in the proper sense."[16] Second, canonical exegesis is done through a "Christological hermeneutic, which sees Jesus Christ as the key to the whole and learns from Him how to understand the Bible as a unity."[17] In the same way, as O'Connell notes, Merton emphasized that "the most important principle is not to consider any particular biblical passage in isolation, for 'the mystery of love' that is the heart of the biblical message 'is gradually revealed' (*MIIS*, 40)" (*MIIS*, xxvi). Merton believed that "the Bible as a whole can and should be seen as imparting a unified, or unifiable, theological message" (*OB*, 61). The message culminates in Christ's incarnation, crucifixion, and resurrection, "in which God makes use of [our] hatred to save [us] by divine Love, of [our] ignorance to enlighten [us] with divine Truth" (*MISS*, 41). Merton argued that Christ mapped out for us how to read and interpret the Scriptures and continues to point out and to teach us how to reach deeper meanings (*MISS*, 127). Canonical exegesis guided by a Christological hermeneutic is so central to Merton's theology, and to theology today, that a particular example of it, pertinent to a theology of religious pluralism, ought now to be considered.

---

16. Ratzinger, *Jesus of Nazareth*, xix.

17. Ratzinger, *Jesus of Nazareth*, xix. The point here is that while modern exegesis helps reveal an *ascending* Christology within the early Jesus movement through the stages of (1) the earthly ministry of Jesus; (2) the "post-resurrection" and pre-composition stage of liturgical worship and proclamation; and (3) the composition stage ranging from early epistles through John's Gospel, the Canon as a whole proclaims a high descending Christology, and this Christology establishes the hermeneutic lens for subsequent reading, so theology in its "proper sense" adheres to the Faith given witness by the whole of the Canon.

Dogma, Dialogue, and Dialectics

Canonical Exegesis and John 14:6

The question regarding the possibility of salvation for non-Christians generated debate within the Catholic Church for centuries, and it still does within ecumenical or interdenominational dialogue. Often enough the debate can get reduced to interlocutors speaking past one another, simply buttressing their own positions by selectively referencing biblical passages. Those with the more universalist view might quote 1 Timothy 2:4, "God wills the salvation of all people," while those emphasizing the narrowness of the gate of heaven may favor John 14:6, "I am the way and the truth and the life. No one comes to the Father except through me." Reconciling the apparent contradiction requires a genuine exegetical effort that goes well beyond selectively referencing preferred passages.

A canonical exegesis of John 14:6 requires a reading of the totality of John and of John in light of the whole, especially Genesis. John's Gospel establishes at the outset that when Jesus speaks he is not speaking as a merely human subject, but as the incarnate Word, the divine power "though whom all things were made" and who, even whenever John's Gospel is being read, is creating, sustaining, ordering everything that exists. He *is* the Logos fully present and speaking as a friend to Thomas and Philip (John 14:1–14) but who is also and always omnipresent with God the Father the Unbegotten and Invisible. To see Jesus rightly is to see God. In one sense, nothing that exists is outside of or cut off from the Logos. Every temporal and conditional being is *already* "through him" and exists in him. Indeed, the whole context of the conversation with Philip and Thomas is "Do not be troubled." In this way, the words of Jesus are not a warning with an emphasis on a threatening "except" or "unless" but a consoling reassurance. Jesus is inviting Thomas and Philip to see that they are already with the Father in the Son. Believing in Jesus amounts to recognizing and accepting his real presence, which is omnipresence. Even face to face with Jesus, Philip did not recognize it! "Have I been with you for so long a time now and you still do not know me, Philip?" (John 14:9).

As theologians such as Cracknell and Dupuis have pointed out, a critical and contemplative reading of John permits if not requires a surprisingly expansive interpretation of 14:6 and opens the door to a positive theology of religious pluralism.[18] Ironically, the very passage often quoted to

---

18. See Cracknell, *In Good and Generous Faith*, 41–97; Dupuis, *Toward a Christian Theology of Religious Pluralism*, 281–304.

reject more permissive appraisals of the possibility of salvation becomes, through canonical exegesis, a support for the more hopeful position. The universal presence of the Word means that there is nowhere where Christ is not, and where Christ is so too the Unbegotten, and the Holy Spirit, not merely present, but always *operative*. He is with the Muslims, the Hindus and the Buddhists, even if the presence of the One who became flesh is not recognized. Philip was "through Him, with Him and in Him" and did not recognize Him, even face to face. Philip's not knowing did not change the fact. There is no doubt that Merton read John in these expansive terms, even correlating the Zen Master Hui Neng's universal presence of the Unconscious with "the Light which enlightens all human beings" from John 1:9 (*ZR*, 533; *MZM*, 40–41).[19]

Dogma, Dialogue, and Exegesis

It's not only the process of composing and compiling the Biblical text that required, as Ratzinger noted, the challenge of new situations and new experiences in order for the word to open, but the task of interpreting and appropriating the word is performed today in similarly challenging situations, and is a process by which the word gradually unfolds its meaning, already somehow present like seeds ready to take root and open up in the one who hears scripture or in the one who contemplates dogma. The insight that divine inspiration operates through a historical process applies not only to the composition and interpretation of scripture but also to the development of doctrines and dogmas and to their genuine interpretation. Historical-critical methods, which enable understanding to move forward in an organic way, impact the interpretation of scripture and the interpretation of defined doctrine. It means that there is a legitimate distinction to be drawn between the historically conditioned literary forms of scriptural texts, and the revealed truths they mediate. It brings to light the fact that the permanence of dogma pertains to its *meaning* and not to its formulation.[20]

Historically conditioned thought-forms and patterns of a particular epoch impact the expression of affirmed meanings. In order to preserve the

---

19. John 1:9 provides the hermeneutical key to *NA*, which encourages Christians to recognize the presence of the Logos in other religions, which "often reflect a ray of that truth which enlightens everyone."

20. See Lonergan, "Exegesis and Dogma." See also International Theological Commission, *Interpretation of Dogma* B.ii.2.2–3.

Dogma, Dialogue, and Dialectics

meaning intended by the original formulations, exegetical effort is needed. But the affirmed meaning of dogma is not something that can be entirely reduced to formulaic propositions. The formulation mediates a meaning that has a transcendent quality, correlative with God's own infinite intelligibility. Dogma, as formulated, *becomes* meaningful to persons through an interpretive process illuminated by religious experience and conversion. There can be insight into the meaning—an "aha" type epiphany, but the one who has it will not be able to explain exactly what she or he affirms, because what is affirmed transcends what can be completely comprehended or definitively stated. The meaning begins to be written out qualitatively in a person's life, effecting decisions and patterns of behavior. Merton was no doubt speaking of this when he described his philosophy of life as one which "consists not in statements about a truth which cannot be adequately stated, but in grace and mercy and in the realization of a new life that is in us by the gift of the Holy Spirit" (*TMR*, 17).

His study of early Christian sources and biblical hermeneutics coupled with his own inner experience left him keenly aware of the distinction to be drawn between the propositions *about* God (*fides quae*), and the *sapiential* knowledge *of* God (*fides qua*) emergent through an "experience of *the realities* of the dogmas" themselves (*CFMT*, 238). Again, however, this distinction is no separation since the mystical tradition and the dogmatic tradition form one whole (*ICM*, 15–16).[21] From the time he heard that first homily at Corpus Christi he remained Chalcedonian to the core. While *his* faith (*fides qua*) informed a developing and growing understanding of *the* faith (*fides quae*), his commitment to the faith endured because he trusted it to be true. An anecdotal aside can help to illustrate this.

Near the end of his life he engaged in a challenging epistolary exchange with a young theologian that revealed his commitment to the Christological dogmas.[22] Rosemary Radford Ruether began writing Merton in hopes of finding out whether it was possible to be a person of integrity and remain a Catholic.[23] Together they shared their struggles, at times playfully and sometimes pointedly, with what it meant to be Catholic. Merton related

21. For O'Connell's presentation of Merton's emphasis on the integration of mystical experience and doctrines, see his introduction to *ICM*, xxii–xxxiv.

22. Tardiff, *At Home in the World* (cited hereafter as *AHTW* parenthetically in the text).

23. Rereading her own letters decades later, she saw how they might have seemed like personal attacks levied at Merton, rather than what they were, artifacts of her own quest to resolve an issue of whether she, as a thinking person of faith, could be at home in such a church (*AHTW*, xv–xvii).

to the much younger Ruether as a peer and as an equal, and asked her for recommendations on what to read on the Bible and the church (*AHTW*, 17) and she referred him to Loisy, Barth, and Bonhoeffer (*AHTW*, 21). In her eyes modern exegesis revealed a fully human Jesus who did not appear to intend to found "any separate Christian religion at all, much less any institution with the structure of the Roman Catholic Church" let alone one with "the pretenses of papal infallibility" (*AHTW*, 17). In a letter to Merton from February 1967 she wrote:

> God's incarnation is not a magical new nature—this is the heresy which was condemned as monophysitism, but which we have never been able to purge out of our hellenistic souls. Incarnation, whether Jesus, the Bible, the Church, the Eucharist—this is man's word about God's Word—as God's Word it is really God-with-us. But this happens within or rather *as* words, persons, gestures, "stuff" that remains quite human, fallible, stumbling, imperfect, full of error and sin. Once we get this proper relation . . . (which ultimately means rethinking Christology all over again) . . . the historical Jesus will cease to scandalize us, not to mention church history. (*AHTW*, 19–20)

She then closed her letter by teasing Merton a bit and pushing him to ask himself "whether you want to be a Christian or not . . . to be an authentically creational, incarnate, flesh and blood man, or whether you want to be an abstraction, zen mystic" (*AHTW*, 21).

In his response dated February 14, 1967, Merton shared Ruether's irritation over exaggerated ecclesiologies that tended to ignore the all-too-human limitations that forever plagued the church. He wrote that he was rather uneasy about Catholics dictating to all the "other religions" that "we are the one authentic outfit that has the real goods" (*AHTW*, 22), but he was more cautious about a suggested need to rethink Christology. He wrote:

> What I don't know about is the Christology. I am not arguing about it. It is just that my coming into the Church was marked by a pretty strong and dazzled belief in the Christ of the Nicene Creed. One reason for this was a strong reaction against the fogginess and subjectivity and messed-up-ness of the ideas about Christ I had met with up and down in various types of Protestantism. I was tired of a Christ who had evaporated. (*AHTW*, 22)[24]

---

24. As he wrote to June J. Yungblut, "The knowledge of Jesus as a man who 'was' a Jewish mystic is to me somewhat irrelevant. That is knowledge 'about' Christ, not knowledge 'of' Christ, and not (what interests me more) knowledge 'in' Christ" (*HGL*, 643).

Dogma, Dialogue, and Dialectics

It is incumbent upon any theologian to think about Christology, but Merton is reticent here about any rethinking that would undo or erode either side of Chalcedon's paradoxical affirmation. The formulas reveal the mystery they affirm; they do not resolve it. Implicit in Merton's words to Ruether is the idea that a rejection of monophysitism, though absolutely necessary and meant to *affirm* the humanity of Jesus, cannot amount to a rejection of his divinity. So too, the rejection of subordinationism, meant to affirm the full divinity of Jesus, cannot amount to a denial of his full humanity. The lion roars in both directions, against monophysitism and against all shades of subordinationism. Rather than reading the formulas as positive propositions *about* God, Merton read them as apophatic denials that, if taken seriously, could facilitate an encounter with the living God.

Later in his letter he responded to Ruether's suggestion that he might prefer to become "an abstraction—zen mystic" rather than an incarnational Christian. He wrote: "About Zen: not abstract at all the way I see it. I use it for idol cracking and things like that" (*AHTW*, 24).[25] Zen was for him a way to cultivate an intellectual humility that, as O'Connor said of dogma, "preserves mystery for the human mind."

St. John Henry Newman[26] wrote:

> a believer is sure, and nothing shall make him [or her] doubt that if anything seems to be proved . . . in contradiction to the dogmas of faith, that point will eventually turn out, first, *not* to be proved, or secondly, not *contradictory*, or thirdly, not contradictory to anything *really revealed*, but to something that has been confused with revelation.[27]

Newman was writing in response to geological discoveries indicating the earth was much older that what the Biblical authors knew, and in the

---

25. This letter is also available in *HGL*, 500–501.

26. Merton initially appreciated Newman for the role he played in mentoring Gerard Manley Hopkins through the poet's conversion (*SSM*, 235–36), but as a young monk he did not connect with the Cardinal as a theologian writing: "he is completely alien to me" (*ES*, 79). Later, however, when Merton was going through his own struggles with his religious superiors, he began to admire Newman's dignity and patience as an "inexhaustibly important" model for how to endure trials with ecclesiastical authority (*DWL*, 266). He eventually came to admire Newman's work and found in him a friend whose theology was like a music that spoke directly to his heart and drew him into consonance with God (*CGB*, 188).

27. Newman, *Idea of a University*, 422, italics added (originally published in 1891).

context of a widening acceptance of evolutionary theory.[28] Since Newman trusted the dogmas to be true, he knew that they could not truthfully be contradicted. Yet if something that *seemed* to contradict them were to be proven true, then the relation between what had been proven and what had been revealed had to be reconsidered. The contradiction, upon further examination, would turn out to be apparent, not actual, in which case a higher interpretive synthesis would be possible. If, on the other hand, the contradiction turned out to be actual, then the believer had misunderstood what had been revealed, or had uncritically conflated *obiter dicta* with divine revelation.[29] Newman's imaginative and interpretive approach to the exegesis of dogma recognized both the impermanence and imperfection of human understanding and the security of an enduring truth that must be incessantly re-appropriated by ever-evolving persons of faith within ever changing contexts. Newman's statement above, though originally proposed in relation to the dialogue of faith and science in the context of a university, has translatable relevance for interreligious dialogue and provides insight into Merton's own approach to it.

Merton believed that dogmas are divinely revealed truths. This meant that the contradictions he encountered in his interreligious dialogues were not a source of anxiety and fear but of curiosity and hope. If another person's religious belief contradicted his dogma, he did not worry about *the truth* of dogma, but did begin to wonder if what seemed to be contradictory would turn out, on further examination, not to be so. Furthermore, because he had already learned not to be idolatrous of his own views, he was willing to wonder if he had not perhaps confused his own limited or even faulty understanding of what had been revealed with what had actually been revealed; or if he had taken an *obiter dictum* of non-binding tradition for what had been really revealed. He was willing to be patient, not forceful, and eager to affirm where he could and resist or object where he felt he must.[30]

Merton's faithful commitment to the truth of dogma, which really exemplified his iconoclastic spirit, was not a hindrance but a benefit

---

28. Charles Darwin published *On the Origin of Species* in 1859.

29. Newman believed that the inerrancy of the Bible pertained to its material purpose of salvation and did not extend to the incidental references (*obiter dicta*) that reflected the common-sense views of the world held by the inspired human authors. See Newman, "On the Inspiration of Scripture."

30. As William Apel noted, "Merton never became defensive" in his dialogues: "This hopefully allowed for him to say his 'yes' and his 'no' without fear of jeopardizing the relationship" (Apel, "How to Disagree," 21).

impacting his approach to interreligious dialogue. Ryan Scruggs, for example, perceptively pointed out that the ancient definition of theology as "faith *seeking* understanding" identified Merton's *position* and *purpose* in relation to interreligious dialogue. He wrote: "by recognizing the distance between faith and full knowledge [Merton was] free to seek an understanding of the truth of faith in dialogue with the other and to rejoice in the transformation that new understanding brings."[31]

Merton was not, then, a "pluralist" in the sense of being one who has "assessed as equally valid despite their being different" the world's religions.[32] Such a judgment seems to require a "super-look" by which one can stand outside his or her own tradition, and above all the traditions, and render a universal judgment regarding them all. Absent such a naive realism it would require several lifetimes' worth of attentive and intelligent learning to reasonably render any judgment regarding *all* the religions. He was, however, an advocate of religious plurality because he believed he had found genuine knowledge of God among people who identified themselves with *many* religions, believed that their knowledge was not arrived at independently of their religiously committed lives, and discovered that he could learn from them in ways that enriched his own understanding. In other words, by going deep within his own tradition he found a heuristic openness by which he could discern and affirm the gifts of the Spirit operative, and the fruits of the Spirit manifest, in the lives of non-Christians who had been positively formed within and by their own traditions.[33] This is the case

---

31. Scruggs, "Faith Seeking Understanding," 2. In the same piece Scruggs also explores Barth's influence on Merton and he notes a discrepancy between Barth's objective and *authoritative* perspective on Biblical faith versus Merton's *intuitive* perspective which includes emphasis on religious experience. I would treat that same discrepancy in terms of Merton's emphasis on *fides qua* as a resource and guide informing intelligence on the road to understanding the affirmed *fides quae*.

32. Perry Schmidt-Leukel writes: "'Religious Pluralism' designates a specific theory and evaluation of religious diversity. This theory first assumes that religious truth exists—and in a sense must exist—in a diversity of forms, which are then assessed as equally valid despite their being different" (Schmidt-Leukel, *Religious Pluralism and Interreligious Theology*, 1). Merton never makes a final judgment that the religions are "equally valid," which would seem enormously presumptive given his dedication to *the lion's roar*, but he was eager to discover the one truth "shining out in all its various manifestations" (*CWA*, 206) insofar as that were possible from within his very specific and rich tradition.

33. He could extend this to include non-believers too, who could no longer identify themselves with the traditions that had shaped them. For example, he found profound spiritual wisdom in the writings of "non-believers" such as Albert Camus and Erich Fromm.

Opening New Horizons

with Suzuki, and with many of the ancient Zen Masters he learned about from reading Suzuki and conversing with him.

3

The Dialogue with Dr. D. T. Suzuki

MERTON HAD INDICATED HIS interest in Zen as early as 1938, and began a more intentional study in the early 1950s, but it wasn't until 1955, when he wrote James Laughlin to ask him to send whatever books he could find by Suzuki, that he would settle on a Sensei.[1] That he sought out Suzuki to

1. Cooper, *Selected Letters*, 108.

serve as his teacher is not surprising since no one else in Japan writing on Zen at the time was half as prolific in a language accessible to Merton. In addition to "nearly ninety titles in Japanese," Suzuki published "over thirty volumes in English."[2] The basic message of non-duality, approached from different angles and considered under different aspects remained the same, but Suzuki found it "inexhaustibly new with each new book" and made it so for Merton (*ZBA*, 65).[3]

It is difficult to overestimate Suzuki's role as a harbinger of Zen to the West. Martin Heidegger, referring to D. T. Suzuki's work, is reported to have said, "If I understand this man correctly, this is what I have been trying to say in all my writings."[4] Masao Abe credited Suzuki with "sparking a radical change in Western ways of thinking." The fundamental message of Suzuki's work, Abe claimed, was to return "to the basic experience prior to the dichotomy between subject and object, being and non-being, life and death, good and evil—in order to awaken to the most concrete basis for life and the world."[5] Abe clarified that Suzuki's emphasis on this experience of a primordial unity existing prior to and beyond the "separation between self and other, subject and object, man and God" does not exclude the subjective operations of consciousness that think, analyze and discriminate, "but gives the proper foundation to them and makes them alive and energetic."[6] Suzuki's obsession with an experiential unity that precedes and transcends, but does not destroy the world characterized by diversity and multiplicity, becomes the focus of their dialogue.

2. Abe, *Zen Life*, xv.

3. Merton's library at the hermitage contained eleven of Suzuki's books. Jonathan Montaldo, former director of the Thomas Merton Studies Center at Bellarmine University, informed me that some of these eleven books were found by monks of Gethsemani in their common library with Merton's marginalia. Some are now available online (see Thomas Merton Center, "Thomas Merton's Marginalia"). Montaldo also suggested that Merton could well have read more by Suzuki than these eleven books because Merton often used inter-library loan. The eleven books by D. T. Suzuki in "Merton's library" are *An Introduction to Zen Buddhism*; *Essays in Zen Buddhism, First Series*; *Essays in Zen Buddhism, Second Series*; *Essays in Zen Buddhism, Third Series*; *Manual of Zen Buddhism*; *Studies in Zen*; *The Training of the Zen Buddhist Monk*; *The Zen Doctrine of No-Mind*; *Zen Buddhism: Selected Writings of D. T. Suzuki*, edited by William Barrett; *Zen and Japanese Buddhism*; and *Zen and Japanese Culture*. Thomas Merton Center, "Books Cited by Merton," has references in Merton's journals and letters to Suzuki books.

4. Barrett makes this claim in his introduction, "Zen for the West," in Suzuki, *Zen Buddhism*, xi.

5. Abe, *Zen Life*, xv.

6. Abe, *Zen Life*, xvi.

The Dialogue with Dr. D. T. Suzuki

Robert E. Daggy suggested that the most comprehensive picture of the dialogue between Merton and Suzuki could be gleaned from three primary sources: Daggy's collection of the Merton/Suzuki letters,[7] Merton's essay "D. T. Suzuki: The Man and His Work," and "Wisdom in Emptiness: A Dialogue by Daisetz T. Suzuki and Thomas Merton" (*Encounter*, xviii–xix).[8] These materials help to create the picture of the dialogue that I offer in this chapter.[9] I generally withhold my own commentary and interpretations regarding their dialogue and save them for my analysis in the following chapters.

Merton initiated his written correspondence with Suzuki while he was working on a compilation of sayings of the Egyptian desert monks and hermits of the fourth century. Preparing the manuscript, he was struck by similarities he found in the *verba seniorum* and the sayings of many Zen masters. By this time Merton had been reading Zen literature quite steadily for several years. He decided to write Suzuki and ask him if he would write an introduction to what would later be published as *The Wisdom of the Desert*.[10]

Merton Makes Contact

On March 12, 1959, Merton wrote to Suzuki and began his letter by confessing his ignorance of Zen and claiming very little knowledge of Christianity.[11] He then wrote:

---

7. Robert E. Daggy compiled a collection of extent letters between Merton and Suzuki as well as Merton's journal entries relating to the Merton and Suzuki meeting in New York in 1964 as *Encounter: Thomas Merton and D. T. Suzuki* (cited hereafter as *Encounter* parenthetically in the text).

8. Merton, "D. T. Suzuki: The Man and His Work," first appeared in Japan in *Eastern Buddhist* 11 in 1967; and "Wisdom in Emptiness" (which is comprised of a "Prefatory Note" by Merton; "Knowledge and Innocence" by Suzuki; "The Recovery of Paradise" by Merton; and "Final Remarks" by both Suzuki and Merton) first appeared in *New Directions in Prose and Poetry* 17 in 1961.

9. The Merton/Suzuki dialogue is discussed in topical and summative fashion by Park, *Thomas Merton's Encounter with Buddhism and Beyond*, 76–83. Lipsey provides an astute analysis of their relationship, including some of their correspondence, in his essay "Merton, Suzuki, Zen, Ink," in Thurston, *Merton & Buddhism*, 137–75. See also Zyniewicz, *Interreligious Dialogue between Thomas Merton and D. T. Suzuki*.

10. Suzuki's introduction was prohibited by the censors of the order from inclusion in *WD*, but it would eventually be published in *Wisdom in Emptiness* and later in *ZBA*. See *TME*, 535; *CT*, 128.

11. He approached his elder as a disciple does a master, and their whole conversation

All I know is that when I read your books—and I have read many of them—and above all when I read English versions of the little verses in which the Zen Masters point their finger to something which flashed out at the time, I feel a profound and intimate agreement. Time after time, as I read your pages, something in me says "That's it!" Don't ask me what. I have no desire to explain it. . . . I have my own way to walk and for some reason or other Zen is right in the middle of it wherever I go. So there it is, with all its beautiful purposelessness, and it has become very familiar to me though I do not know "what it is." Or even if it is an "it." . . . I'll simply say that it seems to me that Zen is the very atmosphere of the Gospels, and the Gospels are bursting with it. It is the proper climate for any monk, no matter what kind of monk he may be. If I could not breathe Zen I would probably die of spiritual asphyxiation. But I still don't know what it is. No matter. I don't know what the air is either. (*Encounter*, 5–6; *HGL*, 561)

Suzuki Replies

Dr. Suzuki responded enthusiastically on March 31, 1959, by inviting Merton to send his manuscript on the sayings of the desert elders. Suzuki acknowledged that the temperament, insight, and detachment expressed in some of the writings reminded him too of "stories told in the annals of Zen" (*Encounter*, 11). However, Suzuki also warned that:

Zen is misunderstood by American and European writers in various ways. To grasp Zen thoroughly a certain course of discipline is needed along with the reading knowledge of Japanese and Chinese literature on the subject. While Zen abhors bookishness, the masters have not neglected writing book after book and talking one thing after another. (*Encounter*, 12)[12]

Suzuki ended his letter by sharing some of his own judgments concerning Christianity that he listed as follows: "We have never been driven out of

---

would become a mondo.

12. With the benefit of hindsight it is not difficult to see the irony in Suzuki's statement here. Whatever misunderstanding there was of Zen in the "West" was due, at least in part, to his own work. Suzuki would later be criticized by Robert Sharf and John P. Keenan for neglecting to emphasize the very features that Suzuki says here are necessary to appreciate in order to get a sufficient grasp of Zen. See Sharf, "Zen of Japanese Nationalism"; Keenan, "Limits of Thomas Merton's Understanding of Buddhism."

Eden; We still retain our innocence; We are innocent just because of our sinfulness; Paradise and original sin are not contradictory; God wanted to know himself, hence the creation; When we know ourselves we know God; etc. etc." (*Encounter*, 13).

Merton to Suzuki

The apparent paradoxes concluding Suzuki's letter especially excited Merton and the letter in general inspired his desire to discover to what degree he and Suzuki understood one another, though he supposed that they understood each other quite well. Merton's reply of April 11, 1959, is long (eight pages in *Encounter* and four pages in *HGL*). Merton wrote:

> We in the west are always ready to talk about things like Zen and about a-hundred-and-one other things besides, but we are not so eager to do the things that Zen implies: and that is what really counts. . . . At the moment, I occasionally meet my own kind of Zen master, in passing, and for a brief moment. For example, the other day a bluebird sitting on a fence post suddenly took off after a wasp, dived for it, missed, and instantly returned to the same position on the fence post as if nothing had ever happened. A brief, split second lesson in Zen. . . . The birds never stop to say "I missed" because, in fact, whether they catch the wasp or not they never miss, and neither does Zen. (*Encounter* 18; *HGL*, 563)

After thanking Suzuki for his "deeply moving and profoundly true intuitions on Christianity" and referring Suzuki to his own and others' works that deal specifically with some of the ideas Suzuki expressed in his letter, Merton shares his own insights and convictions about the new creation in Christ that further affirm Suzuki's paradoxical assertions. Merton wrote:

> In Christ the world and the whole cosmos has been created anew. . . . The whole world has risen in Christ, say the Fathers. If God is "all in all" then everything is, in fact, paradise because it is filled with the glory and presence of God, and nothing is anymore separated from God. Then comes the question whether or not the resurrection of Christ shows that we had never really been separated from Him in the first place. Was it only that we *thought* we were separated from Him? But that thought was a conviction so great and so strong that it amounted to separation. It was a thought that each one of us had to be god in his own right. . . . Each one slaved in the service of his own idol—his consciously fabricated

social self. Each one then pushed all the others away from himself, and down, beneath himself: or tried to. This is original sin. In this sense, original sin and paradise are directly opposed. In this sense there is exclusion from Paradise. But yet we are in paradise, and once we break free from the false image, we find ourselves what we are: and we are "in Christ." . . . But Christ Himself is in us as unknown and unseen. We follow Him, we find Him (it is like the cow-catching pictures)[13] and then He must vanish and we must go along without Him at our side, why? Because He is even closer than that. He is our self. O my dear Dr. Suzuki I know you will understand this so well, and so many people do not, even though they are "doctors in Israel." (*Encounter,* 20–21; *HGL,* 564)

He goes on then to warn Suzuki that if he wants to write about Christianity he should beware of the "theological watchdogs" who will hound him if he tries to speak in any sense definitively about Christian doctrine.

Merton then acknowledges that his own understanding of Zen is enriched by the Christian doctrine of grace. He sees relations between the qualities of Zen koans as they are generative of insight and Christian sacraments as they are efficacious for salvation, between the breakthrough of Zen awakening and the gift of divine life that erupts in freedom and indeterminacy as the offer of salvation (*Encounter,* 22–23; *HGL,* 565).

Merton ends his letter in a search for reconciliation of a different sort. Lamenting the tragedies of Hiroshima and Nagasaki, he apologizes on behalf of the Christian tradition for a history of mission work and theory riddled with bias and oversight from which no part of Asia had been spared:

> If I wept until the end of the world I could not signify enough what this tragedy is. If only we had thought of coming to you to *learn* something. . . . If only we had thought of coming to you and loving you for what you are in yourselves, instead of trying to make you over into our own image and likeness.[14] For, to me it is clearly

13. Merton is referring here to the "Ten Stages of Spiritual Cow-herding" that Suzuki interprets in his *Essays in Zen Buddhism, First Series,* 363–76. Johnston also discusses the ox-herding pictures in *Silent Music,* 80–81; *Inner Eye of Love,* 113–14. See also Park, "Christian Contemplative Approach."

14. The sentiments Merton is expressing here shaped his ecclesiology and his notions of evangelization. Sharing the Gospel, for him, could never be aimed at the goal of making others into some conventional image of a Christian, a goal he regarded as a form of cultural imperialism. Furthermore, he was convinced that the Church of Christ, both visible and invisible, was made up of those who "with all their deficiencies and limitations, seek only truth and love, as best they can" regardless of their "official" religious or non-religious standing. See his letter to Doña Louisa Coomaraswamy (*HGL,* 132–33)

The Dialogue with Dr. D. T. Suzuki

evident that you and I have in common and share more intimately precisely that which, in the eyes of conventional westerners, would seem to separate us. The fact that you are a Zen Buddhist and I am a Christian monk far from separating us makes us most like one another. (*Encounter*, 24; *HGL*, 566)

During the summer of 1959 Merton continued his study of Zen. He considered another koan that asked, "what is the power with which a lion seizes its prey?" He thought "sincerity, or non-deception," total and un-self-consciously focused action. He wrote in his journal: "I find it, by intuition, related to Christ's words . . . 'Do not think of how to speak or what to say. It will be given you in that hour what to say.' . . . I have the seeds of it, but I do not let them grow. I begin to want to assure people of my sincerity, and then I deceive myself. And, of course, I am trying to deceive them—that I am sincere" (*SFS*, 292).

While Merton crunched on koans at Gethsemani, Suzuki had been attending the Third Conference of East-West Philosophers in Honolulu, Hawaii. Partly due to this, and perhaps to his advanced age (Suzuki was eighty-nine years old at this point), five months passed before he responded to Merton's letter. On September 25, 1959, Suzuki replied briefly, keeping to the business of questions concerning the preface to Merton's book that he was writing. Two more letters to Merton follow that remain on the level of practical considerations concerning the length of the preface, and the date by which it ought to be submitted (*Encounter*, 27–35).

The conference in Hawaii had made Suzuki more aware of Western misunderstandings of Zen, especially regarding questions of morality. Suzuki became concerned with clarifying that Zen was not about condoning moral relativism under the guise of spiritual freedom from conventional norms, and he was disturbed that so many Westerners, whether they were attracted to Zen or repulsed by it, were understanding it thus. The preface to Merton's book became an avenue to address this issue for a Western audience, and so the manuscript he sent Merton dealt largely with the Zen Buddhist take on the dynamic of freedom and responsibility. Yet Suzuki's presentation is novel and he uses the Genesis narrative of the Fall of Adam and Eve to elucidate points concerning a Zen morality.

---

and his essay "A Letter to Pablo Antonio Cuadra concerning Giants" (*SE*, 113–26).

Opening New Horizons

Suzuki's Preface

Near the beginning of "Knowledge and Innocence" Suzuki shared with his readers a question posed to him at the conference in Hawaii. In the paper Suzuki presented at the conference he stated: "All the moral values and social practice come out of this life of Suchness which is Emptiness" (*ZBA*, 104). One of the participants at the conference asked: "If this is so, then 'good' and 'evil' are secondary differentiations. What differentiates them and how do I know what is 'good' other than 'evil'? In other words, can I—and if so, how can I—derive an ethics from the ontology of Zen Buddhism?" (*ZBA*, 104).

Suzuki takes up this question in part one of his essay as a point of departure for elucidating a Zen-Buddhist "ethics." He then explained Zen "ethics" in the light of the Christian understanding of Adam and Eve's innocence before the fall, and the Desert Fathers' quest for a post-lapsarian recovery of Paradise. He emphasized that although the practitioner of Zen must be concerned with social and ethical values, his/her primary concern is with the recovery of "innocence" through the interior life.[15]

> [The Zen person] wants to have the heart thoroughly cleansed of all impurities issuing from "Knowledge" which we acquired by eating the fruit of the forbidden tree. When we return to the state of "Innocence" anything we do is good. St. Augustine says, "Love God and do as you will."[16] The Buddhist idea of *Anabhoga Carya* corresponds to Innocence. When Knowledge is awakened in the Garden of Eden where Innocence prevails, the differentiation of good and evil takes place. In the same way, out of the Emptiness of the Mind a thought mysteriously rises and we have the world of multiplicities. The Judeo-Christian idea of Innocence is the moral interpretation of the Buddhist doctrine of Emptiness. (*ZBA*, 104)

---

15. Throughout this essay, Suzuki identifies the Christian ideas of "Knowledge" and "Innocence" with the Buddhist ideas of "Ignorance" and "Emptiness." For Suzuki, Christian "Knowledge" (of good and evil) and Buddhist "Ignorance" or *avidya* refer to a "fallen state" in which Christian "Innocence" and Buddhist "Emptiness" or "the original light of suchness" is lost or obscured in some sense. The acquisition of "knowledge" in this sense means falling into a falsely dichotomous or dualistic frame of mind (*ZBA*, 105). Merton describes *avidya* as an "invincible error" causing one to "treat the ego as an absolute and central reality and refer all things to it as objects of desire or repulsion" (*ZBA*, 82). Merton also brings the concept of *avidya* into his consideration of ignorance in relation to Guigo the Carthusian and St. Bernard in *CFMT*, 82, 109.

16. Merton refers to the same line from Augustine in *CF*, 112; *ICM*, 160.

The Dialogue with Dr. D. T. Suzuki

Suzuki contrasts Innocence with Knowledge only to establish them in proper relation to one another. From one point of view Knowledge and Innocence appear in oppositional conflict, but Suzuki suggests that their relation is actually of a different sort. So our task is to "have a thoroughly penetrating insight into the relationship between the two"(*ZBA*, 105). Suzuki explains:

> The so-called opposition between Innocence and knowledge . . . is not the kind of opposition we see between black and white, good and evil, right and wrong. . . . The opposition is, as it were, between container and the contained, between the background and the stage, between the field and the players moving on it. . . . It is like the rain that falls on the just and the unjust. It is like the sun rising on the good and on the evil, on your foes and on your friends. (*ZBA*, 106)[17]

Zen practice aims at recovering the "inner goodness" of Innocence out of which we can operate authentically in the world of Knowledge, which requires a discerning and discriminating mind. For Suzuki it is a matter of becoming free from "self," "for all evils and defilements start from our attachment to it" (*ZBA*, 109). It is through liberation from the "self" that one begins to act out of "suchness" or "emptiness" un-self-consciously. *Anabhoga Carya*, which Suzuki translates as "effortless action" or "no striving" act, names the realization of authenticity.[18] Suzuki then uses examples from the stories of the Desert Fathers and quotations from Meister Eckhart to further illustrate and support his basic insights.

Using the proper relation between Knowledge and Innocence as a hermeneutical tool Suzuki makes ethical evaluations. If one sets Innocence and Knowledge up in contradictory opposition, one ends up with the legalistic enslavement to an ungrounded "knowledge" on the one hand, or the misguided license of a false "innocence" on the other. Knowledge without Innocence is the fallen state of alienation from the ground of one's being. Innocence without knowledge is illusory; it is the quietism of

---

17. Suzuki implies that "black and white, good and evil" may be legitimate *contradictory* oppositions, but argues that the opposition between innocence and knowledge is not of this sort. To put this in Lonerganian terms, Suzuki is suggesting that from the standpoint of a recovered paradise consciousness, the opposition between knowledge and innocence ceases to be regarded as *contradictory* and begins to be regarded as *genetic* in that Innocence is a pre-condition that gives rise to knowledge, but knowledge now, instead of eliminating innocence, includes it.

18. Suzuki refers readers to his *Lankavatara Sutra*, 32, 43, 89.

empty-headedness, or the reversion to infancy. The proper relation of the two leads to mindfulness and wisdom, or *prajna*. But even in the recognition of their complementarity, the responsibility of realizing the balance between the two falls on the acting subject. Suzuki sees the story of the "great hermit" as an example of a failure to maintain the balance.[19]

> The "great hermit" is guilty of not realizing Emptiness, that is, Innocence, and Abbot Poemen commits an error in applying Innocence minus knowledge to the affairs of the world. The robbers are to be consigned to prison, for the community will suffer; as long as they are outlaws they must be deprived of their liberty. (*ZBA*, 107–8)

Whereas in part one of his essay Suzuki focused on the relation of Buddhist Emptiness to Christian Innocence, in part two he discusses it in relation to poverty. He begins, "The metaphysical concept of Emptiness is convertible in economic terms into poverty, being poor, having nothing: 'Blessed are those who are poor in spirit'" (*ZBA*, 108–9). Suzuki spends the remainder of part two attempting to convey the utterly radical nature of the kind of poverty he is talking about. It is a poverty so great that there remains no-self to be poor, or to be proud of one's spiritual emptiness. In order to communicate this idea he draws on the sayings of some Zen masters, but he ends the second part with a quotation from Eckhart:

> If it is the case that a man is emptied of things, creatures, himself, and God, and if God could find a place in him to act, then we say: as long as that (place) exists, this man is not poor with the most intimate poverty (*eigentlichste Armut*). For God does not intend that man shall have a place reserved for him to work in, since the true poverty of spirit requires that man shall be emptied of God and all his works, so that if God wants to act in the soul, he himself must be the place in which he acts—and that he would like to do. (*ZBA*, 110)

---

19. The "great hermit" was attacked by robbers and when other hermits heard his cries they rescued him and marched the robbers off to jail. "But then the brothers were very ashamed." They went to Abbot Poemen for counsel and he said: "Remember who carried out the first betrayal, and you will learn the reason for the second. Unless you had been betrayed by your own inward thoughts you would never have ended by turning those men over to the judge." The hermit who had been attacked, "touched by these words, got up at once and went into the city and broke open the jail, letting out the robbers and freeing them from torture" (See *WD*, xxxvii, 38).

The Dialogue with Dr. D. T. Suzuki

Finally, in the third part of his essay, Suzuki discusses the virtues a Buddhist attempts to actualize. "They are: (1) *Dana*, 'giving'; (2) *Sila*, 'observing the precepts'; (3) *Virya*, 'spirit of manhood'; (4) *Ksanti*, 'humility' or 'patience'; (5) *Dhyana*, 'meditation'; and (6) *Prajna*, 'transcendental wisdom'" (ZBA, 111–12). He clarifies that each of these virtues is fundamentally related to the others. Although *Prajna* is most commonly considered the goal of practice, it is also the basis of authentic practice itself. So the "Paramita moves in a circle with no beginning and no ending. The giving is possible only when there is Emptiness and Emptiness is attainable only when the giving is unconditionally carried out" (*ZBA*, 112). Suzuki relates *Dana* to *Prajna* citing these words of Eckhart:

> St. Peter said, "We have left all things." St. James said, "we have given up all things." St. John said "we have nothing left." Whereupon Brother Eckhart asks, When do we leave all things? When we leave everything conceivable, everything expressible, everything audible, everything visible, then and then only we give up all things. When in this sense we give up all, we grow aflood with light passing bright with God. (ZBA, 113)

Suzuki then develops the idea of *Dana* as a kind of total giving unto death, a spiritual death. He cites a seventeenth-century poem by the Zen-master Bunan Zenji:

> While alive, be dead
> thoroughly dead—
> All is good then,
> Whatever you may do. (ZBA, 113)

However, he is careful to make one final point that he emphasizes as the goal of all Zen training. And that is to get beyond the possibility of "a distorted interpretation of the experience" of enlightenment. In other words, when a person experiences enlightenment in the break-through of satori, "the Zen Master ... will tell us to transcend or 'to cast away' the experience itself—to be absolutely naked.... Then and only then do we find ourselves to be the ordinary Toms, Dicks, and Harrys we had been all along" (*ZBA*, 114).

Suzuki concludes "Knowledge and Innocence" with the suggestion that the gravest question that faces modern humans is "how to actualize the transcendental wisdom of *Prajna* in a world where the growth of Knowledge is everywhere encouraged in a thousand and one ways" (*ZBA*, 115). And he suggests that both Buddhist and Christian monks seek the solution by cultivating the virtues of "poverty, tribulation, discretion, obedience, humility, not-judging others, meditation, silence," and he suggests that the most fundamental is poverty. "Poverty corresponds ontologically to Emptiness and psychologically to selflessness or Innocence" (*ZBA*, 115).

Merton Responds

On October 24, 1959, Merton writes Suzuki after having received the latter's proposed preface.

> Your commentary is excellent, but I am convinced that most readers will have no grasp of its real and intimate relation to the Desert Fathers, and will think it is a rather "unrelated" excursus on Zen. ... Hence, in order that they may grasp the import of your distinction between innocence and knowledge, which is so fundamental for the Desert Fathers and for ancient Christian tradition, I will absolutely have to bring to light some clear Christian texts which show conclusively that what you are saying really belongs to the authentic Christian tradition and is not merely something that you, as a Buddhist, have read into it through Eckhart. Your use of Eckhart, of course, puts the whole study on a much more sophisticated level than the Desert Fathers sayings originally suggest. (*Encounter*, 40)[20]

In response to his own concern for Suzuki's material to be received openly, and understood correctly, Merton writes his "Prefatory Note" and his essay "The Recovery of Paradise" that later become, along with Suzuki's "Knowledge and Innocence," parts that make up "Wisdom in Emptiness" in *ZBA*.

However, Merton takes issue with Suzuki's interpretation of the story of the great hermit.

> I particularly value your astute remarks about the necessity of combining spiritual ("recovered") innocence with a kind of practical, matter-of-fact acceptance of our necessity to deal with good and evil ... and your observations about the failure of some of the Desert Fathers to combine them is very illuminating. I am grateful for this insight. ... However, I do think that you are unjust to the "great hermit." What had happened was that the monks failed to do what your Zen hermit did quite properly when he helped the robber with the ladder. These monks being "sick" with attachment

---

20. For O'Connell's concise overview of Merton's evolving attitude toward Eckhart, from mild, almost ambivalent, admiration to enthusiastic embrace, see *ICM*, xliii–xlv.

to self and with fixation on their own proprietorship and security, had seized the robbers with anger and turned them over to the police—and thus put them in danger of torture.... Now behind the action of the "great hermit" in liberating the robbers is the deep truth that the violence, attachment, and sickness of the righteous is what causes, to a great extent, the delinquency of the unrighteous.... This does not mean that laws ought not to be enforced, but it means that the obligations and responsibilities of the ones who make and enforce the laws are beyond all comparison with what is actually thought. (*Encounter*, 41–42)[21]

However, Merton goes on to say: "I believe I understand why you insisted on this point—that robbers should go to jail—because America is now full of people who think that Zen is mere yielding to irrational impulses, and who do not know the difference between satori and being dead drunk" (*Encounter*, 42).[22]

In *ZBA*, however, Merton suggests that perhaps Suzuki's reading of the "great hermit" is distorted by a preoccupation with his desire to dispel the misconceptions that Zen advocates a kind of moral chaos. In his "Prefatory Note" Merton recognizes that "Zen is at present most fashionable in America among those who are least concerned with moral discipline" (*ZBA*, 101). Knowing that Suzuki is well aware of this, in "The Recovery of Paradise" Merton writes: "I am tempted to wonder if there is not, in this reaction of his, a touch of what might be called 'overcompensation'" (*ZBA*, 121). Merton ends his letter thanking Suzuki for his "admirable study ... by which I hope to profit spiritually in many ways." Merton tells Suzuki, "I shall send you a copy of whatever I write further on the subject" (*Encounter*, 44).

---

21. This is a more candid and nascent version of his interpretation of the "great hermit" found in *ZBA*, 122. Merton's own reading of the parable evokes the third chapter of the *Daodejing* (or *Tao te Ching*), where the sage opines: "Not praising the deserving prevents envy. Not valuing possessions prevents theft. Not displaying what is desirable prevents confusion of the senses."

22. Merton never mentions who these people are, but he likely has in mind the beat writers Allen Ginsberg and Jack Kerouac who were interested in Zen in the mid-to-late 1950s and who were well known for their "licentious" living. Kerouac's *Dharma Bums* was published by Viking Press in 1958 and it chronicled, in slightly fictionalized fashion, the exploits of these "Zen Buddhists."

Opening New Horizons
Recovery of Paradise

"The Recovery of Paradise" (*ZBA*, 116–33) is Merton's response to "Knowledge and Innocence" and a careful attempt to further elucidate, along with Suzuki, the points of convergence and divergence between the spiritual wisdom of the Desert Fathers and Zen Buddhism. But Suzuki's use of Eckhart has moved the discussion well beyond the *Verba Seniorum* into the more fundamental dialogue concerning Buddhist Emptiness and Christian "Paradise" consciousness. So Merton, following Suzuki, reaches into the writings of later Christians to further develop the dialogue.

"We do not understand that life is paradise, for it suffices only to wish to understand it, and at once paradise will appear in front of us in its beauty." Merton begins by referring to these words of Zosima, a character in Dostoyevski's *The Brothers Karamazov*, in order to suggest that this is precisely what motivated early Christians to enter deserts. They were inspired "by the hope that by so doing they might return to paradise" (*ZBA*, 116). However, Merton first takes care to distinguish paradise from heaven. He writes: "Paradise is not 'heaven.' Paradise is a state, or indeed a place, on earth. Paradise belongs more properly to the present than to the future life. . . . It is the state in which man was originally created to live on earth. It is also conceived as a kind of antechamber to heaven after death—as for instance at the end of Dante's *Purgatorio*" (*ZBA*, 116).

While Merton is intent here on keeping paradise distinct from heaven, it seems odd that he does not even acknowledge that Dante's treatment of heaven in *The Divine Comedy* is called, *Paradiso*. Still, in and through the transformative power of Christ humans can recover paradise. Merton writes: "In the beginning Adam was 'one man.' The fall had divided him into 'a multitude.' Christ had restored man to unity in Himself. Christ was the 'New Adam' and in Him all men could return to unity, to innocence, to purity and become 'one man.' *Omnes in Christo unum*"(*ZBA*, 117). But the recovery of this lost unity requires the individual to die with Christ "to his 'old man,' his exterior, egotistical self, and [rise] in Christ to the new man" (*ZBA*, 117).

Where Suzuki had employed the Genesis account of The Fall to demonstrate that "good and evil" are indeed "secondary differentiations," Merton communicates the Patristic understanding of "the Fall" as a support to Suzuki's argument.[23] He writes:

---

23. See *TME*, 153–54, 349–51, for the entries on "Fall" and "Paradise."

The Dialogue with Dr. D. T. Suzuki

> First of all, the state in which man is created is one of un-self-conscious "reaching out" to what is . . . higher than himself, but nevertheless intimately present within his own being, so that he himself is hidden in God and united with him. . . . The knowledge of good and evil begins with the fruition of sensible and temporal things *for their own sakes*, an act which makes the soul conscious of itself, and centers in on its own pleasure. It becomes aware of what is good and evil "for itself." As soon as this takes place, there is a complete change of perspective, and from unity or wisdom (identified with emptiness and purity) the soul now enters into a state of dualism. It is now aware of both itself and God, as separated beings. It now sees God as an object of desire or of fear, and is no longer lost in Him as in a transcendent subject. (*ZBA*, 126–27, italics added)

Merton suggests that the Augustinian interpretation of St. Paul's dictum, *scientia inflat*, applies to this fallen state. It is in the fallen state that emptiness is lost in an illusory fullness which is only the false self having become full of itself, "puffed up" with a knowledge of its own "fictional substantiality" (*ZBA*, 128).

Throughout his essay Merton contrasted the fallen state of knowledge to the wisdom born of emptiness, poverty, and purity of heart. But Suzuki's radical interpretation of Innocence, supported by Eckhart, seemed to him to amount to a denial of distinctions altogether, even between God and human beings (a kind of innocence without knowledge).[24] By relying on the Christian concept of purity of heart, as it is discussed in the works of John of the Cross and John Cassian, Merton maintains the distinction between God and human beings in his own essay. The self, for Merton, whether illusory or authentic, can be legitimately distinguished from its ultimate ground and goal. He communicates his understanding of the problem, and of the value behind both the Christian and Buddhist perspectives on this point. "Buddhism seems to take 'emptiness' as a complete negation of all personality, whereas Christianity finds in purity of heart and 'unity of spirit,' a supreme and transcendent fulfillment of personality" (*ZBA*, 117–18). He acknowledges that he is not prepared to discuss this problem in his essay but he does make a couple of observations regarding it:

---

24. Zen's apparent denial of distinctions was an issue of central concern for Merton, and he struggled to understand what Suzuki and others meant by their apparent denials. Merton later dealt concretely with this problem in his essay "The Zen Revival," which I will comment on in the following chapter.

> Very often, on the Christian side, we identify "personality" with the illusory and exterior ego-self, which is certainly not the true Christian "person." On the Buddhist side there seems to be no positive idea of personality at all: it is a value which seems to be completely missing from Buddhist thought. Yet it is certainly not absent from Buddhist practice.... The Main difference is that the language and practice of Zen are much more radical, austere, and ruthless, and that where the Zen-man says "emptiness" he leaves no room for any image or concept to confuse the real issue. The Christian treatment of the subject makes free use of richly metaphorical expressions and of concrete imagery, but we must take care to penetrate beyond the exterior surface and reach the inner depths. In any case the "death of the old man" is not the destruction of personality but the dissipation of an illusion, and the discovery of the new man is the realization of what was there all along.... I wonder if what Dr. Suzuki has said about "emptiness" ought not to help us to go deeper than we usually do into this doctrine of our mystical unity and purity in Christ. (*ZBA*, 118–19)

Finally, Merton ends his essay by communicating what he believes the real difference between Christianity and Zen to be. Using John Cassian's understanding of the two-fold goal of the monastic life he suggests that Zen stops at the intermediary end of the recovery of paradise in "emptiness" while the Christian journey anticipates a further ultimate end which is not purity of heart but heaven itself, "which eye hath not seen, ear hath not heard, nor hath it entered into the heart of man to conceive." The Christian anticipates a fullness in the Holy Spirit, which is realized eschatologically, not in paradise which is the original state of creation, but in heaven. This eschatological fullness does not result from "an object that enters into emptiness to 'fill' it. It is nothing else but God's own suchness" (*ZBA*, 133).[25]

---

25. Even before the decision was made by the censors to exclude Suzuki's essay from *WD* Merton worried about its reception in a letter to Sister Theresa Lentfoehr, SDS. dated November 20, 1959, where he wrote: "The Desert Fathers are coming along—that Zen Man, Suzuki, wrote a provoking article and I wrote another to help explain it. People may be interested, and challenged, and maybe shocked. I don't know. I think the dialogue is lively and interesting, and hope it will have the right effect. Of course, there are always narrow minded people to be taken into account" *(RJ,* 235).

The Dialogue with Dr. D. T. Suzuki

Suzuki to Merton

On November 22, 1959, Suzuki wrote Merton after having read "The Recovery of Paradise." He thanked Merton for his "illuminating letters" and for the manuscript itself. Suzuki wrote: "As you say, one's 'intellectual antecedents' are bound to condition everything one desires to elucidate either Christianity or Buddhism. . . . The only thing we can do in the circumstances is to be tolerant toward each other" (*Encounter*, 47). Suzuki then informed Merton that he would be sending him some comments that he would like to have follow Merton's essay. He ended his letter: "I wonder if I shall have a chance to meet you personally" (*Encounter*, 47).

Final Remarks: Suzuki

The comments Suzuki sent to Merton appear as "Final Remarks" in *ZBA* (133-34). In them, Suzuki begins by recognizing his lack of knowledge regarding Christian doctrine and tradition, and that what he says regarding such "may miss the mark entirely" but he nonetheless risks voicing his opinion. He writes:

> I would like to say that there are two types of mentality that fundamentally differ one from another: (1) affective, personal, and dualistic, and (2) non-affective, non-personal, and non-dualistic. Zen belongs to the latter and Christianity naturally to the former. The fundamental difference may be illustrated by the conception of "emptiness." (*ZBA*, 133)

He then writes that Merton's use of the term "emptiness" does not go "far and deep enough" because it is still on the level of God as Creator, which Suzuki understands to be dualistic, because of the distinction made between creator and creation, or creature. Zen anticipates an experience of emptiness, or no-mind, before thoughts arise, before thoughts of God and self, good and evil, etc. Attempting to push the discussion further, using Christian terminology to communicate his idea, Suzuki invokes the distinction between God as Creator, and the Godhead. He equates the Godhead with Zen emptiness.[26]

---

26. Suzuki seems to erect a dichotomy between mentalities that "differ fundamentally" which leads him to erect another distinction between God as Creator and the Godhead—a distinction that Merton considers "dualistic" (*ZBA*, 135). See also Merton's letter to Lawrence Ferlinghetti where he is critical of this distinction (*CT*, 271). Merton's

Opening New Horizons

> Zen emptiness is not the emptiness of nothingness, but the emptiness of fullness in which there is "no gain, no loss, no increase, no decrease," in which this equation takes place: zero = infinity. The Godhead is no other than this equation. In other words, when God as Creator came out of the Godhead he did not leave the Godhead behind. . . . For creation is out of inexhaustible nothingness. (*ZBA*, 134)

Suzuki then continues to say that the eschatological fullness is "something never realizable and yet realized at every moment" (*ZBA*, 134). Recognition of this reality is The Great Mystery, or Divine Wisdom, when questions cease and we simply live.

Merton Responds

On November 30, 1959, Merton writes in a letter to Suzuki, "I am so glad that you have added a few comments to your article. They are very wise and I do hope that they can lead to further exchange of views, because really we have only *begun* to get into the subject" (*Encounter*, 51). And further on, "I recognize the validity of your criticism of my treatment of 'emptiness' . . . it must wait for further development." Merton then cautions Suzuki that his use of the distinction between God and Godhead "runs into technical theological difficulties" but he refers Suzuki to John Ruysbroeck whom he believes develops Suzuki's idea quite well.[27] He then informs Suzuki that he too will be appending some notes to Suzuki's final remarks. The latter half of Merton's letter is more personal and considers the value of their discourse.

> Once again I thank you warmly for your collaboration in this work. It has been very interesting and challenging and I feel that such contacts are of great importance. Certainly I know that I have profited personally from your remarks. For we have been discussing our common interests on two levels: first as writers, but then as monks or Zen-men or whatever you would like to say. That level is to me

---

suggestion that Christianity anticipated a superior realization to that of Zen likely put Suzuki on the defensive.

27. Ruysbroeck was a fourteenth-century mystic and spiritual writer whom Merton greatly admired. Merton included a biographical note on Ruysbroeck in *The Ascent to Truth* where he calls him "one of the greatest Christian mystics" who "dominated the golden age of German and Flemish mysticism" (*AT*, 325). See also *NM*, 141–47. Contemporary translations spell the Flemish mystic's name Ruusbroec rather than Ruysbroeck.

The Dialogue with Dr. D. T. Suzuki

much more important, though alas I have been compelled to stay more on the first level in order to get out this book. (*Encounter*, 52)

Merton then conveys the difficulties he experiences in trying to understand and communicate that which is at the heart of their dialogue concerning "emptiness." In seriousness and jest, he writes:

> I am glad you are far away or you would settle the question with thirty blows of the hossu.[28] But at any rate I thought you would be happy to know that I struggle with the—not problem, but koan. It is not really for me a serious intellectual problem at all, but a problem of "realization"—something that has to break through. Every once in a while it breaks through a little. One of these days it will burst out. (*Encounter*, 52)

Final Remarks: Merton

Merton's final remarks introduce the thought of John Ruysbroeck as a possible tool for establishing a mutually acceptable communication of the experience of "emptiness." Ruysbroeck wrote of an experience of God, or the ground of being, as "emptiness without manner," beyond all manner, beyond all conceiving. Merton quotes Ruysbroeck, though without a reference, as saying:

> For God's impenetrable lack of manner is so dark and without manner that in itself it comprehends all the Divine manners . . . and in the abyss of God's namelessness it makes a Divine delectation. In this there is a delectable passing over and a flowing away and sinking down into the essential nakedness, with all the Divine names and all manners and all living reason which has its image in the mirror of divine truth; all these fall away into the simple nakedness wanting manner and without reason (*ZBA*, 135–36).[29]

Merton suggests that this "essential nakedness" corresponds more closely to Zen emptiness than did his earlier concept of purity of heart,[30] and he

---

28. Daggy has a footnote here that reads: "The *hossu* was part of the traditional equipment of the Zen Master, a whisk or a stick with hair on it, originally used to brush away flies and mosquitoes. It was also used to whack disciples; Ummon, for example, frequently prescribed thirty blows for a questioning disciple" (*Encounter*, 99n26).

29. This quotation comes from Ruusbroec's *Spiritual Espousals*. See Wiseman, *John Ruusbroec*, 52.

30. In his essay "The Study of Zen" (*ZBA*, 1–14), written almost a decade after this

remarks that if this "essential nakedness" is what Suzuki means by "suchness of the Godhead" then it is "thoroughly acceptable."

Merton continues making some important comments concerning grace that perhaps reach the heart of the difference between the interlocutors regarding their comments concerning the experience of "emptiness." Merton writes: "If in my own exposition I have not spoken so much of 'sinking down into the essential nakedness' of God it is not because I have insisted on man's awareness of God as Creator but rather, at least implicitly, on man's dependence on God as Savior and giver of Grace" (*ZBA*, 136).

Merton contends that the experience of "Divine Mercy" is grace, "not as a reified substance given to us by God from without, but grace precisely as emptiness, as freedom, as liberality, as gift. This giving without reason, without limit, without return, without self-conscious afterthought is, perhaps, the real secret of God who 'is love.'" Merton surmises that everything Suzuki has talked about he would tend to see from the point of view "of freedom and of gift" (*ZBA*, 136–37).

Merton concludes by acknowledging that despite the many differences in the doctrines of the two religions he is grateful that he and Suzuki can communicate so easily. He writes: "I feel that in talking to him I am talking to a 'fellow citizen,' to one who, though his beliefs in many ways differ from mine, shares a common spiritual climate. This unity of outlook and purpose is supremely significant"(*ZBA*, 138).

The Meeting

Several years after this dialogue, on June 1, 1964, Suzuki's secretary, Mihoko Okamura, wrote to Merton to inform him that Suzuki would be in New York for most of June 1964 and would like, if possible, to meet Thomas Merton in person (*Encounter*, 57). Merton, rather unexpectedly, secured

---

dialogue, Merton recognizes Cassian's "purity of heart" as an inadequate correlative to Zen emptiness. He wrote: "My choice of Cassian's 'purity of heart' as a Christian expression of Zen-consciousness was an unfortunate example. . . . Cassian's idea of 'purity of heart,' with its Platonic implications, while it may or may not be mystical, is not yet Zen because it still maintains that the supreme consciousness resides in a distinct heart which is pure and which is therefore ready and even worthy to receive a vision of God. It is still aware of a 'pure,' distinct and separate self-consciousness" (*ZBA*, 9). In other words, Merton later accuses himself of using Cassian in a way that promotes "mirror-wiping Zen." He then goes on to affirm the very same quote from Eckhart that Suzuki had used in their dialogue as a superior expression of Zen emptiness.

The Dialogue with Dr. D. T. Suzuki

permission from his Abbot to go to New York, "under strict obedience not to see anybody but Suzuki."[31] Merton was excited about the prospect of meeting the man he so much admired, whose books he had been reading for almost ten years, but he was ambivalent and reticent about going to New York. On June 12, 1964, he recorded in his journal that he "can think of nowhere [he] would less like to go than New York." Yet he was also pleased by thoughts about going to the Guggenheim Museum, and that he might "slyly get to a concert" (*Encounter*, 77–78). Merton found upon arrival that he loved being in New York, seeing the lively people, noticing what had changed and what had not.

On June 16 Merton records some sketchy notes regarding his meeting with Suzuki that he returns to and develops in his June 20 entry after their second meeting. In the June 16 entry he notes: "We could not get anywhere definite on the idea of 'person.' We are all different expressions (words) of the same emptiness" (cf. Pessoa).[32] And "the thing he insisted on most—in Xtianity and Buddhism—love more than enlightenment" (*Encounter*, 82–83).

Though Suzuki was ninety-four years old when he and Thomas Merton met, and deaf to the point of having to use an ear-horn in order to hear Merton, the two had some mutually gratifying discussions. In his June 20, 1964, journal entry Merton provides a more extensive picture of their meetings. They sat and drank green tea while they talked about their lives and work. Merton seemed surprised to discover that "quite a few Zen people read the *Ascent to Truth*. This is somewhat consoling though it is . . . in some ways my emptiest book . . . and in writing it, I was not fully myself. Suzuki was especially pleased with my essay on Zen in *Continuum* (1) and thought it was one of the best things on Zen that has been written in the West" (*Encounter*, 84–85).[33]

Suzuki expressed his love for Eckhart and told Merton more stories from the annals of Zen lore and Merton translated and read to Suzuki from Octavio Paz's translations of Fernando Pessoa's poetry.[34] "There

---

31. Merton also writes: "I certainly did not think that Dom James would give this permission, and yet, very hesitantly he did" (*Encounter*, 77).

32. Merton's translations of Fernando Pessoa's poems can be found in *CPTM*, 987–96.

33. Merton is referring here to "The Zen Revival." I will be examining this important essay in the following chapter.

34. Paz's translations were from the original Portuguese into Spanish. Merton was translating them on the spot into English for Suzuki. Merton's own translations of Pessoa in *CPTM* were based both on the original Portuguese and on Paz's translations. I am

were a few things (in the poem) he liked immensely (especially 'praise be to God that I am not good'—'that is so important!' said Suzuki with great feeling." (*Encounter*, 85).[35]

Merton concludes that this meeting was "profoundly important" and he appreciated the opportunity it provided him to affirm, first-hand, the "deep understanding" between them. Although he comments that perhaps he had "tried to explain things that did not need explaining," he was nonetheless gratified that this encounter gave him "a renewed sense of being situated in the world." And with Suzuki, and his secretary Mihoko Okamura, Merton felt "for once in a long time" that he "had spent a few moments with (his) own family" (*Encounter*, 85–86).[36] Finally meeting his Sensei face-to-face was a joyful experience. As Roger Lipsey noted: "The recognition we need here is that he met in Dr. Suzuki, at last, a living spiritual father . . . with whom he felt instinctively at home."[37]

Later that summer Merton thought back fondly on his trip to New York. He recalled the meals he ate, the museums he visited, the Van Gogh paintings that impressed him, and although there was too much of everything, it was all very good. He wrote in his journal on July 10, 1964: "The people walking on Fifth Ave. were beautiful and there were those familiar towers of hotels above the park. . . . New York is feminine. It is she, the city. I am faithful to her. I have not ceased to love her to the last gasp of this ball point pen (*Encounter*, 88–89). Concluding his recollections he writes: "Literature, contemplative solitude, Latin America, Asia, Zen, Islam, etc., all these things come together in my life. It would be madness for me to attempt to create a monastic life for myself by excluding all these. I would be less a monk. Others may have their way of doing it but I have mine" (*Encounter*, 89–90).

---

grateful to Patrick F. O'Connell for providing clarity on this.

35. The whole stanza reads: "Praise be to God I am not good and have / The natural selfishness of flowers / And rivers, going on their way / Concerned only, and not knowing it, / To flower and go. / This is the only mission in the world: / This—to exist clearly / And to know how / Without thinking about it" (*CPTM*, 993).

36. Merton and Suzuki continued to correspond after this visit (*Encounter*, 65–74). They sent one another books and other items of interest. Suzuki sent Merton a Japanese calendar and a scroll of calligraphy he had written (which Merton hung in his hermitage). Merton's final letter to Suzuki, dated May 3, 1965, ends with these words, "There is only one meeting place for all religions, and it is paradise. How nice to be there and wander about looking at the flowers. Or being the flowers" (*Encounter*, 74).

37. Lipsey, *Make Peace before the Sun Goes Down*, 199–200.

The Dialogue with Dr. D. T. Suzuki

Merton Remembers Suzuki

Three years after their meetings in New York, and one year after Suzuki had passed away at the age of ninety-six, Thomas Merton wrote "D. T. Suzuki: The Man and His Work" (*ZBA*, 59–66).[38] In this essay Merton remembered their earlier dialogue and subsequent meetings with the benefit of hindsight. Merton wrote:

> There is no question that Dr. Suzuki brought to this age of dialogue a very special gift of his own: a capacity to apprehend and to occupy the precise standpoints where communication could hope to be most effective.... This of course is an advantage in any dialogue, for when men try to communicate with each other, it is good for them to speak with distinct and personal voices, not to blur their identities by speaking through several official masks at the same time....
>
> I had the great privilege and pleasure of meeting him. One had to meet this man in order to fully appreciate him. He seemed to embody all the indefinable qualities of the "Superior Man" of the ancient Asian, Taoist, Confucian, and Buddhist traditions. Or rather in meeting him one seemed to meet that "True Man of No Title" that Chuang Tzu and the Zen masters speak of. And of course this is the man one really wants to meet. Who else is there? ... I did feel that I was speaking to someone who, in a tradition completely different from my own, had matured, had become complete and found his way. One cannot understand Buddhism until one meets it in this existential manner, in a person in whom it is alive.... I am sure that no alert and intelligent Westerner ever met Dr. Suzuki without something of the same experience. (*ZBA*, 60–62)

Suzuki had shown Merton that at the foundation of all the images, doctrines, rituals, etc., which can be "very confusing to a westerner," Buddhism was "very simple." In its simplicity Merton understood it in relation to Christian, Muslim, and Jewish contemplative traditions, as they all contain elements within them that anticipate a recovery of lived union "with Absolute Being, Absolute Love, Absolute Mercy, or Absolute Void" (*ZBA*, 62), though their methods for attaining this and their interpretations of what is actually going on all differ in some ways. Merton observes, however, that deep similarities continue to exist between the iconoclasm of Zen and the Christian *via negativa* of "knowing in unknowing" as well as regarding the

---

38. First published in *The Eastern Buddhist* (New Series) 2 (1967).

transformation of consciousness and radical self-transcendence they anticipate. But he concludes with a concern for love: "the last words I remember Dr. Suzuki saying (before the usual good-byes) were 'The most important thing is Love!' I must say that as a Christian I was profoundly moved. Truly Prajna and Karuna [compassion] are one (as the Buddhist says), or Caritas (love) is indeed the highest knowledge" (*ZBA*, 62)

4

From Communication to Communion

THE DIALOGUE BETWEEN MERTON and Suzuki began without a clear focus but with a mutual desire to discover and understand what each suspected to be profound affinities among the sayings of the early Christian desert monks and the ancient Zen masters of Buddhism. As their dialogue advanced the focus crystallized, and it concerned nothing less than the ultimate, transcendent ground and potential of human existence, or what Karl Rahner called the "whither and term of human transcendence." More specifically, their dialogue concerned the correlation of (a) the Judeo-Christian term of Wisdom realized as union with God in Christ through the Holy Spirit by grace, and (b) the Zen-Buddhist term of *prajna* or "transcendental wisdom" realized in "suchness" or "emptiness" through satori, enlightenment, or what Merton prefers to call in his later writings the "Zen insight." In short, their basic terms were "wisdom" and "emptiness," and they explored the meanings of these terms from the contemplative Christian and Zen-Buddhist perspectives.

The recorded dialogue between Merton and Suzuki transpired over a five-year period, but its impact extended beyond that. To appreciate that impact, not only for Merton's growing understanding of Zen, but also for how that impacts his thinking about religious pluralism more broadly, requires a careful analysis. This chapter has six parts. By focusing on the basic terms of their dialogue I attempt to highlight (1) Suzuki's understanding of the terms; (2) Merton's understanding of Suzuki's position; (3) Merton's own understanding of the terms; (4) Suzuki's understanding of Merton's position; and (5) developments in Merton's understanding of Suzuki's position as they are evident in their dialogue;[1] I include in my presentation of Merton's development not only the published dialogue with Suzuki but also (6) Merton's essay "The Zen Revival" to illustrate how Merton finds new ways to communicate his understanding of Zen that Suzuki finds sufficiently non-dualistic.[2]

Suzuki on Prajna

Suzuki's main concern in the dialogue was to communicate the radical dimension of self-transcendence that is at the heart of Zen sayings and the basis of those sayings. It is important to remember that while Suzuki presents a Zen-Buddhist's perspective on enlightenment, he is purposefully writing to a non-Zen audience, so he expresses a special interest in presenting his position in a way that addresses the once typical, occidental concern that Zen advocates moral relativism and nihilistic world-denial (*ZBA*, 103–4).

After distinguishing Knowledge from Innocence[3] in his essay, Suzuki suggests that only in the "fallen state" (for Christians) or in the ordinary

---

1. Since their dialogue centered on ultimate concerns both Merton and Suzuki employed several terms interchangeably. For example, they both used "God" and "ground of being" (Merton also used "Love which is the ground of all being") interchangeably. Suzuki used "emptiness," "Prajna" and "Enlightenment" as univocal terms for "ultimate reality" as well. I also will use several ultimate terms, interchangeably at first, but which I will distinguish from one another later regarding how the meanings of these terms relate to one another from the standpoint of intentionality analysis.

2. "The Zen Revival" was first published in *Continuum* in 1964. A more extensive version of this essay appears in *MZM*, 3–44, entitled "Mystics and Zen Masters." I, however, will be using the 1971 edition of this essay published by the Buddhist Society, London, with a foreword by Christmas Humphreys. This essay, written five years after their initial correspondence, became for them a topic of discussion when they met in June of 1964.

3. As a reminder to the reader, Suzuki interprets "Innocence" as the state in which humanity was originally created in God's image and likeness. This corresponds to a state of consciousness preliminary to the emergence of the subject/object distinction. "Knowledge" designates humanity's lost likeness through sin and alienation. "Innocence" corresponds, for Suzuki, to the Buddhist term "Emptiness," and "Knowledge" corresponds to the Buddhist term "Ignorance." Suzuki suggests that Knowledge is contradictory to innocence, and Ignorance is contradictory to emptiness when the subject/object distinction is taken to be primary and amounts to a division. However, the recovery of paradise through Emptiness establishes a proper relation between Innocence and Knowledge in which the world of explicit subjects and objects is understood to be secondarily derivative and emergent from of a primary unity that is Emptiness or Innocence, wisdom is precisely the transcendent realization of this and the proper reordering of the relationship between innocence and knowledge.

state of *avidya* (for Buddhists) do we see Knowledge and Innocence as divided, separate states. From within this fallen perspective one must discipline his or her actions, and live under laws, struggle to resist the temptations to do evil. But, according to Suzuki, this highly "moral" perspective is not enough. One must transcend the moral concern by purifying the heart. Suzuki cites verse 183 from the *Dhammapada* in the attempt to elucidate what he means by actualizing this freedom:

> Not to do anything that is evil,
> To do all that is good,
> To thoroughly purify the heart:
> This is the teaching of the Buddhas. (*ZBA*, 107)

He interprets this as suggesting that persons alienated from Innocence take the first two lines as moral prescriptions, but from the standpoint of Prajna (suggested by the third line) the first two lines become simply descriptive of how Prajna is manifested (*ZBA*, 106–7). In other words, when the heart is pure, one will do good and avoid evil without undue worry over every choice and action. In this context, Suzuki compares Prajna to the wisdom expressed by St. Augustine's dictum "love God and do as you will" (*ZBA*, 104).[4]

In Prajna, Innocence and Knowledge are not two separate states. Suzuki writes:

> It is out of this zero [out of Emptiness] that all good is performed and all evil is avoided. The zero I speak of is not a mathematical symbol. It is the infinite—a storehouse or womb (Garbha) of all possible good or values. zero = infinity, and infinity = zero. This double equation is to be understood not only statically but dynamically. It takes place between being and becoming. For they are not contradicting ideas. Emptiness is not sheer emptiness or passivity or Innocence. It is and at the same time it is not. It is Being, it is Becoming. It is Knowledge and Innocence. The Knowledge to do good and not to do evil is not enough; it must come out of Innocence, where Innocence is Knowledge and Knowledge is Innocence. (*ZBA*, 107)

---

4. Invoking the same line from Augustine, Merton asserted that such love means "humility and fraternal union without envy, in pure love of [one's] brother, the doctrine that I share all my brother's good by charity, and he mine. Love is everything: *Dilige et quod vis fac* (Love and do as you will)" (*ICM*, 160).

Further on, Suzuki suggests that transcendence of self in Prajna "is no more, no less than the seeing into the nonexistence of a thingish ego-substance" (*ZBA*, 109). It is the "self" that must be transcended that endeavors to do good and avoid evil under the demands of law. But Prajna is effortless action that arises from absolute poverty of spirit. He continues,

> This is the greatest stumbling block in our spiritual discipline, which, in actuality, consists not in getting rid of the self but in realizing the fact that there is no such existence from the first.... Being poor means to be from the very beginning not in possession of anything... to be just so, and yet to be rich in inexhaustible possibilities.... To be absolutely nothing is to be everything. When one is in possession of something, that something will keep all other somethings from coming in. (*ZBA*, 109)

Merton's Initial Understanding of Suzuki's Viewpoint

Merton's essay "The Recovery of Paradise" communicates his own understanding of Zen-Buddhist Prajna not as an ultimate realization of the human journey but as an intermediate one. While Merton and Suzuki could both speak of Wisdom as a kind of return to paradise consciousness, Merton now adverts to John Cassian's distinction between a Christian monk's intermediary goal of paradise consciousness and his ultimate goal of heaven.[5] By distinguishing paradise from heaven at the beginning of his essay Merton is able to conclude at its end that Dr. Suzuki's Prajna is correlative with what Christians recognize as an intermediate end, namely the return to paradise, and not correlative with the ultimate anticipation of human life as recognized by Christians as the eschatological fullness of the Kingdom of Heaven.[6]

---

5. Merton described Cassian as "*the* great monastic writer—the Master of the spiritual life par excellence" and saw him as a bridge between Oriental (Greek) and Occidental (Latin) contemplative traditions. For his lectures on Cassian, see *CF*, 97–259; *PBM*, 44–72.

6. While it is clear that Merton distinguishes between a recovered "paradise consciousness" and the "eschatological fullness of heaven" in his early dialogue with Suzuki, in other writings he seems to understand "paradise consciousness" fully in terms of the "new creation" in Christ that itself is eschatological, and so the distinction in Merton's own thinking never amounts to a separation. On Eschatology, see *TME*, 139–41. In Merton's letter to Rosemary Radford Ruether dated March 9, 1967, he wrote: "I am in the line of the paradise tradition in monastic thought, which is also part and parcel of the

Merton writes:

> The intermediary end, or scopos, is what we have been discussing as purity of heart, roughly corresponding to Dr. Suzuki's term "emptiness." . . . The concept [Cassian's purity of heart] in actual fact, corresponds rather to the Stoic apatheia than to Zen suchness. But at any rate there is a close relationship. It is the *quies*, or rest, of contemplation—the state of being free from all images and concepts which disturb and occupy the soul. . . . One thing, and this is most important, remains to be said. Purity of heart is not the ultimate end of the monk's striving in the desert. It is only a step towards it. . . . The monk who has realized in himself purity of heart . . . is ready for a new work "which eye hath not seen, ear hath not heard, nor hath it entered in to the heart of man to conceive." . . . This is a dimension which does not enter into the realm of Zen. (*ZBA*, 131–32)[7]

For Merton, the eschatological fullness of the Kingdom of God is a "superior and more vigilant innocence . . . an emptiness that is enkindled by the glory of the Divine Word and enflamed with the presence of the Holy Spirit. That glory and that presence are not objects that 'enter into' emptiness to 'fill' it. They are nothing other than God's own suchness" (*ZBA*, 133).

Merton on Wisdom[8]

Merton's own understanding of Wisdom is heavily influenced by the conceptions of Desert monks and Patristic and medieval mystical literature. As such, "The Recovery of Paradise" relies on the specialized terms of doctrines. For Merton, Wisdom "means unity in Christ, so that each one who is in Christ can say, with Paul: 'it is now not I that live but Christ that lives in

---

desert tradition and is also eschatological, because the monk is supposed to be living the life of the new creation in which the right relation to the rest of God's creatures is fully restored"(*AHTW*, 33–38), the point being, from the standpoint of a realized eschatology, there is no division between "recovered paradise" and the fullness of heaven. The idea recalls the mystic and physician Adrienne von Speyr (1902–1967) who received a locution "*Tu vivra au ciel et sur la terre*" (you shall live in heaven and on earth) which shaped the remainder of her life. See Balthasar, *First Glance at Adrienne von Speyr*.

7. Suzuki's use of the quote "to thoroughly purify the heart" from the *Dhammapada* likely prompted Merton to think of John Cassian and then use Cassian as a lens for reading Zen.

8. For a more extensive study of Merton's understanding of wisdom in the context of this dialogue, see Zyniewicz, *Interreligious Dialogue*, 72–92.

me.' It is the same Christ who lives in all. The individual has 'died' in Christ to his 'old man,' his exterior, egotistical self, and 'risen' in Christ to the new man, a selfless and divine being, who is the one Christ, the same who is 'all in all'" (ZBA, 117). For Merton the person who has become empty of all things and dead to his or her ego self is "moved in all things by the grace of Christ" as "action out of emptiness, springing from the mystery of the pure freedom which is 'divine love'" (ZBA, 119). The highest realization of this is a complete emptiness of self "where all is done in us but without us, *in nobis et sine nobis*. But before we reach that level, we must also learn to work on the other level of 'knowledge'—scientia—where grace works in us but 'not without us'—*in nobis sed non sine nobis*" (ZBA, 121).[9]

In reference to this latter level Merton also talks of the necessity to understand Innocence and Knowledge not as dialectically opposed, but interrelated. The rejecting of Knowledge in favor of Innocence is dangerous. One ends up with "an emptiness that is merely blank and silly: an absence of knowledge without the presence of wisdom" (ZBA, 121). The person who is truly empty of all things has no self-concern, is free, and "all he knows is love" (ZBA, 129). The ultimate realization of Wisdom for Merton, is life in Christ through the gift of the Holy Spirit, in "God's own suchness."

Suzuki's Understanding of Merton's Viewpoint

In Suzuki's final remarks he points out that "Father Merton's emptiness, when he uses the term, does not go far and deep enough, I am afraid. . . . Father Merton's emptiness is still on the level of God as creator and does not go up to the Godhead. So is John Cassian's" (ZBA, 133). Suzuki then reiterates his conception of Zen emptiness as a contrast both to the Christian

---

9. Merton seems to be suggesting here that the perfect realization of emptiness is purely "operative grace" which is received without any cooperation on the part of the subject. Merton here may still be using the categories of acquired and infused contemplation, in which case the grace that "works in us but without us" would refer to "infused contemplation." Carr, however, has argued that Merton later dropped the distinction between infused and acquired contemplation, a distinction correlative with the distinction between operative and cooperative grace, and began to conceive grace more broadly. For my purposes, and in light of intentionality analysis, I would affirm that as long as grace is operative "in us" it cannot be operating entirely "without us." For help on this issue, see Carr, *Search for Wisdom and Spirit*, 277–79. For Lonergan's clarification concerning operative and cooperative grace, see *Method*, 106–8. Lonergan suggests that the dynamic state of being in love without limits or conditions or qualifications "of itself" is operative grace. But *the same state* as principle of acts of love, etc. . . . is cooperative grace.

emptiness of Merton and Cassian and to Merton's misconception of Zen emptiness. For Suzuki it is Zen emptiness that is ultimate:

> Zen emptiness is not the emptiness of nothingness, but the emptiness of fullness in which there is "no gain, no loss, no increase, no decrease." . . . Eschatology is something never realizable and yet realized at every moment of our life. We see it always ahead of us though we are in reality always in it. This is the delusion we are conditioned to have as beings in time or rather as "becomings" in time. This delusion ceases to be one the very moment we experience all this. It is the Great Mystery, intellectually speaking. In Christian terms, it is Divine Wisdom. The strange thing, however, is: when we experience it we cease to ask questions about it, we accept it, we just live it. (*ZBA*, 134)

At this point in the dialogue, Suzuki concludes that Zen is non-affective, non-personal, and non-dualistic, while Christianity is the opposite in all regards (*ZBA*, 133). Thus, Suzuki continues to understand Merton as striving for a kind of "subjective" emptiness that enables the pure experience of the "objective" reality which is somehow apart from and over against the emptiness of the subject. This is correlative with what Suzuki would call "mirror-wiping" Zen rather than authentic Zen insight.[10]

Merton's Understanding Develops

In late 1959 Merton responded to Suzuki's final remarks (*ZBA*, 135–38), and nearly five years later he published "The Zen Revival." These writings are integral to the Merton/Suzuki dialogue and examined in that context reveal significant refinements in Merton's own thinking.

Merton begins his "Final Remarks" by confessing that "the strongly personalistic tone of Christian mysticism, even when it is 'apophatic,' generally seems to prohibit a full equation with Zen experience" (*ZBA*, 135). This is because Zen ultimately professes to be trans-personal, while Christianity seeks the fulfillment of the person in the love of God. However, Merton now suggests that if Christian emptiness and Zen emptiness are at all correlative then he and Suzuki need to find new terms to discuss this other than the terms Suzuki proposes.

---

10. I will elucidate the concept of "mirror-wiping" Zen in my discussion of Merton's essay "The Zen Revival," in section 6 of this chapter.

Opening New Horizons

For Merton, the way to avoid the semblance of dualism in his accounts of emptiness, a dualism that Suzuki links with the personalistic nature of Christianity, is not to invoke the distinction between God and Godhead in reference to levels of "experience" as Suzuki does, which Merton claims is itself a distinction "of a clearly dualistic nature" and "technically condemned by the Church." Rather, Merton prefers to seek new mutually satisfying forms of expression.

The distinction that Suzuki is trying to articulate by the terms God and Godhead "must be treated in other terms." Merton suggests that perhaps Suzuki's distinction is more accurately stated, from a Christian point of view, as a distinction between "divine energies" and "divine substance" or "Trinity of Persons" and the "Unity of Nature." In this regard, Suzuki's concept of experiencing the "Godhead" might correlate with Ruysbroeck's orthodox term of the climax of mysticism as an "emptiness without manner" or knowing God "beyond all conceiving" in God's "transcendent, ineffable reality," a knowledge that transcends knowing God in his works (*ZBA*, 135). From this point of view, Merton announces, Suzuki's distinction is "thoroughly acceptable."

Merton's second point of concern in his final remarks is to affirm Suzuki's understanding of "eschatological fullness" (*ZBA*, 137). This affirmation is significant because it contrasts with his earlier judgment that Zen only anticipated an intermediate end, rather than the ultimate, eschatological fullness. Suzuki's comments on the "already" and "not yet" quality of the eschatological fullness of the Kingdom of God persuaded Merton that Suzuki had a firm grasp of these Christian concepts and related them accurately to his Zen-Buddhist tradition (see *ZBA*, 134).

Finally, Merton articulates his understanding of the difference between Zen and Christianity in new terms. Earlier he had suggested that Christian contemplation anticipated a realization superior to that anticipated by Zen. He supposed that while Zen anticipated an intermediate "paradise consciousness" the Christian went further anticipating the eschatological fullness of heaven (*ZBA*, 131–32). Now, however, he suggests that the difference is not a matter of one anticipating or attaining an ultimate experience and the other an intermediate one, rather the difference has to do with how each understands the ultimacy that they both intend or attain (*ZBA*, 136–37). This insight brings Merton to the affirmation that the "emptiness" that both he and Suzuki intend (not as a counterpart to some imagined fullness "standing over against it in metaphysical isolation") will be affirmed by the Christian as "having the character of a free gift of love." This affirmation does not erect divisions between giver, gift, and receiver, but stems from the understanding of emptiness *as grace*, "not as given to us by God from without, but grace precisely as emptiness, as freedom, as liberality, as gift" (*ZBA*, 136–37). Merton, however, does not develop this line of thinking, but the shift in his own thinking is important; no longer is he imagining Christianity as superior to Zen in virtue of the former having some experiential state of consciousness or promised fullness "that does not enter into the realm of Zen" (*ZBA*, 136).[11] Rather, Merton is identifying the fundamental difference now as a matter of understanding and interpretation.[12]

This development is key. From what I can tell, it is precisely this move that accounts for Merton's gradual shedding of his reservations about recognizing any "supernatural" element or quality in non-Christian contemplative traditions. As Roger Lipsey noted, "It isn't easy to detect Merton growing and changing, we can see him grown and see him changed" but the changing reveals his ambivalence and his contradicting himself.[13] He never sheds those reservations entirely, and remained guarded against a facile and uncritical syncretism, but he was far more comfortable imagining that "the great prophetic and religious figures of Islam, Hinduism, Buddhism,

---

11. Merton does begin to recognize an implicit affirmation of "grace" in different schools of Buddhist thought. For example, he sees it in the Zen "tile-polishing" story, in which a master shows a disciple that he cannot attain enlightenment by his efforts alone (*MZM*, 20), and in "the uncultivated yoga" of Tibetan Buddhism, which recognizes that enlightenment can seize a person who is not looking for it and is not engaged in practices intended to cultivate it but suddenly "identifies the natural spontaneity of all phenomena as the dharmakaya." Merton learned of the latter by reading Evans-Wentz, *Tibetan Yoga and Secret Doctrines*, on his Asian journey. I discuss this further in chapter 7.

12. In other words, Merton is no longer identifying Buddhism with "natural" mysticism and Christianity with "supernatural" mysticism. Lonergan, who is helpful on this score, understood the distinction between the natural and the supernatural as correlative with the distinction between proportionate and transcendent being. He defines being heuristically as that which is "to be known." Being is what judgments affirm. Proportionate being is being insofar as it is sensible, intelligible, and knowable to humans through judgments of fact and probability. Transcendent being, though infinitely intelligible, transcends our finite acts of understanding, though still can be experienced as fulfilling our intentional consciousness in love and freedom and can be known through judgments of value, and affirmed as unknown, or "not yet fully known." These are not two "beings" but a continuum of being insofar as it is proportionate and insofar as it is transcendent, relative to the structure of human consciousness, which is also part of being. See *Insight*, 670–80; *Method*, 309–11.

13. Lipsey, "Merton, Suzuki, Zen, Ink," 140.

etc., *could have been* mystics, in the true, that is, supernatural, sense of the word" (*MZM*, 207).

"The Zen Revival": New Terms for Affirming Mutual Understanding

The first phase of the Merton/Suzuki dialogue[14] ended leaving the partners with feelings of mutual respect, gratitude, and with the desire to continue, but a temporary impasse regarding agreement concerning emptiness and wisdom had also become clear. Merton continued to affirm life in Christ as the gift of the Spirit, as the fulfillment of the person, while Suzuki continued to understand this affirmation as exemplary of Merton's insufficient understanding of emptiness and as ultimately divisive and dualistic in light of the Buddhist doctrines of *anicca* (impermanence) and *anatta* (no self).

In the "Postface" to ZBA written several years after "Wisdom in Emptiness" Merton commented that he was "tempted to cut out" his "Final Remarks" from their published dialogue. They seemed to him to serve as "an example of how *not* to approach Zen." Not that the theological terms of Christian doctrine were wrong or false but because "any attempt to handle Zen in theological terms was bound to miss the point" (*ZBA*, 139). The back-and-forth challenges from Suzuki compelled him to be a better listener, and, as Pramuk put it, to resist the tendency to "too quickly appropriate (and thus effectively silence) the other's reality into [his] own frame of reference."[15] Instead, Merton wanted to approach Zen on its own terms, and to see if he could relate to those terms solely on the basis of his own spiritual experience, his own interior life, without adverting to the terms of his own theological tradition. This was the impetus behind his essay "The Zen Revival."[16]

Christmas Humphreys noted that through this article, which Suzuki had read without Merton's prompting, "Merton made clear to Dr. Suzuki the depth and quality of his understanding of Zen, not merely as a scholar

---

14. By "the first phase" I mean the dialogue that led to the publication of "Wisdom in Emptiness" and was completed by November of 1959. The second phase started in June of 1964 immediately prior to their meeting in New York and continued until Suzuki's death in 1966.
15. Pramuk, *Sophia*, 286.
16. Merton, "Zen Revival" (cited hereafter as *ZR* parenthetically in the text).

but in terms of his own enlightenment."[17] Indeed, it was this article that Suzuki praised, saying "there is more true understanding of Zen in this article than anything I have ever read by a Western writer."[18] The article became a brief topic of discussion when the two men met in 1964, and it evinces further development in Merton's thinking.

"The Zen Revival" is partly a review of Heinrich Dumoulin's *A History of Zen Buddhism* and partly Merton's own contribution to answering the question "what, exactly, is Zen?" (ZR, 526). Though Merton suggests that Dumoulin's book is "probably the best and most comprehensive history of Zen that has appeared in any western language," he takes issue with Dumoulin for his tendency to characterize Zen as a kind of natural mysticism (ZR, 524). Any advanced reader of Merton's oeuvre can't miss the irony here; nonetheless, Merton tries rather to treat the question of Zen without having to employ the distinction between the natural and supernatural. He approaches the question as a phenomenologist rather than a theologian.

Before hazarding answers to the question "what is Zen?" Merton undermines and subverts inadequate responses by asserting what Zen is not. In doing this he not only distinguishes his position from Dumoulin's but also from his own previous judgments regarding Zen. As soon as Merton poses the question "what, exactly, is Zen?" he asserts that the "Zen tradition absolutely refuses to tolerate any abstract or theoretical answer" to the question (ZR, 526). Merton informs his readers that Zen is "not a religion, not a philosophy, not a system of thought, not a doctrine and not an ascesis" (ZR, 526).[19] He insists that the insight anticipated by Zen cannot

---

17. From Christmas Humphreys's foreword to Merton, *Zen Revival*.

18. Mr. Lunsford Yandell met with D. T. Suzuki the day after Merton had met with him. Mr. Yandell remembers Suzuki saying these words as he handed him a copy of Merton's article. See Humphreys's foreword to Merton, *Zen Revival*.

19. Merton explains that the word "Zen" comes from the Chinese *Ch'an* which designates a certain kind of meditation, "and is based on the Sanskrit word *dhyana*" (ZR, 526). But *dhyana* is not meant to be an acquisitive form of meditation that anticipates the practitioner coming into possession of a kind of experience; rather it is meant to bring the extinction of "seeking" when anticipation finds fulfillment. Thus, Zen is not an ascesis. In this regard the word Zen itself becomes synonymous, in a sense, with *Prajna, Emptiness*, and the other ultimate terms.

The Chinese Ch'an School was originally introduced into China by Bodhidharma in the early part of the sixth century. Its distinctive element was the teaching of the four principles: "A special transmission from spirit to spirit, out with the Scriptures; no dependence as far as words were concerned; to aim directly for the mind; to discover one's true nature in order to reach buddhahood." When the Ch'an tradition of Bodhidharma made its way into Japan in the eighth and ninth centuries it became Zen. Zen in Japan

be communicated in a doctrinal formula nor fully or precisely described. This is not because Zen is Gnostic or esoteric in doctrine, but because any description or explanation might imply that the Zen insight "is 'an experience' that a 'subject' is capable of 'having'" and such terms "contradict all the implications of Zen" (*ZR*, 526). So employing any language that may imply a primary division of the world into subjects (who have experiences) and objects (of experience), essences and appearances, matter and spirit, is liable to perpetuate misunderstanding.

After Merton asserts that the "most elementary fact about Zen is its abhorrence of . . . dualistic division(s)" he attempts to communicate Zen's fundamental affirmation in positive ways (*ZR*, 527). Merton elucidates his basic assertion that "Zen is the awareness of pure being beyond subject and object" (*ZR*, 527), and later writes:

> Zen enlightenment is an insight into pure being in all its actual presence and immediacy. It is a fully alert and super conscious act of being which transcends time and space. . . . Zen insight is at once a liberation from the limitations of the individual ego, and a discovery of one's "original nature" and "true face" in "Mind" which is no longer restricted to the empirical self, but is in all and above all. Zen insight is less our awareness than being's awareness of itself . . . (it) is a recognition that the whole world is aware of itself in me . . . (and) that my identity is to be sought not in separation from all that is, but in oneness with all that is. This identity is not the denial of my own personal reality but its highest affirmation. (*ZR*, 529)

Although he employs metaphysical language to elucidate his meaning he also reminds his readers that the language of the Zen masters is ordinarily not explanatory nor theoretical but poetic, descriptive and common sensical (*ZR*, 530).[20] The intention of Zen is not to explain to others an understanding of enlightenment but to facilitate for others the experience of it.

In view of emphasizing Zen's "abhorrence of division" Merton comments on what is known to the "Southern school" of Chinese Zen as

---

flourishes primarily in two forms: the Soto school, founded by Hsing-su (d. 740), and the Rinzai school, attributed mostly to the leadership of Lin-chi (d. 867). See Brosse, *Religious Leaders*, 34–35.

20. Merton actually says that Zen language "is *not metaphysical* but poetic and phenomenological. The Zen insight is a direct grasp of being, not a formulation of the nature of being" (*ZR*, 532).

"mirror-wiping" (ZR, 530–32).[21] He explains that mirror-wiping Zen is regarded as a kind of heresy by Zen masters of the Southern school. The heresy affirms that ultimate consciousness is realized or attained by one who empties the mind, frees his or her mind of thoughts, and thereby achieves a state of enlightenment. In this view an individual must continually wipe the mirror, keeping it clean, empty and pure, so that the mind becomes a perfect reflection of ultimate emptiness. But the Zen masters of the Southern school reject such conceptions because (a) the image of a mirror reflecting suggests primordial divisions, and (b) because the abstraction of a self as custodian of the mirror mind is problematic because it erects an illusory self as primary, who is capable of "possessing" a mind, purifying it, attaining enlightenment, etc. Hui Neng's solution to the problem is radical denial of such divisions. There is nothing to reflect, no mirror to reflect, no self to wipe the mirror.[22] Thus, Hui Neng exclaims "fundamentally not one thing exists." Merton, however, quickly cautions that "the western reader . . . is likely to seize upon the phrase 'not one thing exists' to account for his anxieties: but if he thinks this is a fundamental principle, a declaration of pantheism, he is wrong . . . statements about the 'nothingness' of beings and of 'oneness' in Buddhism are to be interpreted just like the . . . terms of western mystics describing their experience of God" (ZR, 530). In other words, the language is poetic and not theoretical. However, Merton acknowledges that the problem of expressing the Zen insight might also be solved not only by emphasizing denial and the withdrawal from objectification, but by taking care to make further distinctions, in this case by distinguishing between

---

21. Merton explains that the Chinese school of Zen (or Ch'an) split into Northern and Southern schools in the seventh century, over the choosing of the Sixth "Patriarch." The Sixth Patriarch was to be chosen among the disciples of the Fifth Patriarch, Hung-Jen, on the basis of poems written by them that communicated the highest degree of enlightenment. Shen-hsiu, a senior and most revered monk, composed a poem that likened the mind to "a clear mirror standing." Hui Neng composed a poem that proclaimed "the clear mirror is nowhere standing / Fundamentally not one thing exists" and his poem was preferred and Hui Neng was chosen as the Sixth Patriarch. Shen-hsiu, however, was apparently endorsed by enough disciples to constitute a kind of schism in the Chinese Zen school and the Northern school remained faithful to him.

22. In a letter to Heinrich Dumoulin dated July 20, 1964, Merton takes issue with Dumoulin's interpretation of Hui Neng, writing: "I cannot get anything from your words except that Zen is the suppression of concepts by concentration and effort directed precisely to suppression. . . . I am unable to see how this can be the Zen of Hui Neng, when this is what Hui Neng says Zen is not" (HGL, 171).

the "ego self" and the genuine "person" actualized in self-transcendence through grace (ZR, 528).[23]

Merton attempts to offer an account of the genuine person actualized through self-transcendence from a Zen perspective. He clearly affirms the inadequacy of mirror-wiping Zen and is able to say, now in accord with Hui Neng and Suzuki, that "to speak of the mind as a mirror which is 'owned' by the ego and which must be kept pure by the extinction of all thought" is "sheer nonsense" (ZR, 532–33). Merton writes:

> As Bodhidharma said, the "Unconscious" (prajna) is a principle of being and light secretly at work in our conscious mind making it aware of transcendent reality. But this true awareness is not a matter of the empirical ego standing back and "having ideas," "possessing knowledge," or even "attaining to insight" (Satori). Here we are not dealing with a Cartesian awareness of a thinking self but with a vastly different realm of prajna-wisdom. Hence what matters now is for the conscious to realize itself as identified with and illuminated by the Unconscious, in such a way that there is no longer any division or separation between the two. It is not that the empirical mind is "absorbed in" Prajna, but simply that Prajna is, and nothing else has any relevance except as its manifestation. Indeed it is not the empirical self which "possesses" prajna-wisdom, or owns "an unconscious" as one might have a cellar in one's house. In reality the conscious belongs to the transcendental Unconscious, is possessed by it and carries out its work, or it should do so. Its destiny is to manifest in itself the light of that Being in which it subsists, as a Christian philosopher might say. It becomes one, as we would say, with God's own light, and St. John's expression, the "Light which enlightens every man coming into this world" (John 1:9), seems to correspond fairly closely to the idea of Prajna and of Hui Neng's "Unconsciousc" [sic]. (ZR, 533)[24]

Here Merton makes room for a positive understanding of the person. His interpretation of Hui Neng's idea of Prajna is correlative with his own conception of authentic personhood as the gift of the Holy Spirit. Here again

23. Merton is making a familiar move here, one he continuously makes when differentiating the true and false selves. Jacques Maritain's distinction between the "individual" and the "person" underpins what he is now contrasting as the "ego-self" and the "person." See Carr, *Wisdom and Spirit*, 28–32; WCT, 17.

24. It is interesting that Merton is identifying Prajna here with a kind of Christ-consciousness, becoming one with God's own light, which is to say, becoming one with Christ. *Nostra Atatae* uses the same scriptural passage to affirm that non-Christian traditions often "reflect a ray of that truth which enlightens all men and women."

Merton would advert, as he often does, to the words of St. Paul who professed "I live, no longer I but Christ lives in me." But Merton understands Paul's qualifier "in me" not as an affirmation of a "Paul" who exists *apart from* the "Christ" who lives in him, but expressive of the necessary distinction between the absolute ground of consciousness and of being (Hui Neng's "Unconscious")[25] and the provisional, contingent consciousness that comes to know itself as an expression of the former.

Merton comments further on Zen enlightenment:

> This state of "enlightenment," then, has nothing to do with the exclusion of external and material reality, and when it denies the existence of the empirical self and of external objects, this denial is not the denial of their reality but of their relevance insofar as they are isolated in their own forms. They have become irrelevant because the subject-object relationship that existed when the empirical self regarded them and cherished its thoughts about them, has now been transcended in the "void." But this void is by no means a mere negation. It would be helpful for western minds to call it a pure affirmation of the fullness of positive being . . . the Unconscious as manifest and conscious in us. (*ZR*, 535)

He dedicates the remaining few pages of "The Zen Revival" to emphasizing the importance of understanding Hui Neng's rejection of mirror-wiping Zen. His own grasp of Hui Neng demonstrates a movement beyond his own prior understanding of Zen enlightenment, which he previously characterized as an intermediate experience and clearly in line with what Suzuki and Hui Neng reject as an emptiness that does not go far and deep enough (namely as a kind of mirror-wiping Zen). Ironically, in the first phase of the dialogue both Merton and Suzuki were, in a sense, suspicious of the other as advocating a kind of mirror-wiping Zen. That is to say, Merton thought Zen anticipated "the *quies*, or rest, of contemplation—the state of being free from all images and concepts which disturb and occupy the soul"(*ZBA*, 131), but not the radical self-transcendence actualized by grace and characterized as "an emptiness without manner" (*ZBA*, 132). Suzuki, on the other hand, concluded that Christianity, and Merton's conception of emptiness, remained always on a level of division and separation, because of the distinctions Merton made, which for Suzuki were "divisions,"

---

25. In "The Zen Revival" Merton frequently employs Hui Neng's term "Unconscious" as correlative with "Prajna," the "fullness of being" and "Ultimate Mind." Merton himself, however, is careful to point out that Hui Neng's "Unconscious" "is totally different from the unconscious as it is conceived by modern psychoanalysis" (*ZR*, 533).

between humans and God, and because distinctions belong to the world of knowledge and are always secondary to experience and inner innocence.

Perhaps their own "intellectual antecedents" initially hindered each one's capacity to hear what the other was attempting to say. Surely Merton's reference to "God's own suchness" as a corollary for "emptiness" was not intended as a reference to God as a "something" that creates something else out of a "nothing" that exists in opposition to "God's own suchness." Rather, Merton was speaking of an eschatological and primordial recognition of God as *All in all*, paradoxically identical with Absolute emptiness. Suzuki decision to utilize the distinction between God as Creator who comes out of the "Godhead" seems like an attempt to illustrate a point that Merton already gets, namely, that the truly absolute has no conditions whatsoever. However, by the close of the second phase both Merton and Suzuki seem mutually satisfied that they had understood one another and mutually affirmed the validity of one another's positions.

5

Interiority and the Meanings of "God"

MERTON HAD MOVED TO a position where he could affirm that both he and Suzuki were familiar with the same Ultimate Reality and anticipated and inchoately realized the same fulfillment of consciousness. The move eroded much of his suspicion that non-Christian contemplative traditions where more properly understood as "natural" means and methods than as genuine purveyors of "supernatural" wisdom. The dialogue concerning religious experience required him to draw upon interior events within consciousness to ground meanings of "God" that both he and Suzuki could affirm and it generated the insight that enabled his movement.[1] It led him, I will argue, to recognize a series of successively related meanings of "God" that illustrate his enduring commitment to Christ as the fullness of divine revelation while still affirming *genuine knowledge* of God in other religious traditions.[2]

---

1. Some of the content in this chapter regarding the meanings of "God" and their successive relation first appeared in Raab, "Insights from the Inter-Contemplative Dialogue."

2. There are similarities here to what the theological tradition refers to by the distinction between "general" and "special" revelation. General revelation considers creation itself as God's first revelation, whereby "God gives . . . an enduring witness to Himself in created realities" (*DV* 3) and regards human consciousness as capable of coming to know *that* God is by the use of reason (such as Aquinas argues through his "five ways" in *Summa Theologiae* I, q.2, a.3). Special revelation, whereby God speaks through the prophets in a human voice, and becomes flesh in the Person of Christ, is required in order for humans to know *Who* God is. This distinction, however, is not quite sufficient for mapping the three meanings of God discussed in this chapter since Merton and Suzuki freely utilize not only "reason" but more fundamentally "religious experience" as a source for knowledge of God, a move that blurs the line somewhat between general and special revelation. Personal (or private) supernatural revelation is recognized by Catholicism

Opening New Horizons

Meanings of "God" in and beyond the Merton/Suzuki Dialogue

Bernard Lonergan's work disclosed a ground for metaphysical and theological language, whose terms purport to mediate what is actually true and not merely *refer* to internally imagined images or externally sensible objects. In these realms of discourse Lonergan argued that for "every term and relation there will exist a corresponding element in human consciousness."[3] The term "God," for Lonergan, carries three distinct and successively related true meanings. The first correlates with the transcendental intending of consciousness itself, or consciousness as operative and as given. The second meaning correlates with the *experienced fulfillment* of consciousness in unrestricted love and freedom. The third meaning is one that does not *immediately* correspond to human consciousness, rather it depends upon *belief* in God's own self-communication, revelation in word, so the meaning corresponds only mediately to human consciousness.

The First Meaning of God: The Absolute, Eternal, Infinite Mystery

Karl Rahner, when speaking of what I am calling "the first meaning of the word 'God,'" wrote:

> The word refers to the "ineffable one," the nameless one who does not enter into the world we can name as a part of it. It means "the silent one" who is always there, and yet can be overlooked, unheard, and because it expresses the whole in its unity and totality, can be passed over as meaningless. It means that which really is wordless, because every word receives its limits. . . . For it is the final word before we become silent, the word which allows all the individual things we can name to disappear into the background, the word in which we are dealing with the totality which grounds them all.[4]

The first meaning is the most general and might be expressed as the ultimate ground and goal of intentional consciousness. The meaning correlates with the dynamism of unlimited wonder manifest in human consciousness through questions. As Lonergan put it:

---

and falls under the category of "religious experience" (see *CCC*, 67).

3. Lonergan, *Method*, 21.
4. Rahner, *Foundations of Christian Faith*, 46–47.

Interiority and the Meanings of "God"

> The question of God . . . is not a matter of image or feeling, of concept or judgment. They pertain to answers. It is a question. It rises out of our conscious intentionality, out of the *a priori* drive that promotes us from experiencing to the effort to understand, from understanding to the effort to judge truly, from judging to the effort to choose rightly. In the measure that we advert to our own questioning and proceed to question it, there arises the question of God. . . . It follows that, however much religious or irreligious answers differ, however much there differ the questions they explicitly raise, still at their root there is the same transcendental tendency of the human spirit that questions, that questions without restriction, that questions the significance of its own questioning, and so comes to the question of God. The question of God, then, lies within [our] horizon. Our transcendental subjectivity is mutilated or abolished, unless [we are] stretching forth towards the intelligible, the unconditioned, the good of value. The reach, not of [our] attainment, but of [our] intending is unrestricted.[5]

The question of God typifies the intentional consciousness of human subjects. The question arises naturally for a person who adverts to his or her own questioning and proceeds to question it. This adverting, in a sense, leads one to the discovery of one's self *as* a question. So there is a direct correlation between the self as question and the question of God. This question allows one to grasp the possibility of transcendent reality; and so it is by the question that the term God, in this sense, becomes meaningful.[6] That is to say, this meaning is not determinate; rather it corresponds with my intention, so the meaning is one of mystery. In other words, if I affirm that the horizon of my questioning is unrestricted, I can infer that I ultimately intend the absolute, and that by this intending I am already in relation to that ultimate reality. Now this reality that I become aware of can be objectified, among other ways, as "Absolute Mystery" "Absolute Being" or "Absolute Void."[7]

---

5. Lonergan, *Method*, 103.

6. For Merton on what Lonergan calls "the question of God," see *NSC*, 1–14; *NM*, 3–4. Lonergan's position here is also thoroughly consonant with that of Keiji Nishitani of the Kyoto School of Buddhist philosophy. Nishitani wrote, "When we have become a question to ourselves, the religious quest awakens within us." See Nishitani, *Religion and Nothingness*, 1–4.

7. These are just some of the terms both Merton and Suzuki employ in their dialogue in mutually agreeable ways.

Opening New Horizons

The question of God establishes a horizon of transcendence and once this horizon is established a person can articulate more specific questions. As James Price wrote:

> Once the question of God has emerged . . . and the possibility of a horizon of transcendence glimpsed, the issue of religion arises in a second, more specific way. The horizon of transcendence becomes the specific focus of attention and a new set of questions emerges: What is the ground of consciousness? How is it experienced? How is it related to human consciousness? In what sense can it be known? How can it be most adequately expressed? Note that this set of questions (albeit articulated in terms of interiority) addresses the major issues raised by the [contemplatives] of the various traditions.[8]

Perhaps a few examples will help to illustrate how glimpsing the horizon of transcendence generates expressions consonant with this first meaning of the term "God." Merton's friend, the Jewish mystic Abraham Joshua Heschel, wrote: "Awe is a sense for the transcendence, for the reference everywhere to *mystery* beyond all things. It enables us . . . to feel in the rush of the passing the stillness of the eternal. What we cannot comprehend by analysis, we become aware of in awe."[9] The Muslim theologian and scholar of Islam, Seyyed Hossein Nasr, described Allah as "the Beyond-Being about which nothing can be said without delimiting His Infinite and Absolute Essence, which is beyond all determination."[10] The sacred Sanskrit text, the *Svetesvatara Upanishad*, addresses God in terms of the first meaning by saying that Brahman is "beyond time. Indivisible, infinite . . . womb and tomb of the universe and its abode."[11] The Chinese classic the *Tao Te Ching* begins with this meaning by asserting that "The Tao that can be told is not the eternal Tao . . . the *nameless* is the beginning of heaven and earth."[12]

---

8. Price, "Typologies and the Cross-Cultural Analysis of Mysticism," 185.

9. Heschel, *I Asked for Wonder*, 3.

10. Nasr, "Islam," 456.

11. *Upanishads*, 127. Generally speaking, in the Upanishads *Brahman* names the ultimate reality *as it is transcendent*, while *Atman* names the ultimate reality *as it is immanent*.

12. *Tao Te Ching*, 1. Commenting on this very passage in his essay "Christian Culture Needs Oriental Wisdom," Merton wrote: "[The *Tao*] is the formless form, the imageless image. It is 'the fountain spirit' of inexhaustible life and yet never draws attention to itself. It does its work without remark and without recognition. It is utterly elusive: if you think you have seen it, what you have seen is not the *Tao*. Yet it is the source of all, and all things

Interiority and the Meanings of "God"

Commenting on the Mahayana Buddhist philosopher Nagarjuna (c. 150–c. 250 CE) Masao Abe wrote of *Sunyata* as the *immeasurable unfathomable absolute* emptiness "an emptiness that empties even itself" and makes all things truly be.[13]

Since the question of God is a question and not an answer, my "knowing" of what is intended by my question is apophatic, indeterminate, and only by anticipation. So the first meaning of God is *negative* in the sense that it negates limitations from the transcendent reality and points back to the limitations of human consciousness. First-meaning terms for God say what God is not. "Absolute Being" says that God is *not* conditioned by anything. "Eternal" says that God is *not* limited by time and space, and "mystery" that God is *not* proportionate to our comprehension so cannot be fully known or understood. The first meaning of God correlates directly with the raising of the question. It is, as Merton says, a discovering of one's self in "existential mystery" (*NSC*, 9). Both Merton and Suzuki have glimpsed this horizon, which establishes for them a common realm of meaning for the term God.

Outside the context of their dialogue, Suzuki commented on the orientation of the "mind" toward Ultimate Reality and spoke of a meaning of "God" from the horizon of transcendence as "eternity" and "eternal abyss." Suzuki wrote that "in the working of the ... mind there is something calm, quiet, silent ... which appears as if always looking into eternity. This quietude, however, does not point to mere idleness.... It is the silence of an eternal abyss.... It is the silence of God."[14]

When Suzuki characterized enlightenment as transcending the reach of intentional consciousness, he was affirming the transcendent ground and goal of consciousness itself. He wrote:

> So we see that Enlightenment is not the outcome of an intellectual process in which one idea follows another in sequence finally to terminate in conclusion or judgment. There is neither process nor judgment in Enlightenment, it is ... more fundamental, something which makes a judgment possible, and without which no form of judgment can take place. In judgment there are a subject and a predicate; in Enlightenment ... they are ... merged as one, but not as one of which something can be stated, but as one from

return to it 'as to their home'" (*SE*, 106).
13. Abe, "Kenotic God and Dynamic Sunyata," 27.
14. Suzuki, *Introduction to Zen Buddhism*, 35.

> which arises judgment . . . all intellectual operations stop here. This is the wall against which all philosophies have beaten in vain. This is an intellectual terra incognita, in which prevails the principle, 'Credo quia absurdum est.' This region of darkness, however, gives up its secrets when attacked by the will, by the force of one's entire personality. Enlightenment is the illuminating of this dark region, when the whole thing is seen at one glance, and all intellectual inquiries find here their rationale. The Buddha must have experienced something that went far deeper into his inmost consciousness than the mere intellectual grasping of empirical truths. . . . He must have come in touch with that which makes our intellectual operations possible, in fact that which conditions the very existence of our conscious life.[15]

Implicit in this passage is the distinction between individual human consciousness as intentional, manifested in its operations, and the transcendent ground and goal of consciousness itself. The fundamental affirmation that Suzuki makes here is that God grounds and transcends all conscious operations, yet Suzuki is still employing those operations in order to affirm this ultimate ground and to write about it (as of course he must). So one might suggest that although enlightenment is certainly experience-based, and not simply identical with the operations of consciousness, it necessarily involves subsequent operations of consciousness in its realization and in the attempt to understand and to say something about it.

Suzuki is also asserting here that enlightenment is more than the raising of the question of God. For the question of God brings one to the region of darkness, the *terra incognita*, where trust must prevail over understanding. But enlightenment is the "illuminating of this dark region" where, to speak in terms of a faculty psychology, the "will" must transcend what can be grasped by the "intellect." To put this in terms of transcendental method, Lonergan says that "besides the factual knowledge reached by experiencing, understanding, and verifying, there is another kind of knowledge reached through the discernment of value . . . on the existential level of intentional consciousness and in the dynamic state of being in love."[16] Lonergan calls this knowledge "faith" or "the knowledge born of religious love" and he compares it to Pascal's reasons of the heart, "which reason does not understand." This knowing "illuminates" the region that remains dark to human understanding and brings us to the second meaning of "God."

15. Suzuki, *Essays in Zen Buddhism, First Series*, 68–69
16. Lonergan, *Method*, 115.

Interiority and the Meanings of "God"

The Second Meaning of "God": Identifying the Absolute with Light, Love, and Freedom

Merton too makes a basic affirmation of Ultimate Reality as the ground and goal of consciousness, even before he begins to treat Zen in these general terms, especially in his own accounts of understanding himself as a "question."[17] This basic affirmation constitutes a common horizon and realm of meaning for Merton and Suzuki that partly accounts for their "unity of outlook and purpose." There is, however, a further, and more important meaning of Ultimate Reality shared by Merton and Suzuki, and Merton calls this a "second level of awareness." Merton writes:

> The life of contemplation implies two levels of awareness: first, awareness of the question, and second, awareness of the answer. Though these are two distinct and enormously different levels, they are in fact an awareness of the same thing. . . . We awaken not to find an answer absolutely distinct from the question, but to realize that the question is its own answer . . . The contemplation of which I speak is a religious and transcendent gift. . . . It is the gift of God Who, in His mercy, completes the hidden and mysterious work of creation in us by enlightening our mind and hearts. (*NSC*, 4–5)

Merton here moves beyond the question of God to an answer. The answer comes through the enlightening of the mind and the heart. It perfectly parallels Suzuki's enlightenment, which goes beyond "the question of God," a question that opens out into the intellectual *terra incognita* and discovers an answer through the "illuminating of this dark region." Within the horizon of transcendence the first meaning of "God" centers around "question, darkness, intention, mystery" and emphasizes God's transcendence. The second meaning of "God" appears in the language of "illumination and fulfillment" and emphasizes intimacy, immanence, and union.

Lonergan would characterize the second meaning of "God" as established by "religious experience" and "religious conversion." For Lonergan, this further meaning is established by an affirmation made in light of the experience of the incipient total fulfillment of intentional consciousness. That is to say, the first meaning of Ultimate Reality is correlative with our anticipation and intention while the second correlates with the basic

---

17. For example, Merton wrote, "It is as if in creating us, God asked a question" (*NSC*, 3), and in *Untitled Poem* Merton wrote, "Each one who is born / Comes into the world as a question" (see Merton, *Eighteen Poems*).

fulfillment of our unlimited intending discovered through the experience of unrestricted love or freedom.

Lonergan writes:

> The transcendental notions, that is our questions for intelligence, for reflection and for deliberation, constitute our capacity for self-transcendence. That capacity becomes an actuality when one falls in love. Then one's being becomes being-in-love ... as the question of God is implicit in all our questioning, so being in love with God is the basic fulfillment of our conscious intentionality. ... Being in love with God, as experienced ... is being in love without limits or qualifications or conditions or reservations.[18]

This experience is not the product of knowledge or decision. It is an experience that leads to further questions.

The experience of being in unrestricted love leads to a richer meaning of the term "God" or "Ultimate Reality." This experience is what the mystics, who are generally apophatic and withdraw from objectification, rely upon for their positive affirmations regarding God. With the objectification of God, or Ultimate Reality, as "love, goodness, holiness," the human person is faced with the decision of whether he or she will love in return, live out of this Ultimate Love committed to its often hidden invitations and demands. The decision to do so, for Lonergan, constitutes religious conversion. In this sense "conversion" is non-sectarian and religiously converted persons can and do exist in every religion and some claim no religious affiliation. The experience of unrestricted love "dismantles and abolishes the horizon in which our knowing and choosing went on." The acceptance of this love "sets up a new horizon in which the love of God will transvalue our values and that love will transform our knowing."[19]

This second meaning of God or "Ultimate Reality" is one that Merton understands as mutually affirmed by both Suzuki and himself in their dialogue. Suzuki makes this affirmation in the context of their dialogue by endorsing St. Augustine's dictum "love God and do as you will" and by his insistence that "the most important thing is Love" (*ZBA*, 62).[20] While

---

18. Lonergan, *Method*, 105–6.

19. Lonergan, *Method*, 106. Lonergan's words are in reference to religious experience but I am emphasizing the necessity of commitment, which corresponds to decision-making, because (and Lonergan supports this) the experience of unrestricted love is still open to acceptance or rejection on the part of the human subject. It is acceptance and commitment that actualizes religious conversion.

20. Merton also wrote in his journal on June 17, 1964, reflecting on his meeting with

Interiority and the Meanings of "God"

Merton affirms the second meaning of "God" in nearly everything he writes, a clear articulation of this appears in *Conjectures of a Guilty Bystander* where he wrote: "Absolute truth is then grasped as love. . . . Only he who loves can be sure that he is still in contact with the truth, which is in fact too absolute to be grasped by his mind" (*CGB*, 44). This richer meaning of Ultimate Reality, shared by Merton and Suzuki, adds to the establishment of their "unity of outlook and purpose." Because the first two meanings of "God" or "Ultimate Reality" are immediately correlative with human consciousness, and therefore transcultural[21] in their simplest expressions, Merton and Suzuki could find themselves occupying the precise standpoints where communication about ultimate concerns could prove most effective (*ZBA*, 60).

At this point, I ought to say something about religious conversion facilitating or advancing the transvaluation of values. For Lonergan, falling in love without limits transforms the human subject, first of all with respect to his or her apprehensions of value.[22] Judgments of value involve the person at the apex of subjectivity (they are "fourth level" operations). But the person who falls in love will also be opened to new experiences, will understand, and will make judgments in light of this transformative love. In other words, even though Lonergan "locates" religious conversion as a response of the subject at the height of his or her subjectivity, the commitment that one makes on this level transforms one's whole way of being in and with the world. Metaphorically speaking, one begins to see with the eyes of faith, with the "inner eye" of love. The "unity of outlook and purpose" that Merton and Suzuki share can also be demonstrated with respect to their apprehensions and judgments of value.

Even while Merton continued to be puzzled by divergent points in the "doctrines" of Christianity and Buddhism regarding their understandings

---

Suzuki in New York, that "the thing he insisted on most—in Xianity and Buddhism—love more than enlightenment" (*DWL*, 115). In light of the meanings of "God" discussed here, I take this to mean that Suzuki holds the second meaning as supremely important. *Karuna* (compassion) is the fruit of *Prajna* (transcendental wisdom).

21. For a more complete presentation of this position, see Lonergan, *Method*, 105–12; "Prolegomena," 55–74.

22. For Lonergan, feelings can be understood in terms of "apprehending value." Apprehensions of value indicate why we are, say, offended by something we see, or moved by something we hear. Apprehensions are not yet "judgments of value" which compel decisions and actions. When we fall in love, what once made us cringe and recoil may now make us feel pity, compassion, or mercy. But judgment and decision are required to affirm what is right and to act accordingly.

of the human person, he was continually heartened by a mutual radical affirmation of the value of human life, affirmed by the Buddhist, if not in creed, certainly in code. Merton wrote that "on the Buddhist side there seems to be no positive idea of personality at all: it seems to be a value that is completely missing from Buddhist thought. Yet it is certainly not absent from Buddhist practice" (*ZBA*, 118). And in the context of remembering Suzuki he wrote: "One cannot understand Buddhism until one meets it in this existential manner, in a person in whom it is alive. Then there is no longer a problem of understanding doctrines which cannot help being a bit exotic for a Westerner, but only a question of appreciating a value which is self-evident" (*ZBA*, 62).

It is in the terms of the transvaluation of values that we can appreciate why Merton so readily connects the Christian conception of the "New Man" and the Taoist and Buddhist conceptions of the "Superior Man" and the "True Man" (*ZBA*, 60–62). The realm of meaning correlative with the further horizon constituted by this acceptance of unlimited love, which is also an experience of liberation and of radical freedom, enabled fruitful and effective communication between them. However, when Merton employed a further meaning of Ultimate Reality which is not immediately correlative with intentional consciousness, communication proved most difficult.

Lonergan contends that religious experience does not occur with "labels attached." Experience can be properly distinguished from meaningful mediation of same, whether it is experience of sensory data, or the data of one's own interior conscious operations, or of feelings rising up from within or seemingly out of nowhere. But experiences and subsequent understandings lead to expressions, and he talks about this as a movement from infrastructure to suprastructure. He distinguishes between "an infrastructure of insights as discoveries or of feelings as felt and . . . a suprastructure of insights as formulated in hypotheses or of feelings as integrated into conscious living."[23] Religious *experience* is on the level of infrastructure (what Merton calls the "inner experience") and its communication is through formulation and objectification on the level of suprastructure. When communities mediate religious experience in language, doctrines and deeds and are bound by shared understandings and affirmations, or confessions, we have religions. Any religious tradition is a community of shared meanings and values and it mediates its affirmed meaning of Ultimate Reality to its adherents, and the adherents shape and fill out that meaning.

23. Lonergan, "Prolegomena," 58.

Interiority and the Meanings of "God"

Buddhism and Christianity provided Suzuki and Merton with their "intellectual antecedents" that sometimes made communication very difficult. While they were nonetheless able to mutually affirm, on the level of suprastructure, many common understandings regarding Ultimate Reality and the ultimacy of Love, understandings immediately correlative with their inner experience, they also met with difficulty on the level of suprastructure when it came to dealing with the idea of persons. Part of that difficulty can be explained by the fact that Merton affirms a meaning of "God" as radically *personal*, in the fullest sense, where the Second Person of the Tri-Personal God assumed a full humanity and dwelt among us.

The Third Meaning of "God": The Trinity

Affirming the truth of Christian doctrines is dependent upon accepting *the testimony* of a community that carries with it a meaning of "God" that is *not* immediately correlative with intentional consciousness. It is formulated in the doctrine of the Trinity, which emerges from an affirmation of Christ's divinity.[24] This meaning depends upon the acceptance of Jesus Christ as the Word of God, and the acceptance of the testimony of the Christian tradition (*fides ex audito*) as the historical extension of that Word, explicated and affirmed. This community's belief, its *fides quae*, is preserved and passed on through its creeds and its worship which bear the Trinitarian structure of its faith.

In other words, the Christian understanding of God is one *that purports to be dependent upon* God's self-communication in word and deed. Creation comes into being through the Logos, who gathers a people, speaks through the prophets, and becomes flesh in Jesus Christ, and continues to speak through sacred scripture and tradition, and through the community of disciples. This further meaning of "God" emerges only mediately, and correlates only mediately with human consciousness. That is to say one hears the testimony of a community's confession and trusts in and affirms its ultimate meaning and value. A person cannot arrive at this meaning of

---

24. While it is possible to discover on the basis of interiority an internal *analogue* for the terms of the Trinity, this gives us only a shadowy image, while Christ reveals the reality of God and what the fullness of Love is and means. In other words, to move from recognizing that distinct cognitive operations generate knowledge and love, and disclose something of the divine reality, to affirming that (dis)similar relations in God constitute Persons, one of whom became human and dwelt among us, requires more than interiorly differentiated consciousness.

Opening New Horizons

"God" by acknowledging and affirming their basic orientation to the transcendent and its potential implications for the discovery of the ultimately real, or even by experiencing a fulfillment of that orientation in love and freedom without limits or conditions or qualifications, though one can come remarkably close to it.[25] No doubt these lead to genuine meanings of "God" but Christian doctrines and dogma make claims about *Who* God is by the accepting of the revelation of the Divine Word. As Lonergan wrote: "If I have concluded that there is a common element to all the religions . . . I must now add that there is a specific element proper to Christianity . . . the outward expression of God's love in Christ Jesus dying and rising again."[26]

Merton suggests that in Christianity, the experience of God (an experience initially objectified as one of "Absolute Being, Absolute Love, or Absolute Void") is "through *word and love*" while for the Buddhist it is "through *insight and emptiness*" (ZBA, 62, italics added). That is to say, the Christian *ordinarily* comes to know God through the *mediated word* though contemplatives can find God also through insight and emptiness.

Merton's early account of a profound experience in Cuba illustrates not only how his particularly Christian belief mediated for him this particular religious experience, but also suggests that he believed religious experience to be transcultural, trans religious, available to "everybody." On Monday, April 29, 1940, Merton reflected in his journal on the experience he had had at mass the previous day at the Church of San Francisco in Havana, Cuba. He wrote:

> Before my head was raised again the clear cry of the brother in the brown robe cut through the silence with the word "*Yo Creo . . .*" "I believe" which immediately all the children took up after him with such loud and strong and clear voices, and such unanimity and such meaning and such fervor that something went off inside me like a thunderclap. . . . I knew with the most absolute and unquestionable certainty that before me, between me and the altar, somewhere in the center of the church, up in the air (or any other place because in no place) . . . was at the same time God in all His Essence. . . . It was as much an experience of loving as of knowing . . . and in it love and knowledge are completely inseparable . . . the same kind [of experience] that millions of Catholics, Jews and

---

25. E.g., Suzuki's disciple Masao Abe said that his teacher often emphasized that "the most concrete fundamental wisdom" is one in which "Knowing, being, and loving (compassion) are united" (Abe, *Zen Life*, 16).

26. Lonergan, *Philosophy of God and Theology*, 10.

Interiority and the Meanings of "God"

Hindus and everybody . . . has felt; . . . absolutely everybody, in some degree or another (*RM*, 217–18).

The reference to knowing and loving again evokes the meanings of God universally shared. But this particular encounter was facilitated by the creedal confession in the context of the mass.

The Meanings of "God" as Successively Related

Emptiness, interiority, and the experience of unrestricted freedom and love yield meanings of God immediately correlative with human consciousness. When Merton wrote "The Zen Revival" he was speaking primarily from within the horizon of their "unity of outlook and purpose" and their "common spiritual climate." When Merton and Suzuki communicated from within this horizon, Merton called this their dialogue as "monks and Zen men" and he found it profoundly important to be able to occupy these precise standpoints. But when he attempted to treat Zen in the language of Christian theology, employing distinctions between the natural and the supernatural, between the recovery of Paradise and the eschatological fullness of Heaven, he met with the realization of a communication breakdown. What I find most significant here is that Merton did not judge points of divergence in his dialogues as things to be ignored, or trivialized, rather he asserted that "differences must remain until moments of greater insight." His ability to say "yes" to the other whenever he could, while remaining faithful to his own position at points of apparent impasse indicated his understanding of how these meanings of "God" are related.

I want to look now at two instances where Merton begins to hint at his own model for understanding the accounts of other contemplatives in relation to his own faith. The first is found in his essay "Final Integration: Towards a 'Monastic Therapy'" from *Contemplation in a World of Action* and the second is a selection from "Contemplation and Dialogue" in *Mystics and Zen Masters*. These are by no means the only examples out there—there are many places where he does this—but these two are succinct and sufficiently clear for our purposes. He writes in the first:

> The infant who lives immersed in a symbiotic relationship with the rest of nature . . . must be "born" out of this . . . and acquire an identity as a responsible member of society. . . . But once one has grown up, acquired an education, and assumed a useful role . . . there is still another birth to be undergone. In Sufism, Zen

> Buddhism and in many other spiritual religions, emphasis is placed on the call to fulfill certain obscure yet urgent potentialities in the ground of one's being.... The man who is "fully born" ... apprehends his life fully and wholly from an inner ground that is at once more universal than the empirical ego and yet entirely his own.... He has attained to a deep inner freedom—the Freedom of the Spirit we read of in the New Testament.... The state of insight which is final integration implies ... the void, poverty and nonaction which leave one entirely docile to the "Sprit." ... The man who has attained final integration ... is fully "Catholic" in the best sense of word. He has a unified vision and experience of the one truth shining out in all its various manifestations, some clearer than others, some more definite and more certain than others.... It is suggested also in the "Degrees of Truth" and the "Degrees of Love" in St. Bernard's tracts on humility and on the love of God.[27]
> ... However for a Christian, a transcultural integration is eschatological. [It is the] rebirth of man and of society ... into the transformed and redeemed time, the time of the Kingdom, the time of the Spirit.... A disintegration of the social and cultural self, the product of merely human history, and the reintegration of that self in Christ, in salvation history, in the mystery of redemption, in the Pentecostal "new creation." But this means entering into the full mystery of the eschatological Church. (*CWA*, 205–7).

Within the framework of the three meanings of "God" we could say that "void, poverty, and non-action" evoke the transcendent mystery of the first meaning, while the attainment of the deep inner freedom, the freedom of the Spirit,[28] speaks to the second meaning of "God," born out of the expe-

---

27. Merton's extensive lectures on St. Bernard of Clairvaux are available in *CFMT* (for his comments relative to what he references here, see esp. 68–80).

28. Merton's clear reference to the Holy Spirit, which is a term of Trinitarian doctrine, might beg the question why I consider the expression here correlative with the second meaning of "God" and not the third. The distinction in Christian theology between the inner word of God written in the hearts of all people (the gift of the Holy Spirit) and the "outer" Word, Jesus, crucified, risen and proclaimed by the apostles and disciples provides the answer from the horizon of theological discourse. Still, since the Word is both Incarnate and eternal—the distinction between the inner and outer Word is not so sharp. For a theological explication of the position that affirms the experience of the Holy Spirit as one that is transcultural see Crowe, "Son of God, Holy Spirit and World Religions." For a Zen Buddhist's affirmation of the approach to interreligious dialogue with Christians in light of the experience of the Holy Spirit, see Nhat Hanh, *Living Buddha, Living Christ*, 13–25. Thich Nhat Hanh believes that the safest way for a Buddhist to approach the doctrine of the Trinity "is through the door of the Holy Spirit" and he believes "all of us have the seed of the Holy Spirit in us, the capacity of healing, transforming, and loving."

rienced fulfillment of human consciousness. Finally, coming to understand this as a participation in salvation history, in "the mystery of redemption," requires "entry into the full mystery of the eschatological Church" and this fills out a third and Trinitarian meaning of "God." The fact that Merton treats these three successively, each flowing into and built upon by the other, suggests that entering into the full mystery of the eschatological Church is not something peripheral for him but focal in his own vision. It is clear that the realization of "final integration" as this deep inner freedom is not dependent upon confessing Christian faith, yet he still presents his Christian faith as offering something important to it. He sets it up as an augmentation of religious meaning, a more complete expression of the truth.

Furthermore, in his essay "Contemplation and Dialogue" Merton suggests a way in which the third meaning of "God" unites genuine knowledge of God with the spiritual experience expressed in the paradox of "fullness and emptiness, *todo y nada*, void and infinity, which appears at the heart of all the great traditional forms of contemplative wisdom" (*MZM*, 212). He suggests that the revelation of God at work in history through Christ's cross and resurrection offers something profoundly important to this contemplative wisdom. He asserts that the mysteries discovered in contemplation find their ultimate meaning and validation in "the Cross of Christ, which is the mystery of *kenosis*, the self-emptying of God, the sacrificial submission of the 'Suffering Servant' (Isa 52) who became obedient 'even unto death' (Phil 2:5–19)" (*MZM*, 212). He continued:

> Here too we paradoxically encounter, in the "word of the cross," the emptying of all human wisdoms (1 Cor 1:18–25). . . . Texts such as these . . . will then be seen as . . . Christian answers to the profound questions raised by all these ancient traditions, which seem to have been grasping at the central truths in their own way. Thus, the full idea of Christian contemplation is a *theoria* that powerfully unites and fuses both "incarnational" and "eschatological" Christianity and then opens out into the realm of divine illumination, the *theologia* in which the highest mystery, the Trinity of Persons in one Nature, is not contemplated as "object" but is celebrated in the hymn of the Spirit, "Abba, Father!" (*MZM*, 213)

By casting Christ crucified and risen as the pivotal point of history and the fullness of divine revelation, he is offering a view that the gospel is both the perfect complement to these *sapiential* traditions and the answer to further questions raised by them. The rightful role of the Christian contemplative in the dialogue is to learn from the other, to discover and affirm the light of God in all its various manifestations, and to continually *point to Christ* crucified and risen as the answer to the profound questions raised by these traditions.

For the later Merton this had nothing to do with triumphalism, or to a presumed superiority of Christian *contemplation*, but had only to do with whom he believed Christ to be. The mature Merton was consistently critical of triumphalism and prescribed humility as the proper dialogical stance, with an openness to discovering the light of Christ in the voice of the stranger. But the fact that Merton continued to hold the "Trinity of Persons in One Nature" as "the highest mystery" should not surprise anyone. One of Merton's beloved Church fathers, Evagrius Ponticus, was fond of saying "if you pray you are a theologian,"[29] and by theologian Evagrius meant "one who contemplates the Trinity."[30]

This contemplation of the Trinity, the highest mystery, is the focal point of Cistercian monastic life, and for more than a quarter-century, and up to his death, Merton was steeped in the rhythms of Catholic liturgy, the Divine Office, the Liturgy of the Hours, the celebration of the Mass. As the old Catholic adage has it, *lex orandi, lex credendi*, how one prays informs one's beliefs. Since Merton never left the church or the monastic life no one should be surprised that he never quit trying to understand the other from within his own tradition. And for those who share his faith, this is not a lacuna but to his credit. As a young monk he was often concerned to assure himself of his orthodoxy by offering merely pejorative accounts of any tradition other than Catholic. However, he eventually learned to understand others by allowing them to speak for themselves, without first imposing his own categories upon their language. But even the elder Merton would try to integrate his newly acquired understandings within the framework of his own religious commitments. He had little choice really about taking the final step. Merton's mind was habitually moving toward higher forms of synthesis; he was always striving for a further horizon capable of integrating seemingly opposing and disparate views, if at all possible.

When Merton expanded "The Zen Revival" to become the first chapter in *Mystics and Zen Masters* he went even further in his consideration of Hui Neng's "Unconscious as manifest and conscious in us." He boldly

---

29. Evagrius, *De Oratione* 60 (see *ICM*, 107).
30. *ICM*, 109–10, 117–18.

Interiority and the Meanings of "God"

asserted that the "Unconscious" exhibited a "Trinitarian structure" isomorphic with human consciousness:

> And the "Trinitarian structure" is this: the ground of all Being is pure Void (*sunyata*–emptiness), which is *prajna*, light illuminating everything in a pure Act of being–void without any limitation. The ground–Being is not distinct from itself as Light and as Act. And to this basic constitution of being there corresponds the threefold disposition of the mind in illumination. First, the ground which is Void, second the emptiness and nowhereness of no-mind which is *dhyana* (right meditation) and illumination; and third, the act of realization or *prajna*, in which the void and light are so to speak let loose in pure freedom and power to give and spend in action. . . . This means inevitably a fulfillment in love, which is what one seemingly least expects in Hui Neng, but it is an ineluctable consequence of the Trinitarian structure of being which his Zen perceives and reveals. (*MZM*, 40–41)[31]

Merton may appear guilty of some eisegesis here, but his own Trinitarian vision of reality was not something he could step out of, and surely he saw this as an *affirmation* of the truth of Buddhism, rather than an *imposition* of his Christian doctrine upon it.[32] In this way he is acknowledging not only the given omnipresence of the Trinity, and its isomorphic relation with creation and with human consciousness, but also a kind of awareness, even apprehension, of the Trinity in Buddhist contemplative wisdom. And though the Buddhist may *never* employ or adopt the same suprastructure, affirm the same *fides quae*, Zen "reveals" the same truth and grows out of it.

---

31. After meeting Suzuki in person, which he mentions in this context, Merton was convinced that the Zen teacher exhibited the fruits of the Holy Spirit, and that he was sincere in his assertion that "the most important thing is love" (*MZM*, 41). This emboldened Merton to write directly about "a fulfillment in love" and an implicit affirmation of the Trinity in Hui Neng's writing.

32. Though not Trinitarian in the technical theological sense, many Hindu mystics speak of God, or Ultimate Reality as having the *trinary* structure of Being–Consciousness, and Bliss (Sat–Chit–Ananda) and Buddhists of Emptiness, Wisdom, and Compassion (Sunyata, Prajna, and Karuna). Pramuk has brilliantly elucidated that for Merton Christ is the incarnate divine wisdom (Sophia/Prajna) and this sapiential Christology, grounded in religious experience, offers a bridge to "the dialogue of theological exchange." In this way, dialogue between Christian contemplatives and Buddhists at the doctrinal level most effectively begins, from the Christian side, *with* the doctrine of the Trinity and Christ as divine wisdom incarnate; a Christological approach that terminates in the undeniable historical particularity of Jesus of Nazareth, and lets Jesus ask in a way he can best be heard: "Who do you say that I am?" (see Pramuk, *Sophia*, 285–88).

I have discussed Merton's synthesis with reference to three distinctive meanings of the term "God," each of which he affirms to be true but which he tends to prioritize in successive relation, so that he continues to hold the Trinity as the highest mystery. This means that his understanding of religious pluralism will be one that tends to account for the transcultural phenomenon of "final integration" in terms of the work of the Spirit which he did not see as restricted to the Christian community.

However, because he held a Trinitarian faith he could not separate the work of the transforming Spirit from the Unbegotten Origin or from the Begotten Word. He stood firmly within a theological tradition that reaches back to the Hebrew Scriptures in their portrayal of God's immanence through the images of Word/Wisdom and Spirit.[33] Irenaeus, the pre-Nicene theologian, read God's Word and God's Wisdom as the "two hands" of the transcendent and ineffable God, then identified them as God's Son and God's Spirit. As O'Collins noted, Irenaeus used the image like a potter's hands whereby God's Word/Wsidom and God's Spirit bring forth creation and shape, form, and intimately order all of creation toward its telos.[34] Since God the Word/Wisdom and God the Spirit are omnipresent and ever operative as God's immanence, God the Unbegotten and Invisible is everywhere speaking to everyone all the time. For Merton, wherever the Spirit is working, so too Christ is present. He was convinced that there is a presence of Christ to every person and this *"is perhaps the deepest most cogent mystery of our time"* (CGB, 298).

---

33. Gerald O'Collins wrote: "Naming God as Father, Son (Word or Wisdom), and Spirit found its roots in the OT. There Wisdom, Word, and Spirit functioned, frequently synonymously, to acknowledge the transcendent God's nearness to the world and to the chosen people—a nearness that did not, however, compromise the divine transcendence, or that otherness that sets God 'beyond' all other beings" (O'Collins, *Tripersonal God*, 32).

34. O'Collins, *Tripersonal God*, 215n11.

6

Anatman and the Reality of *Persons*

THEIR DIALOGUE PROGRESSED INTO the area of doctrines whereby Merton realized that without a clearer understanding of "person" he could not adequately show that while he affirmed the Buddhist doctrine of *anatman* as he understood it, he also affirmed the Christian doctrine of *theosis* and that this was not for him an irreconcilable opposition.[1] Suzuki's enthusiastic reception of "The Zen Revival" suggested that he approved of Merton's efforts to articulate a positive idea of the "person" commensurate with Zen. Yet Merton's comment in his journal that "we could not get anywhere definite on the idea of a 'person'" (*DWL*, 115) in their casual conversations in New York, suggested Merton was still not totally satisfied. The move to interiority yielded true and transcultural meanings of "God" and the same move was beginning to yield a more satisfactory meaning of "person." Though Merton does not explicitly define a *human* person as a "subsistent relation" he basis his own anthropology on the meaning of "person" as employed in Trinitarian discourse and this approaches, I argue, a true and transcultural meaning of "person" acceptable to Buddhists.

His dialogue with Suzuki left him wanting to show that while he accepted the radically iconoclastic rejection of "the self" exhibited by Hui Neng, he was nonetheless committed to affirming the reality of the person in the concrete and the person's fulfillment as a divinization within the life

---

1. The doctrine of *anatman* (the Sanskrit for "no soul") is also commonly referred to as *anatta* (the Pali for "no soul" or "no self"). It is one of the three "marks of existence" along with impermanence (*anicca*) and suffering (*dukkha*). When the Buddha contemplated his own interior consciousness he did not find a substantial or essential nature in himself (*atman*), that enjoyed any permanent existence; instead he found no-soul.

of the Trinity. Roughly a year after his meeting with Suzuki in New York, the Vatican promulgated *Nostra Aetate* and he was heartened by its exhortation to Catholics to engage in "dialogue and collaboration with followers of other religions" (*NA* 2, 3). As he began to hope for more opportunities for fruitful dialogues he remained acutely aware that the notion of *person* "will require considerable clarification before a real dialogue can begin . . . on the level of doctrine or of metaphysics" (*MZM*, 210). He wrote, "Christian contemplatives must be able to show the Asian contemplative that the Christian too is aware of the religious dimension of the Person and . . . does not confuse the person with the individual" (*MZM*, 213–14).

Merton had already contributed to that clarification, but he was often more helpful in clarifying what the person was not. He was certain that the "self-conscious self" is born through a differentiation within consciousness and is therefore secondary (*MZM*, 22–23). The problem, however, is that without the insight that the subject/object distinction is secondary, humans take their "self-conscious selves" to be absolutely primary, or fundamental. The self-conscious self is not *de facto* the false self. It is "not by nature evil, and the fact that it is unsubstantial is not imputed to it as some kind of a crime" (*NSC*, 295), but it becomes the false self when it is "isolated in a lie" and takes itself to be primary along with an "objective" world that exists outside and apart from it. The false self is the self-conscious self insofar as it is "alienated from its spiritual depths" and considers itself to be, or even desires to be, absolute. But what did Merton mean by a "person"?

Body/Soul and Person

Anne Carr's work deftly disclosed the ways in which Jacques Maritain's metaphysical anthropology influenced Merton's thinking about the person and what he commonly referred to as the true self.[2] Maritain relied on Aquinas's view that the human being was a composite of matter and spirit.[3] For Maritain, the material pole accounted for one's individuality, particularity, and finitude, while the spiritual pole constituted one's orientation to the eternal and transcendent, and reached out for communion with God

---

2. See Carr, *Search for Wisdom and Spirit*, esp. chapter 1, "The Seeds of the Self."

3. Merton begins *ZR* by invoking R. C. Zaehner's work *Matter and Spirit* as a kind of foil for illustrating how modern westerners dismiss Zen as a tradition that fails to take the material world seriously. Merton searched for a grasp of this distinction that could exonerate Zen but also ground a positive notion of the person.

and others. The spiritual pole is the principle, as Carr put it, "for creative unity, independence, freedom, and especially for love."[4] In a virtuous *person* the material pole is disciplined and conditioned by the spiritual pole, enabling her or him to manifest increasing kindness, generosity, compassion, and self-control. When the polar relation is imbalanced and inverted, however, the material pole, which is good and natural insofar as it is given, becomes a corrupting and dominating force making an *individual* more selfish, cruel, and vicious. Maritain's view of the person served Merton well for a long time, but it came up a bit short for him when trying to find common ground with Suzuki on "a positive idea of the person" which seemed totally absent from Zen doctrine but not from Zen ethics.

The difficulty becomes focused when we consider that Maritain's metaphysical anthropology rests on a distinction between matter and spirit that is vulnerable, if not properly grasped, to become a dualistic division. Just as the "self-conscious self" becomes a problem absent the insight that it is the result of a secondary differentiation within consciousness, so too the distinction between matter and spirit is something secondary, and can become problematic if taken to be basic and primary. Since Zen, at least as Merton understood it, was profoundly allergic to erecting any kind of metaphysic that presupposed the validity of necessary distinctions, the challenge, as he recognized it, was to articulate a positive meaning for the human person prescinding, as it were, from the matter/spirit distinction.[5]

In Platonist doctrine the soul (spirit) is in the body (matter) the way a charioteer is in a chariot. The soul is the subject, the operator, the one who is conscious and who experiences and understands; it is "the self." The body is the shell, the flesh, the matter to be controlled in life and escaped and left behind at death.[6] Merton himself noted the heretical tendencies

---

4. Carr, *Search for Wisdom and Spirit*, 28–29.

5. When Merton wrote that "Christian contemplatives must be able to show the Asian contemplative that the Christian, too, is aware of the religious dimension of the Person" (*MZM*, 213–14), he implied that he was prepared to start from that "religious dimension" in future dialogues and that this would be preferable to beginning with notions of the human person that presuppose the validity of the body/soul, matter/spirit distinction. I am working out some implications of that here.

6. See Lonergan, "Theology as a Christian Phenomenon," 244–72, at 251. Lonergan asserts that "the notion of soul in general was unknown to Athanasius." Athanasius's assertion that Christ had a human soul, according to Lonergan, was simply aimed against the Apollinarists who rejected it on the basis of their Platonic anthropology. Athanasius's refusal to diminish Christ's humanity propelled his assertion of a human "soul" in Christ, though he did not have, or need, according to Lonergan, a clear idea of what he meant by *soul*.

of body/soul dualism that plagued the early church through the Hellenizing influences of Platonic and Neoplatonic thought, writing: "Nowhere in the New Testament do we find such an ideal of complete deliverance of the soul from the body. On the contrary, the New Testament envisages the spiritualization of the whole [person], body and soul together, pointing to the Resurrection of the Flesh" (*CF*, 19). The clearly dualistic implications of Platonic anthropology, in which souls and bodies are ultimately separable, make it utterly unsuitable as a basis for dialogue with Zen Buddhism. However, Aquinas's concept of "soul," which Maritain and Merton adopt, relies on Aristotle, not Plato, and for "the philosopher" the soul is something far more complicated and, at first blush, elusive.

For Aristotle the soul is not a thing, and not a substance, but "the form of the body." Form (soul) is what makes matter a substance, or a thing "an intelligible unity." Form (soul) does not exist outside and apart from the body, but is a component of the person, distinct from the body and together with the body constituting the person. Aristotle did, however, regard the intellect (*nous*), which is an aspect unique to human souls, as capable of existing beyond the body.[7] Aristotle's view of the human person is more resistant to the charge of dualism, and resists the strict identification of either matter or spirit with the human person, but it nonetheless relies on the body/soul (matter/spirit) distinction.[8] Aquinas, in his Christian appro-

---

7. Aristotle, *De Anima* iii.4 (429a9–10); cf. iii.3 (428a5); iii.9 (432b26); iii.12 (434b3). See also Shields, "Aristotle's Psychology."

8. Merton did affirm the truth of the distinction between matter and spirit, though he would reject the idea that it committed him to some kind of dualism. For him, God is united with matter as its source and sustainer, and indissolubly with it via the Incarnation of the Word, and the Resurrection of the Body. Though many Christians *are* dualists, Christian doctrine has always maintained a resistance against it, e.g., in the orthodox denial of Gnosticism and Manichaeism. The Christian doctrinal tradition had to part ways with the Platonic concept of the soul, which is dualistic, initially due to Christological reasons. Christ could not be conceived as a divine subject simply operating a human body, and still be regarded as fully human. Affirming Christ's full humanity required affirming his human consciousness, mind and will—not just his body. The tradition maintained that "whatever was not assumed" by the Incarnation "could not be saved," and given a dualistic separation of minds and bodies, if the One Christ had only assumed a human body, then human bodies could be saved but not their souls. Nor could Christ have both a divine soul and a human soul from within the Platonic framework, or He would be two subjects, two persons, inhabiting a single body. The Platonic frame was insufficient for expressing the faith that affirms the *one* Person Jesus Christ is both fully human and fully divine. In "Christian Culture Needs Oriental Wisdom," Merton suggests that just as "the Greek Fathers" utilized Platonic thought to the extent they could, without compromising revealed truth, the nondual wisdom of the *Tao Te Ching* might provide a complementary way to penetrate "the

priation and reinterpretation of Aristotle, explicitly identified the uniquely human soul with "*nous*" and regarded it as immortal.[9]

Merton was fully aware that the notion of "a soul" posed a difficulty in the dialogue with Buddhists. He humorously recalled that Francis Xavier, the great missionary to Asia, was totally confused by his conversations with the Zen master Ninshitsu because the "good old man did not seem to know whether or not he had 'a soul.' In fact, to him the concept of 'a soul' as a sort of object that one could be considered as 'having' and even 'saving' was completely unfamiliar" (*ZR*, 528; *MZM*, 16). He further noted that though the texts of Bodhidharma do speak of "the mind," what is rendered there as *mind* is not "equivalent to the scholastic idea of the soul as 'the form of the body'" (*ZR*, 528; *MZM*, 16). A conception of the person based solely on interiority can avoid reliance on the body/soul, or matter/spirit distinction, but in order to find a concept of the person that makes no reference to the soul in the Catholic intellectual tradition, one must look to Trinitarian theology.

Interiority and the Meaning of "Person"

Early in the third century, Origen of Alexandria[10] recognized that the failure to appreciate the matter/spirit distinction unnecessarily complicated our understanding of the relation between the Unbegotten Father and the eternally Begotten Word revealed in John's Gospel, causing commentators to imagine the relation in material terms as a "generation by which the offspring of animals and of men are accustomed to come into existence." This misunderstanding is precisely what would lead Arius to reject the idea of the eternal and coequal existence of the Son along with the Father. In order to grasp the idea of an *eternal* generation, where the Unbegotten source does not temporally precede the Begotten Word, Origen "remove[d] all notions of corporeality" and said that "the Word and Wisdom is generated from the invisible and incorporeal God apart from any corporeal passion,

---

depths of the revealed mystery of Christ" (*SE*, 112).

9. Thomas Aquinas, *Summa Theologiae* I, q.89 (110–12) (cited hereafter as *ST* parenthetically in the text). I will provide references by *pars* and *quaestio* as *ST* is traditionally referenced as well as by page numbers that correspond with Timothy McDermott's translation.

10. Merton wrote, "Origen is certainly one of the greatest and holiest of the Church fathers and was certainly the most influential. . . . If he unfortunately did fall into theological errors . . . it is not difficult to separate his errors from the great mass of his orthodox teaching" (*CF*, 23).

as will proceeds from mind . . . as light can never exist without splendor. Therefore, how can it be said that there was a time when the Son was not?"[11]

What Origen did was step back behind the matter/spirit distinction which emerges within consciousness, and adverted to prior operations of consciousness to serve as an analogue for the image of Christ (who is Word and Wisdom) eternally issuing forth from God the unbegotten Father.[12] This move enabled a grasp of the simultaneity of the relation between the mind's thinking and the mind's thoughts. This move enabled a grasp of the idea of an eternal dynamic constancy rather than a temporal sequencing of first A, then B. Origen's move to interiority, which correlated "terms and relations with elements in human consciousness," foregrounded Augustine and Aquinas who did the same in their psychological analogies of the Trinity,[13] and Merton who did it when affirming the "Trinitarian structure" of Hui Neng's Unconscious, or the Trinitarian structure of the ground of being.

In the fourth century, the Cappadocians (Basil, Gregory of Nyssa, and Gregory of Nazianzus), were embattled against another permutation of Arius's subordinationism. Eunomius held that the divine essence (*ousia* or substance) was being "unbegotten." Since only the Father was unbegotten, the Son and the Spirit were necessarily less than God. The Cappadocians argued instead that the essence of God was unknowable, and that unbegottenness was a property unique to one Person (*hypostasis*) but not the shared *ousia* or "substance" of the three Persons. Prior to this move there was no clear distinction *between* substance and person. This move, which LaCugna said is "impossible to overestimate" in terms of its importance, "*made person rather than substance* the primary ontological category" for Trinitarian discourse.[14]

---

11. Origen of Alexandria, *De Principiis*.

12. In a similar way, C. S. Lewis later used the distinction between the "act of imagination" and a "mental picture" noting that "your act of imagination [is] the cause and your mental picture the result" but it is not the case that one precedes the other, since "the moment you do it, the picture is there" (Lewis, *Mere Christianity*, 173).

13. See Augustine, *Trinity*, 382–83; Thomas Aquinas, *ST* I, q.36, a.2 (65–67). Lonergan went beyond the classical categories of a faculty psychology when he wrote: "Can one speak intelligibly of three distinct and conscious subjects of divine consciousness? I believe one can, but to do so . . . one must be able to follow the reasoning from processions to relations and from relations to persons, and one has to think analogously of consciousness. The psychological analogy, then, has its starting point in . . . the dynamic state of being in love. Such love manifests itself in its judgments of value. And the judgments are carried out in decisions that are acts of loving. Such is the analogy found in the creature" (Lonergan, "Christology Today," 93; see also 74–99).

14. LaCugna, "God in Communion with Us," 86.

Anatman and the Reality of Persons

Speaking directly of Gregory of Nyssa in the context of the Eunomian controversy, Merton said: "Gregory stands up strongly for the 'darkness' which obscures the mind of man in the presence of the transcendent mystery of God—this is one of the most important ideas in his mystical theology: to know God by unknowing" (*CF*, 54–55). The Cappadocians clearly understood that "person" implied relatedness to one another, and to creation, and that relatedness belonged to the primary ontology of God; but the meaning of "person" remained rather elusive. However, because of their efforts "person" could now be sufficiently distinguished from "substance" and forge the way forward for a clearer articulation of the doctrine of the Trinity.

Centuries later, when Thomas Aquinas engaged the question of the person, he rightly realized that Boethius's definition of a person as "an individual substance of a rational nature" was insufficient for discussing divine Persons due to the frame set forth by the Cappadocians, since that definition still prioritized substance (*ST* I, q.28 [68]). If each divine person were "an individual substance of a rational nature" Christians would actually be polytheists worshipping three individual substances. If however, the three were *homoousios*, Boethius's definition offered little defense against a non-Trinitarian modalism, since "an individual substance of a rational nature" can simply appear externally as relationally different in three modes or masks. In a stunningly pivotal move Aquinas solved the problem by redefining a Person as a "subsistent relation" which meant that each of the divine Persons could be conceived as one and the same substance yet remain *truly* distinct from one another as Persons by the eternal *relations* that constituted them as such. Each Person distinguishable from each other Person, yet identical to the Ousia, reveals the dark and incomprehensible substance *as the relationship of the Persons in relation to one another*. Aquinas wrote: "In other words such a relationship is really the same thing as God's substance" (*ST* I, q.39 [87]).

The interior analogue is this: the mind knows and the mind wills according to what the mind knows. The mind's knowing and willing are distinguishable from the mind, and from one another, but not separable from it, or from one another. So the Begotten Word (analogous to that which is known), who is the *same substance* as the Unbegotten (analogous to mind that knows) is *distinct* from the Unbegotten by the relationship of *begetting* (knowing). The Holy Spirit, (analogous to that which is willed) is *distinct* from the Unbegotten and the Begotten by the relationship of *proceeding* (willing). In the human mind these two activities yield knowledge and love. In God, these two relations, begetting and proceeding, *constitute* three Persons.[15]

The relations are *primary* and *make* (for lack of a better word) the Persons, so much so that the Persons *are* their relations to one another.[16] They are not individual substances who *have* relationships with other individuals. The question becomes, might this definition of person as a "subsistent relation"—prescinding from the body/soul distinction and prioritizing "relation" as the primary ontological category—apply also to humans, enabling meaningful dialogue between Buddhists and Christians about the reality and value of persons?[17]

Interbeing and Interiority

Merton's "brother" Thich Nhat Hanh[18] illustrated the doctrine of *anatman* ("there is no such thing as an individual") in reference to a sheet of paper.[19]

---

15. St. Augustine had already achieved something similar in his psychological analogy of the Trinity, using *mens* (mind), *notitia sui* (self-knowledge), and *amor sui* (self-love), as analogues for the divine persons, but Aquinas moved everything forward by defining the persons as "subsistent relations." For a clear synopsis of Augustine's psychological analogy, see O'Collins, *Tripersonal God*, 135–41.

16. The theological tradition speaks of the interdependence of Persons constituting relations in the Trinity as *perichoresis* or *circumincession*. Granted, one might see this prioritizing of relation over substance as a potential nullification of personal "freedom"— but it must not be understood in this way. Freedom from the theological horizon is commensurate with love, and love is relational.

17. The question of *value* is key since the *reality* of human persons in the concrete is normally taken for granted in our ordinary daily dealings. Yet an entirely neurobiological account of human consciousness, such as Daniel C. Dennett offers in *Consciousness Explained*, is ill-equipped for handling the question of value. The rejection of the idea of "a soul" can translate in Western minds to a denial of human dignity and transcendent value. In a sense one could argue that the affirmation that humans "have souls," is simply a judgment of value masquerading as a judgment of fact. In other words, to say that humans have souls is to say that humans have value, and that we believe it is important to affirm that they have a transcendent or intrinsic worth, one that is not determined by or reducible to individual attributes or socio-cultural preferences. This is where Lonergan's epistemology is again helpful since "truth" for Lonergan is realized not only in correct judgments of fact (which may include "there is no such 'thing' as a soul" in the naive realist's sense), but also in authentic judgements of value ("the value of unique human beings transcends individual preferences and social and cultural determination").

18. Merton wrote a short homage, entitled "Nhat Hanh Is My Brother," which appeared as a chapter in his larger work *Faith and Violence*, 106–8.

19. Nhat Hanh, *Being Peace*, 45–47.

Anatman and the Reality of Persons

He suggested that if you hold a piece of paper in your hand and look at it with the "eyes of a poet" you can see its relation to the clouds, the sun, and the trees. If you look at it with the "eyes of a bodhisattva" you can see the logger, what he ate for breakfast, his mother, and everything in the universe in that piece of paper—"So much so" that if you return the logger to his mother, the rays to the sun, the rain to the clouds, the tree to the forest you would be left holding nothing! "The paper is empty. Empty of what? Empty of a separate self.... Empty, in this sense, means that the paper is full of everything, the entire cosmos."[20] Not one thing exists absolutely, and everything that exists does so interdependently. He was reflecting on an ancient Buddhist doctrine of "Interdependent Causation" and relating it to the doctrine of *anatman*,[21] but he articulated the insight underpinning both these doctrines as an insight into the "interbeing" of reality.[22]

To understand a human person in this way is to regard a person as an interbeing, *as* a unique nexus of multiple relationships, rather than as an autonomous individual "substance" who *has* relationships. It is to understand a human person in the way Aquinas understood the divine Persons, namely, as *constituted by* their relations. Mihoko Okamura, remembering her "Sensei" Suzuki, recalled that "in his eyes, each individual also reflected the whole of existence while preserving his or her own uniqueness, each was irreplaceable, and for that reason unfathomable, infinitely novel. And thus, for Sensei each individual was endlessly fascinating, and for each he was endlessly grateful."[23]

Merton was already prioritizing *relation* over *substance* in terms defining human persons, often without invoking the concept of the *soul*, long before writing Suzuki. In *Seeds of Contemplation* he wrote:

> All sin starts from the assumption that my false self, the self that exists only in my ego-centric desires, is the fundamental reality

---

20. Nhat Hanh, *Being Peace*, 46–47.

21. Harold Talbott, who served as Merton's guide in India, described Merton's first audience with the Dalai Lama in which His Holiness talked about *"tendrel*, or interdependent causation, as well as suffering, impermanence, and no-self." *Tendrel*, then, is the Vajrayana term for what Thich Nhat Hanh refers to as *interbeing*. It is a way of naming that which unifies the three marks of existence. See Talbott, *Tendrel*, 170.

22. Thich Nhat Hanh founded the Tiep Hien order of Buddhism, which he translates as "The Order of Interbeing." See Nhat Hanh, *Being Peace*, 83–103.

23. Okamura, "Wondrous Activity." As an aside, she also recalled that "Sensei" regularly repeated a French proverb "to know all is to forgive all" as a kind of mantra. "'To understand that' he often said, 'is all you need to know.'"

of life to which everything else in the universe is ordered. Thus I use up my life trying to accumulate pleasures and experiences and power and honor . . . to clothe this false self and construct its *nothingness* into something objectively real . . . but there is *no substance* under the things I have gathered together about me" (*SC*, 22–23, italics added).

Instead, he writes, "To say that I am made in the image of God is to say that love is the reason for my existence: for God is Love. Love is my true identity, Selflessness is my true self" (*SC*, 40). Early on then Merton was asserting that what makes a human person *real* is not a *substance* construed as an invisible *something*, but proper *relations* of a certain quality. In other words, while he could speak meaningfully and affirmatively of specific persons or subjects, human subjects, for him, are never eradicable from the constitutive web of intersubjective relations. As Joseph Bracken argues, "human personhood and human community only make complete sense within an overarching metaphysics of universal intersubjectivity . . . [and] interrelated subjects . . . exist at every level of existence and activity within Nature."[24] This view underscores not only human consubstantiality with all of creation, but also the necessity of human interpersonal exchange and dialogue, since a plurality of personal perspectives potentially broadens and deepens each person's knowledge and love of God the ultimately real.

Later in that same chapter of *Seeds of Contemplation*, "We are One Man," Merton explicitly used the "subsistent relations" model of Trinitarian Persons for his understanding of proper human relations and therefore human identity. Expounding on the notion of Person constituting relations he wrote:

> God in His Trinity of subsistent relations infinitely transcends every shadow of selfishness. For the One God does not subsist apart and alone in His Nature. He subsists *as* Father and *as* Son and *as* Holy Ghost. The Three Persons *are* One, but apart from them God does not subsist also as One. . . . In the Father the infinite Love of God is always beginning and in the Son it is always full and in the Holy Spirit it is perfect and it is renewed and never ceases to rest in its everlasting source. But if you follow the Love forward and backward from Person to Person, you can never track it to a stop, you can never corner it and hold it down and fix it to one of the Persons as if he could appropriate to Himself the fruit of the love of the others, for the One Love of the Three Persons is an

24. See Bracken, "Subjectivity, Objectivity, and Intersubjectivity."

> infinitely rich giving of itself which never ends and is never taken, but is always perfectly given, only received in order to be perfectly shared. (*SC*, 45, italics added)

This is what Merton meant by "the religious dimension of the Person" that he believed to be compatible with Zen (*MZM*, 213-14).

In "Christian Culture Needs Oriental Wisdom" Merton commented favorably on Confucianism as a *personalistic* philosophy that recognizes "that our person is received as a gift from our parents" and gets fully developed by entering "fruitfully and lovingly into the five basic relationships" (*SE*, 110). "To give priority to the person" he argued, "means respecting the unique and inalienable value of the *other* person, as well as one's own, for a respect that is centered only on one's individual self to the exclusion of others proves to be fraudulent" (*WCT*, 17). He also gestured in the direction of defining human persons in terms of their relations when he wrote: "We have the choice of two identities: the external mask which seems to be real and which lives by a shadowy autonomy for the brief moments of earthly existence, and the hidden, inner person who seems to us to be nothing, but who can give himself eternally to the truth in whom he subsists"(*NSC*, 295).

"The truth in whom he subsists" reveals what for Merton is the *primary relation* constituting human *persons* (and the existence of everything else). The Christian, of course, will refuse to claim that we are the *same substance* by *nature* as the Persons of the Trinity since we do not perfectly know and love one another and everything else into being or interbeing. But The Interbeing (The Tripersonal Love) *is* perfectly knowing and loving all of us, and all things into interbeing. There is no being apart from Interbeing, or as Merton would say, everything is a *participation* in God's gift of God's own life.

John Heidbrink, Thomas Merton, and Thich Nhat Hanh.

Ousia and *Homoousios*

St. Athanasius[25] can be credited with rendering a useful grammatical rule, rather than a precise definition, for establishing a heuristic meaning for the term "consubstantial" or *homoousios*. Athanasius claimed that the Nicene Bishops intended the term to mean "that whatever is true of the Father is true of the Son, except the name Father."[26] As Jeremy Wilkins noted, the assertion "is not only heuristic but also apophatic. It is not a claim to comprehend all that may be said of God; it does not pretend to know God's substance . . . it acknowledges the intelligible truth of revealed mystery without claiming to understand it."[27]

The apophatic nature of the assertion is key. It amounts to an affirmation of God's mysterious *ousia* beyond the purview of human understanding.

---

25. While Merton once somewhat dismissively described Athanasius as "a Church politician" (*CF*, 45–46), he clearly revered Athanasius, not only as the biographer of St. Anthony but also as a formidable apophatic theologian in his own right. Merton praised Athanasius for understanding not only just what was at stake in the Arian controversy, but also for his affirming that human divinization is the goal and the fruit of the Incarnation (*ICM*, 60–62).

26. Athanasius, *De Decretis*, 19, 20, 23.

27. Wilkins, *Before Truth*, 275–76.

Anatman and the Reality of Persons

Aquinas, however, identified the *ousia* as love, claiming "relationship is really the same thing as God's substance." Love, for Aquinas, is understood *connaturally*—that is by sharing in it. Since God is *infinite* love, the mystery of love ever remains transcendent of finite acts of human understanding. In his prose poem *Hagia Sophia*, Merton imagined holy wisdom as the "Gift of God" and "God as Gift," and as "the Love" by which God is "given and known, held and loved." He tentatively suggested, while admitting to *not knowing*, that She (*Sophia*) "is the unknown, dark, and nameless Ousia.... One in Father, Son and Holy Ghost" (*CPTM*, 367–68). Of course he knew *that* God is Love (1 John 4:8), but the fullness of Love remained for him a mystery *to be fully known*, so he did *not know* that nameless *Ousia* in a comprehensive and definitive sense.

In order to consciously apprehend and completely participate in the fullness of Love (the *divine substance—which is relation*) we stand in need of a conversion, indeed an ongoing conversion that transforms us in accord with God who is that perfect love. In the view of both Athanasius and Merton, the Incarnation has initiated this process of deification on a universal scale, affecting the entire human family, and birthing the new creation of the new heaven and a new earth (Rev 21:1). For Merton, then, the undeniable reality of *grace* is necessary for the person to be "taken up into the mystery of Christ, by His love, by the Holy Spirit" (*NSC*, 295). Again, however, this grace is not "a reified *substance* given to us by God from without" but is "grace precisely as emptiness, as freedom, as liberality, as gift" (*ZBA*, 136).[28]

In Christian doctrine Christ is *both* consubstantial with the Unbegotten Father *and* consubstantial with us.[29] This means that whatever can be said of us can be said of Christ with respect to his humanity, since he is like

---

28. Throughout his *oeuvre*, it is clear that Merton refuses to bracket or marginalize the centrality of grace. He was happy to critique the subject/object distinction, and the body/soul distinction insofar as these can lead us into naïve realism and dualism if we are not careful. He can even assert that he has not "insisted on man's awareness of God as Creator." But he always insists on our "dependence on God as Savior and giver of Grace" (*ZBA*, 136). What he is insisting on is not that another needs to affirm the truth of the distinction between nature and grace, but his own need to acknowledge his dependence on grace, which he is certain is not only true for himself but for everyone and everything.

29. The Council of Chalcedon (451) formally affirmed: "The same Son, our Lord Jesus Christ, the same perfect in divinity and perfect in humanity, the same truly God and truly man ... the same consubstantial (*homoousios*) with the Father as to the divinity and consubstantial (*homoousios*) with us as to the humanity, like unto us in all things but sin [cf. Heb 4:15]." See Dupuis, *Christian Faith*, 614, 301 (227).

us in everything "except sin." If human persons are also "subsistent relations" then they are, like Thich Nhat Hanh's sheet of paper, consubstantial with "the entire cosmos," yet distinct within it by the relations uniquely comprising and constituting each.[30] Merton expressed the realization of his consubstantiality with all of creation when he wrote of his "recognition that the whole world is aware of itself in me" (*ZR*, 8). He expressed it poetically when he wrote: "I am earth, earth / Out of my grass heart, Rises the bobwhite. / Out of my nameless weeds / His foolish worship" (*CPTM*, 345). But he continued to anticipate the eschatological fullness when grace would elevate his *dependence on* God *to utter union with* God, unencumbered by the burden of sin. This elevation unites our consubstantiality, shared with Christ and the entire cosmos, with the Divine *Ousia* "celebrated in the hymn of the Spirit," when we, as the Eucharistic prayer intends, "come to share in the divinity of Christ, who humbled himself to share in our humanity." It is the supreme *coincidentia oppositorum*, and like the palms united in the *gassho*, there is no separation, no division. The doctrine of *theosis*, as LaCugna pithily put it, is simply this: "'we *become* by grace what God *is* by nature,' namely, persons in full communion with God and with every other creature."[31] For "whoever loves is begotten by God and knows God" (1 John 4:7).

Through his dialogue with Suzuki Merton became satisfied that his Buddhist friend knew God as the ground and goal of consciousness, and as love and freedom. He also inferred that there was in Buddhism an implicit affirmation of grace, for example in what the Tibetans called the "uncultivated yoga" or as suggested by the "tile polishing" mondo of Zen. But he nonetheless continued to faithfully point to the "outer word" Jesus Christ as the corresponding and fulfilling complement to his interior gifts and insights. Put another way, Merton's *mysticism* was married to the *prophecy* of the Incarnate Word who advocates for the poor and oppressed, stands

---

30. To regard human persons as "subsistent relations" has fascinating implications for the doctrine of the *Imago Dei*. It radically prioritizes the fact that being made in God's image means being made by and for loving relationship. The Image is lost by trying to isolate one human person, since just as the divine persons cannot be considered "individually" but only relationally, so too for us. Marjorie Hewitt Suchocki explores some of these implications in her book *Divinity and Diversity*, 57–75. She wrote: "the image of God is not reducible to an individual's intellect alone, nor to freedom, self-transcendence, or any human quality alone. If God is . . . a complex unity that can be expressed through irreducible diversity, then community, rather than individuality, is required for creaturely imaging of God" (67).

31. LaCugna, *God For Us*, 1.

in judgment of our injustices, liberates captives, redeems, heals, calls, and elevates us to greater love and communion. Every aspect of the prophetic side emphatically affirms the value of persons, and the Person who reveals that inestimable worth.

7

Seeds in the Garden of New Growth

THE SECOND VATICAN COUNCIL (1962–1965) marked an enormous advance in Catholic ecclesiological reflection. Commenting on the advances immediately preceding Pope John's call for a council, Joseph Ratzinger wrote: "If until that time we had thought of the Church primarily as a structure or organization, now at last we began to realize that we ourselves were the Church."[1] The church, for centuries, had been on the defensive against threats to its authority, and its response had been to emphasize the very features of itself attacked first by the reformers, then the enlightenment thinkers, and then the modernists.[2] The emphasis on its own authority tended to encourage an ultramontanism and ossify the institutional church as a "perfect society" fully realized. In other words, prior to the council, *distinctions* between the Church of Christ and the Catholic Church, and between the Church of Christ and its visible boundaries, were ignored or at least deemphasized. Ignoring those distinctions makes it far too easy to conflate the church triumphant with the pilgrim church, resulting in an uncritical deification of the pilgrim church in the minds of many Catholics. The institutionalist ecclesiology was not a matter of defined dogma so much as it was an atmosphere shaping attitudes. In that context Catholics often narrowly interpreted the ancient dictum *extra ecclesiam nulla salus* in a juridical way so that "outside" meant not being an official member of the Roman institution.

---

1. Ratzinger, "Ecclesiology of Vatican II."
2. Dulles, *Models of the Church*, 33.

Seeds in the Garden of New Growth

With a renewed humility the church at Vatican II lamented the rifts and dissensions that caused the schism and the Reformation and acknowledged that "often enough, men of both sides were to blame" (*UR* 3). In conciliatory fashion it recognized and affirmed that "many elements of sanctification and truth" exist "outside the visible structure" of the Catholic Church (*LG* 8.2). Elements such as "the written word of God; the life of grace; faith, hope, and charity, with the other interior gifts of the Holy Spirit" (*UR* 3.2). Other Christian traditions, which also cherish the written word of God and adore Christ as the incarnate Word "have been by no means deprived of significance and importance in the mystery of salvation. For the Spirit of Christ has not refrained from using them as a means of salvation" (*UR* 3.4).

While the Council refrained from specifying what such elements could be found in *non-Christian* religions, it did assert that these other religions often "reflect a ray of that Truth which enlightens all men and women" and that the Catholic Church "rejects nothing that is true and holy in these religions" (*NA* 2.2).[3] The church further exhorted Catholics to dialogue with members of other religions and to "recognize, preserve, and promote the good things, spiritual and moral" found among them (*NA* 2.3). All the while the church strongly maintained that the one true Church of Christ *subsists* fully in the Catholic Church, and that the elements of sanctification and truth that exist outside her visible boundaries belong to the Church of Christ and are "forces impelling toward catholic unity" (*LG* 8.2).

The whole presentation of religious pluralism put forth in *Nostra Aetate* follows, implicitly, the three meanings of "God" previously discussed. It begins by presenting the plurality of religious traditions as socio-cultural phenomena understood as objectifications of the universal human quest for the ultimate ground and goal of all existence, and moves toward increasingly personal apprehensions of that ground as love, seeing reflections of the Light which enlightens all human beings in the world's religions; thus framing the whole discussion within a Logos/Sophia Christology (*NA* 2). Gerald O'Collins noted that by reflecting "explicitly and positively" on the world's great religious traditions "*Nostra Aetate* did something no ecumenical council had ever done before." He went on to assert that while "*Nostra Aetate* does

---

3. Merton seems to anticipate *NA* 2 in "Christian Culture Needs Oriental Wisdom" when he wrote, "The 'universality' and 'catholicity' which are essential to the Church necessarily imply an ability and a readiness to enter into dialogue with all that is pure, wise, profound, and humane in every kind of culture" (*SE*, 112). He quotes generously from *NA* in his preface to *Mystics and Zen Masters* (*MZM*, viii–ix).

not expressly state that Christ is both universal Revealer and universal Savior... what it says amounts to that. How can [Christ] 'illuminate' all human beings without conveying to them something of God's self-revelation and hence also the offer of salvation?"[4] In other words, the world's religions are not at all dismissible as merely human projections of wishful thinking but must be taken seriously since the universal Revealer/Savior is mysteriously present and operative, illuminating those who affirm the truth and value, and even identify as members, of those religious traditions.

The church continued to hold that the churches and ecclesial communities spawned by the schism and the Reformation suffered from deficiencies (*UR* 3.1–4), and that the world still suffered from "false or inadequate religious notions" (*GS* 28.2). Still its tone of optimism outweighed apprehensiveness as it recognized "seeds of the word... which a generous God has distributed among the nations" (*AG* 11), which can be "found sown" not only "in minds and hearts" of individual persons, but also "in the religious practices and cultures of diverse peoples" (*LG* 17).

As the council was underway, Merton famously wrote:

> I will be a better Catholic, not if I can refute every shade of Protestantism, but if I can affirm the truth in it and still go further. So, too, with the Muslims, the Hindus, the Buddhists, etc. ... If I affirm myself as a Catholic merely by denying all that is Muslim, Jewish, Protestant, Hindu, Buddhist, etc., in the end I will find that there is not much left for me to affirm and certainly no breath of the Spirit with which to affirm it. (*CGB*, 129)[5]

He had already discovered that there was much truth to affirm in Buddhism (and the others) and holiness to affirm in Suzuki. After Suzuki's death on July 12, 1966, Merton wrote his homage "D. T. Suzuki: The Man and His Work" in which he effusively praised his Sensei as one whose simplicity, authenticity, and intelligence reminded him of "Saint Augustine and Saint Gregory of Nyssa," and whose work stood as "a great gift," a remarkable "intellectual and spiritual achievement" (*ZBA*, 60–65). Rather than seeing Suzuki's Buddhism as inconsequential to his wisdom and virtue, he regarded Suzuki as the living embodiment of a Buddhist tradition, "a person in

---

4. O'Collins, *Second Vatican Council*, 115–16.

5. Although *CGB* was not published until 1966, a year after the close of Vatican II, Merton appears to have completed it, or was at least close to completing it, by February of 1962 when he wrote in his journal, "But there is always of course *Conjectures of a Guilty Bystander*, which may not even get through the censor" (*TTW*, 203).

whom it is alive"; a tradition through which he "had matured, had become complete and found his way" (*ZBA*, 62).

Thomas Merton and Chatral Rinpoche

Passing Over and Polonnaruwa[6]

Merton's engagement with Buddhism did not conclude with the death of Suzuki. It culminated in his final great epiphany in Ceylon (Sri Lanka) and concluded with his mysterious death in Thailand. The narrative of Thomas Merton's *Asian Journal*, if one can seize upon its golden thread, begins with excited anticipation of a great discovery and culminates with the Polonnaruwa experience that confirms and consoles the pilgrim and the reader with the fulfillment of Merton's intense longing just days before his death in Bangkok on December 10, 1968. For many of his Christian readers the Buddhist language Merton employs in his December 4 entry, recounting his experience of December 1, is both intriguing and challenging, for the

---

6. Much of this section was previously published. See Raab, "*Madhyamika* and *Dharmakaya*," 195–205. That article was based on a talk originally delivered as part of a round table plenary session entitled "Merton and the East' at the International Thomas Merton Society conference in Vancouver, Canada, June 5–7, 2003. Bonnie Thurston presided over the panel that included Roger Corless, Lucien Miller, and Joseph Q. Raab.

same reason. It is the writing of a Catholic monk whose account of his intense spiritual vision is shot through with Sanskrit terms and without one explicit comparison or even allusion to a Christian frame of reference. In order to appreciate the extent of his "passing over"[7] into Buddhism I want to consider the Sanskrit terms Merton employed in his journal entry. In accord with Merton's own affinity for integrating seemingly disparate traditions, I would like to consider how this very significant experience can be understood within the context of the larger narrative of his Catholic life.

From the very outset of the *Asian Journal* Merton prepares himself and his reader for the experience that surprises him in front of the stone Buddhas in Polonnaruwa, Ceylon just days before his death. The experience surprised him because he was not especially expecting a great realization on that particular day in that particular place, but still he was anticipating such a breakthrough in an indeterminate way when he left on his Asian pilgrimage months earlier hoping to "settle the great affair" and to discover "the great compassion, the *mahakaruna*" (*AJ*, 4). Indeed, a couple of weeks before he approached those Buddhas in Gal Vihara with his shoes off, Merton was discussing *dzogchen* and *dharmakaya* with Chatral Rinpoche and confessing that he had not yet attained to perfect emptiness, but that he was hoping to go out and get lost in a great realization (*AJ*, 143).[8]

On December 1, as he toured among the artifacts in the park in Polonnaruwa, Merton had a powerful realization. A few days later he recreated the scene and the experience in a detailed journal entry. In his account he characterized the monumental bodies of the Buddha figures as "questioning nothing, knowing everything, rejecting nothing" and filled with "the peace . . . of Madhyamika that has seen through every question." Yet he warned that "for the doctrinaire, the mind that needs well-established positions, such peace, such silence, can be frightening" (*AJ*, 233). Then he recalled the inner event of being "jerked clean out of the habitual half-tied vision

---

7. John S. Dunne uses this term to speak about a form of the spiritual journey that involves temporarily immersing oneself in, or passing over to, a tradition other than one's own in order to deepen one's understanding and appreciation both of the other tradition and of one's own. See Dunne, *Way of All the Earth*, ix–xii.

8. When Merton arrived in Dharamsala he met Sonam Kazi who sparked Merton's interest in Vajrayana (*OSM*, 237). When he met later with the Dalai Lama he asked His Holiness to teach him about *dzogchen* and received some preliminary instructions. Later, Merton began making plans to study *dzogchen* formally under Chatral Rinpoche, a teacher Talbott described as "completely unpredictable." Talbott said of Chatral, "He is savage about the ego and he will put you on the spot," but "he was Merton's Man." See Talbott, *Tendrel*, 281.

of things" when everything became clear and evident and obvious. In an instant he had moved to a total affirmation of a truth, "as if exploding from the rocks themselves." And his affirmation was this: "all matter, all life is charged with *Dharmakaya*, everything is emptiness and everything is compassion" (*AJ*, 234). It is possible when reading Merton's journal to appreciate the impact and the importance he assigned to this experience without having any clue what he meant by the Buddhist terms he employed. But, since the language Merton used was thoroughly Buddhist, it is the language I want to consider, especially the terms *Madhyamika* and *Dharmakaya*.

Madhyamika

At one level *Madhyamika* or "the middle way" is simply another name for Buddhism. It suggests the Buddha's realization of *moksha* by navigating through the dialectical extremes of a self-indulgent adolescence and a self-destructive asceticism that characterized his early adulthood. It also names the method for advancing one's liberation as spelled out in the eight-fold path. But the term is richly over-determined; it also refers to a level of systematic reflection developed within the Mahayana traditions.[9]

Merton's understanding of *Madhyamika* is largely informed by his reading of T. R. V. Murti's *The Central Philosophy of Buddhism: A Study of Madhyamika System*. This is one of the many texts he carted around with him on his journeys from Calcutta, to Darjeeling, to Sri Lanka, and then further east to Bangkok; his journal is generously peppered with quotations from Murti.[10] In this immensely rich work, Murti presents *Madhyamika*, the doctrine of the middle path systematized by Nagarjuna in the second or third century CE, as a denial of both a monistic reading of the Vedanta and a nihilistic reading of Buddhism. For the Mahayana, Nagarjuna's clarification of *Madhyamika* is a recovery of Buddha's original teaching that had been misunderstood by the Theravada. For Murti, and consequently for Merton, *Madhyamika* offers a critique of any and all philosophical positions and aims at a spiritual purification of the mind "freeing it from the

---

9. According to Roger Corless, Mahayana emerges as a distinct tradition on the Indian subcontinent in the first century CE at least in part as a reform movement liberating the Dharma from dogmatic rigidity. Mahayana contains two theoretical traditions: *Madhyamika* and *Yogachara*. I will attempt to elucidate only the former. See Corless, *Vision of Buddhism*, 290.

10. *The Asian Journal* also includes a section for complementary reading (263–92) that incorporates many helpful and poignant snippets from Murti's text.

cobwebs and clogs of dogmatism."[11] No doubt Merton heard the lion roar in *Madhyamika*.

Methodologically, *Madhyamika* is an approach to any philosophical or ideological position that would disclose the emptiness, impermanence, or contingency of that particular view through the dialectical process. The process undermines and exposes the hidden, tacit, or overlooked limitations of any philosophical position. It is avowedly deconstructionist since it offers a negation of the definitive pretensions of any formula; but it is not nihilistic nor agnostic because a commitment to truth still obtains and an ultimate affirmation of life establishes the context within which the deconstruction is carried out. *Madhyamika* espouses the "both/and" and "neither/nor" view always between contraries purporting absolutist positions. *Madhyamika*, then, transcends the "dualistic grasping" inherent in *avidya*.[12] Some of Merton's own notations on Murti's text help to illustrate what he was gleaning from it, or at least what he found complementary to his own way of thinking. Merton commented:

> Madhyamika does not oppose one thesis with another. It seeks the flaw in both thesis and antithesis. It investigates the beginningless illusion that holds "views" to be true in so far as they appeal to us and when they appeal to us we argue that they are not "views" but absolute truth. All views are rejected for this reason. . . . "Criticism is Sunyata—the utter negation of thought as revelatory of the real." The empirical, liberated from conventional thought forms is identical with the absolute. (*AJ*, 115)[13]

And a couple of pages later Merton wrote, "The purpose of Madhyamika is not to convince, but to explode the argument itself. Is this sadism? No, it is compassion! It exorcises the devil of dogmatism" (*AJ*, 118).[14]

The insight that engenders *Madhyamika* grasps that our ordinary language (or unenlightened mind) is falsely dichotomous because it implicitly accepts the subject/object division as foundational, primary, and basic. When one grasps the unity that precedes, transcends, and conditions

---

11. Murti, *Central Philosophy of Buddhism*, 146. While Merton revered dogma, he loathed dogmatism. The first is revealed truth, and the Spirit that gives life, the second is *the letter that killeth* (2 Cor 3:6).

12. See *Dzogchen*, 185–87.

13. Here Merton was reflecting on the material found in Murti, *Central Philosophy of Buddhism*, 140–43.

14. This is Merton's synthesis of the material from Murti, *Central Philosophy of Buddhism*, 145–46.

the subject/object distinction that emerges in consciousness, one discovers a new freedom. When the opposition comes together (or dissolves) in a penetrating insight, it often finds expression in the mystical paradox, the *coincidentia oppositorum*; the *todo y nada* of St. John of the Cross; Suzuki's "zero equals infinity, infinity equals zero" or even Eckhart's prayer to God to be free from God. *Madhyamika* denies the final validity of all other positions in order to affirm the illimitability of *rigpa*, the emptiness of mind that gives rise to each limited view.

There is an affirmation of transcendence that is essentially performed by *Madhyamika* but not explicitly declared and thus translated into a philosophical position. The denying of any particular claim to fully determine the nature of reality amounts to an affirmation of reality as transcendent of any one view. And the affirming of transcendence is simultaneously an affirmation of nature and immanence because *Madhyamika* refuses to set one up against another. It is both a refusal to reduce reality to monism (a single view) and a refusal to fracture reality into a pluralism of many unrelated, mutually exclusive, or irreconcilable views. In his recollection Merton sees the peace of *Madhyamika* exploding from the rocks. He expresses the realization with the final affirmation, "all life is charged with *dharmakaya*, everything is emptiness and everything is compassion."

Thomas Merton and His Holiness Dalai Lama XIV

Opening New Horizons

Dharmakaya

Dharmakaya translates as "the body of truth" or more directly, "truth body" and it can be used in numerous ways. Again, we can search through the many books Merton was toting around with him to find out whence his conception of *dharmakaya* was forming. An important influence seems to have been Evans-Wentz's translations entitled *Tibetan Yoga and Secret Doctrines*; there the term is used in its traditional relation to the two other bodies of the Buddha. In Mahayana Buddhism, Buddha is said to be realized in three distinct ways, or "bodies." This doctrine is called *trikaya*, and the three bodies are: (1) *nirmanakaya*, or a living Boddhisatva, or earthly incarnation of the Buddha; (2) *sambhogakaya*, a bodhisattva inhabiting a celestial sphere, in splendid paradise, who imparts wisdom to pilgrims seeking liberation; and finally (3) *dharmakaya*, or "truth body" which means that the essential nature of Buddha is identical with the non-dual, absolute or ultimate emptiness (*sunyata*).[15] This is the Buddha's first body or, for lack of a better term, his true or essential nature, as well as the essential nature of all beings.[16]

The book that Evans-Wentz calls "Book II," was, according to Donald S. Lopez, Jr., originally written by Padma dkar po (1527–1592) and entitled *Notes on Mahamudra* (Phyag chen gyi zin bris).[17] Here the original author explicates four ways of realizing *Mahamudra*, or the Great Seal, or enlightenment. Padma dkar po speaks of two ordinary ways and two extraordinary ways. The latter of the extraordinary ways is called the "uncultivated yoga" whereby without meditation and prior dispositional practices the one to be enlightened suddenly "identifies the natural spontaneity of all phenomena as the truth body (*dharmakaya*)."[18] This provides a fairly sound avenue for understanding Merton's experience at Polonnaruwa from within the Buddhist frame of reference he employed. Merton's own description that "everything is charged with dharmakaya" resembles this identification.

---

15. While it has become almost commonplace to say that Buddhism is focused on the *teachings* of Siddhartha Gautama and not so much on the person, there is no doubt that a development from the Gautama of history to the Buddha of faith is discernable in the Mahayana tradition.

16. In the Glossary of *The Asian Journal*, the definition of *dharmakaya* is taken from Murti's text and reads, "the cosmical body of the Buddha, the essence of all beings" (372).

17. Evens-Wentz, *Tibetan Yoga and Secret Doctrines*, i.

18. Evans-Wentz, *Tibetan Yoga and Secret Doctrines*, 148–49.

Seeds in the Garden of New Growth

Given this meaning of the term *dharmakaya*, however, it may seem odd for Merton to say, "everything is charged with" it, since this syntax can reify the *dharmakaya* as a "something" that imbues "something else." It is tempting to attribute this odd phraseology to the fact that Merton relied on Evans-Wentz, whose own translations of Tibetan texts were heavily influenced, and in some cases seriously flawed, by his theosophical worldview.[19] In addition, many of the texts Evans-Wentz undertook in translation were texts explicitly reserved for initiated practitioners, and presumably those initiations and practices established contextual parameters for a kind of orthodoxy. However, O'Connell has suggested that Merton's use of "charged with" might simply have been a conscious or unconscious evocation of the opening lines of Hopkins's poem, "God's Grandeur": "The world is charged with the grandeur of God / It will flame out like shining from shook foil"— in which case *dharmakaya* presents not another something but the innermost reality revealed in this epiphany.[20] The stone statues seem to mediate a glimpse of the transcendent.

In other words, Merton attains here a sacramental vision, or an *iconic* vision which goes beyond an iconoclastic refusal of idolatry. This vision does not impose a spiritual emptiness upon a material substance. As Jean-Luc Marion put it: "Whereas the idol results from the gaze that aims at it, the icon summons sight in letting the visible . . . be saturated little by little with the invisible. The invisible seems, it appears in a semblance . . . which, however, never reduces the invisible to the slackened wave of the visible. . . . One would say . . . that the invisible proceeds up into the visible, precisely because the visible would proceed from the invisible."[21] At any rate, *dharmakaya*, for *Madhyamika*, is not a spiritual substance permeating a non-spiritual substance, but is identical with both emptiness and form.

---

19. Donald S. Lopez Jr., in his new foreword to the most recent edition of Evans-Wentz's translations of these seven Tibetan books, makes the flaws and limitations of Evans-Wentz's work very clear to newer readers while still lauding Evans-Wentz for a work remarkable for its time.

20. O'Connell, correspondence with the author, January 11, 2020.

21. Marion, *God without Being*, 17.

Opening New Horizons

Reclining Buddha, Polonnaruwa

Dzogchen and Sacramental Vision

At Polonnaruwa, Merton had a flash of insight into the essential emptiness of nature, and found the insight led to the *mahakaruna*, the great compassion that arises beyond and within the emptiness, and in fact is not separate from the emptiness. Merton's final affirmation that "everything is emptiness and everything is compassion" is clearly consonant with the language of *dzogchen*.[22] Donald S. Lopez Jr. describes the *Mahamudra* realization of the Great Seal, analogously akin to the Great Perfection of *Nyingma*, or *dzogchen* as "a state of enlightened awareness in which phenomenal appearance and noumenal emptiness are unified" in a single vision.[23] Again it is quite easy to see this as correlative with Merton's language concerning his

---

22. It is important here to recall Merton's conversations with Chatral Rinpoche with whom he spoke for a couple of hours about *dharmakaya*, *dzogchen*, and relations among Buddhist and Christian doctrines (*AJ*, 142–44). Indeed, it was this conversation that led Merton to describe *dzogchen* as the "unity of sunyata and karuna" which means the "unity of emptiness and compassion" the precise terms Merton uses later to recall his experience of December 1, 1968.

23. See Donald Lopez's Foreword to Evans-Wentz, *Tibetan Yoga and Secret Doctrines*, i.

Seeds in the Garden of New Growth

experience at Polonnaruwa. Given the linguistic parameters set by the Sanskrit terms, we still wonder about how Merton, who was always concerned to "unite divided worlds" in himself and "transcend them in Christ" might have understood and integrated his Buddhist experience of the "Great Seal" within his own Catholic faith life.

The language of *dzogchen* as the "unity of emptiness and compassion" and the unity of "noumenal emptiness and phenomenal appearance" would remind the Catholic monk of St. Augustine's definition of a sacrament as "the visible form of invisible grace."[24] This correlation would have been natural for Merton to make since he had already, in his dialogue with Suzuki, identified the Buddhist experience of *emptiness* with his Christian experience of *grace*, characterizing grace precisely as emptiness, as freedom, as gift (ZBA, 136–37). In this sense we can understand Merton's experience at Polonnaruwa as a sacramental experience as well as an experience of *dzogchen*.

Christianity affirms the divine Wisdom/Word of the Transcendent Source, who speaks in and through creation itself and the apostolic *kerygma* and the *koinonia*. Buddhism fiercely debunks the false conceptions we tend to erect about ourselves, the world, and even the ultimate source, and reveals the essential emptiness or radical contingency of all individual existents. For Merton, the apophatic or iconoclastic function of Buddhism helped till the soil to receive more deeply the good news of Christ, the Word, who becomes incarnate in history and community through a process of self-emptying, and whose acceptance in the world of "rapacious men" demands the utter humility of self-forgetting. Christ is both the kenosis and expression of God, and through our own self-emptying we are transformed by the Spirit; Christ becomes incarnate in us.

The *karuna* (compassion) that Merton declares in union with *sunyata* (emptiness), was for him not something other than the compassion of the Christ, the one who reveals to him exactly what "compassion" can mean. Apart from the life of Christ, the one who willingly suffers with us and for us, and whose suffering heals us, "compassion" can end up being, as Flannery O'Connor once lamented, "a vague and popular word that sounds good in anyone's mouth ... which no one can put his finger on in any exact critical

---

24. This broad but classic definition of sacrament commonly attributed to St. Augustine of Hippo was also taught by St. Thomas Aquinas and affirmed by the Council of Trent (Session XIII, Decree on the Holy Eucharist, chapter 3). It also reminds the Merton reader of the opening line of Merton's *Hagia Sophia*, "There is in all visible things an invisible fecundity, a dimmed light, a meek namelessness, a hidden wholeness." See *CPTM*, 363.

sense, so it is always safe for anybody to use."²⁵ But for Merton, "compassion" (literally "suffering with") was not a vague or vapid conception at all. O'Connell, commenting on Merton's conception of "compassion" wrote:

> Compassion is the common stream from which all religious traditions drink in their "deep, unutterable thirst for the rivers of Paradise" (*IE*, 130). It is the quality by which we realize that the God of Islam, who "is invoked as the 'Compassionate and the Merciful,'" (*HGL*, 48) is the same God as the Lord of Israel, whose "compassion . . . is for every living thing" (Sir 18:13), and who is also the "compassionate and the merciful" God of Jesus Christ (James 5:11). It was compassion, a recognition of the suffering common to all in sickness, old age, and death that drove Siddhartha Gautama from the security and pleasures of his palace to search for liberation, and it was compassion that compelled the enlightened Buddha to share his experience of the "Middle Way" to salvation. And of course it is compassion that brings Jesus of Nazareth to the crowds on the banks of the Jordan, and then leads him into the desert, the same desert that Merton called "the wilderness of compassion . . . the desert that shall truly flourish like the lily. . . . It is in the desert of compassion that the thirsty land turns into springs of water, that the poor possess all things" (*SJ*, 334). It is compassion that inspires Jesus to preach and to teach and to heal those who come to him: "He had compassion for them, because they were like sheep without a shepherd" (Mark 6:34). Finally it was compassion that brought Jesus to the cross, to take upon himself the suffering and sin and oppression of all humanity, to share our death and invite us, by dying to ourselves, to share his victory over suffering and death as well.²⁶

Within Merton there is a complementary interpenetration of *contexts*, Buddhist and Christian, and his interest in the former always included the faith commitments he had made within the latter.²⁷ The kenotic hymn of Philippians and the passion of the Christ would, for Merton, reveal a profound and personal meaning for the *sunyata* and *karuna* of *dzogchen*.

25. O'Connor, *Mystery and Manners*, 43.
26. O'Connell, "Merton on the Eve of the Third Millennium," 8.
27. Harold Talbott commented that "[Merton] had reached a point—unrecognizable to me and perhaps to you—where the Judeo-Christian theistic tradition of the Mother Church of Christendom and *dzogchen* of Nyingmapa Tibetan Buddhism were not in contradiction." He said, "*dzogchen* was the final bestowal on Merton by a divinely compassionate savior." Helen Tworkov, who was interviewing Talbott, asked: *Do you mean the Dalai Lama?* Talbott replied: "No. The Holy Trinity." See Talbott, *Tendrel*, 285.

Merton's contemplative Catholicism provided him with a place from which to move into the Buddhist world; a first language with which to correlate meanings within a new linguistic frame of reference. It was always to Christ, the Person that Merton would turn to help him define the essential terms and conditions of his own life. The "both/and" and "neither/nor" positions of *Madhyamika* would only support his faith in the paradoxical Christ who is both truly human and truly divine, neither exempt from suffering and death nor defeated by suffering and death.[28]

Such a unifying vision, which can be attributed to Merton, seems to ignore or gloss over the complexity of doctrinal and ritualistic differences between and among religious traditions. He was, however, always on guard against the extremes of a "facile syncretism" and a standoffish apologetics.[29] His studies of non-Christian traditions led him to the conviction "that all truly serious spiritual forms of religion aspire, at least implicitly, to a contemplative awakening both of the individual and of the [community]" (*IE*, 20). He was of the opinion that all the great traditions shared a simple, *functional* core—meant to facilitate for persons a transforming, transcendental encounter, resulting in more compassionate, loving, and honest persons (*ZBA*, 61–62). He considered this functional core to be the focus of the *sapiential* or contemplative traditions within each of the broader cultural traditions identified as *religions*. As he wrote to Marco Pallis,[30] his "sapiential approach" allowed him to see "where other traditions say and attain the same thing, and where they are different" (*HGL*, 465, 469).

He was, however, keenly aware that no religion, not even the Christian religion, was safe from ideological corruption into forms that belied its functional core. He wrote:

---

28. In 1965 Merton had written: "I may be interested in Oriental religions, etc., but there can be no obscuring the essential difference—this personal communion with Christ at the center and heart of all reality, as a source of grace and life. 'God is love' may perhaps be clarified if one says that 'God is void' and if in the void one finds absolute indetermination and hence absolute freedom. (With freedom, the void becomes fullness . . .) All that is 'interesting' but none of it touches on the mystery of personality in God, and his personal love for me. Again, I am void too—and I have freedom, or *am* a kind of freedom, meaningless unless oriented to Him" (*DWL*, 259).

29. Both Scruggs and Clooney emphasize this point. See Scruggs, "Faith Seeking Understanding," 1–16; Clooney, "Thomas Merton's Deep Christian Learning," 50–64.

30. Marco Pallis (1895–1989) was an author, Himalayan mountaineer, and student of Tibetan Buddhism. Merton's letters to Pallis appear in *HGL*, 463–77.

> When religion becomes a mere artificial façade to justify a social or economic system—when religion hands over its rites and language completely to the political propagandist . . . this brings about the alienation of the believer, so that his religious zeal becomes political fanaticism. His faith in God, while preserving its traditional formulas, becomes in fact faith in his own nation, class or race. His ethic ceases to be the law of God and of love, and becomes the law that might makes right: established privilege justifies everything. (CP, 140–41)

So it remains incumbent upon every believer, in any religion, to aspire to a discovery and an appropriation of the tradition at its best, as it cultivates an ever-widening compassion, and positively participates in the new creation which "will be perfected in the end of time" (*NM*, 150).

He was not interested in all aspects of Islam, but in the Sufi wisdom of *fana* and *baqa*; not in every aspect of that diverse spectrum of ritual and beliefs known as "Hinduism," but in *advaita* and the yogas; not all the permutations of Buddhism, but in Ch'an, Zen, and Tibetan *dzogchen*.[31] He valued these traditions insofar as he witnessed their efficacy in the lives of real persons who sincerely practiced them, and with respect to Buddhism that meant especially Suzuki, the Dalai Lama, Thich Nhat Hanh, and Chatral Rinpoche. He was convinced, I believe, that these contemplatives were, in a certain sense, persons of faith, familiar with the revolutionizing *event and encounter* (*fides qua*) that unveils the *semen gloriae*, the *inchoatio gloriae*; and were generously endowed with wisdom, the gift of the Spirit.[32]

---

31. As Clooney noted: "No one should read Merton as their primary source on Hinduism or Buddhism, yoga or zen. . . . Merton's real contribution is to create a space for those of us who are, and hope to remain, grounded where we first met God, even while opening our hearts and minds to God's dwelling in innumerable familiar and unexpected places" (Clooney, "Thomas Merton's Deep Christian Learning," 62).

32. Merton's outlook certainly has affinities with Karl Rahner's "anonymous Christian." Rahner explained his meaning in an interview when he said: "'Anonymous Christianity' means that a person lives in the grace of God and attains salvation outside of explicitly constituted Christianity . . . let us say, a Buddhist monk (or anyone else I might suppose) who, because he follows his conscience, attains salvation and lives in the grace of God; of him I must say that he is an anonymous Christian; if not, I would have to presuppose that there is a genuine path to salvation that really attains that goal, but that simply has nothing to do with Jesus Christ. But I cannot do that. And so if I hold if everyone depends upon Jesus Christ for salvation, and if at the same time I hold that many live in the world who have not expressly recognized Jesus Christ, then there remains in my opinion nothing else but to take up this postulate of an anonymous Christianity" (Egan, *Karl Rahner in Dialogue*, 207). The choice of "anonymous Christian" raises eyebrows but the idea, that a person can be saved and become *Christ-like* and not have

Seeds in the Garden of New Growth

Dominus Iesus and Merton's Complementarity

Merton's positive appraisal of non-Christian contemplative traditions begs the question of how his view holds up in relation to the cautionary parameters laid down decades later by *Dominus Iesus* (*DI*). While the document clarifies certain distinctions that theologians must respect and maintain, it also forbids particular separations that stem from or lead to relativism and indifference. For example, the first three sections center around the assertion that the Jesus of history cannot be separated from the Christ of faith (*DI* 5–15), and the following three around the assertion that Christ cannot be separated from the church (*DI* 16–22). Since the document pinpoints various ways that erroneous separations can sometimes occur it amounts to a clarification of three fundamental affirmations that Catholic theologians must continue to maintain: (1) the distinction between theological faith and belief in other religions; (2) the completeness and perfection of Christian revelation; and (3) the church as *the* way (not one way) of salvation. Interpreting these parameters offers an opportunity to illustrate Merton's orthodoxy as well as the new horizon he opens with his contemplative theology of religious pluralism. The distinctive features of Merton's theological model come in to relief through this interpretive exercise.

First, *DI* asserts:

> The distinction between theological faith and belief in the other religions, must be firmly held. If faith is the acceptance in grace of revealed truth, which "makes it possible to penetrate the mystery in a way that allows us to understand it coherently"[33] (*FR* 13), then belief, in the other religions, is that sum of experience and thought that constitutes the human treasury of wisdom and religious aspiration,

---

explicitly "thematized" that faith as Christian, as Rahner would say, is something Merton himself believed. It was Rahner's meditation on death that won Merton over to Rahner as a theologian (*TTW*, 211). Merton admitted to sometimes wondering why Rahner was considered "so dangerous" (*TTW*, 342).

33. "Coherently" does not mean exhaustively or completely. The fact that the One God who is Three Persons can be understood with some coherence on the basis of interiority (the interiorly differentiated consciousness of a religiously converted subject) does not change the fact that what is proximately grasped is *the interior analogue*, while God remains a mystery more unlike than like human consciousness fulfilled and properly grasped. Aquinas conceded that "reason" could lead to knowledge of God and of "some essential attributes appropriated to the persons such as power, wisdom, and goodness" but without revelation reason could not know the Trinity "by its proper attributes, such as paternity, filiation, and procession" (*ST* I, q.32).

which man in his search for truth has conceived and acted upon in his relationship to God and the Absolute (*FR* 31–32). (*DI* 7.3)

While *DI* refrains from explicitly employing the "natural/supernatural" distinction, the distinction made here can be expressed in those terms. The beliefs of other religions are natural (the human treasury of wisdom) while theological faith is supernatural (the acceptance in grace of revealed truth).

Merton embraces this distinction wholeheartedly and assumes it when he writes that Christian revelation provides "answers to the profound questions raised by all these ancient traditions, which seem to have been grasping at the central truths in their own way" (*MZM*, 213). His insistence on characterizing the kerygma as "supernatural" affirms the faith that transcendent being is Trinitarian, creative, and communicatively gracious. This is the distinction that causes him so much hesitation for so long a time in straightforwardly affirming that non-Christian contemplatives can be regarded as mystics in the "supernatural" sense. It seems clear that for Merton, as long as *explicit* faith in Christ is absent something important is missing.

DI, however, can easily be read as implying or even suggesting that "theological faith" belongs exclusively to explicitly professed Christians, or to *the* Christian religion(s). In other words, only those who embrace the third meaning of God may be said to have theological faith. This can happen because *DI* employs the term "theological faith" as inclusive of both senses of faith (*fides qua* / *fides quae*) without distinction, and this is where Merton would likely roar a cautionary objection.

His own published writings seldom cross the boundary, by which he discerns the actuality, not just potentiality, of "theological faith" among non-Christians,[34] but his private letters often display a greater boldness. For example, when writing to Marco Pallis that he could recognize where other traditions "say and attain the same thing" (*HGL*, 469) he is undoubtedly speaking in ultimate terms and regarding ultimate concerns. He strongly suggested in a letter to Suzuki that he believed him to possess the gift of faith (*fides qua*), enabling him to "penetrate the mystery" in a way that allows him to understand it coherently when he wrote: "The Christ we seek is within us, in our inmost self . . . yet infinitely transcends ourselves. . . . O my dear Dr. Suzuki I know you will understand this so well, and so many people do not, even though they are 'doctors in Israel'" (*Encounter*, 21).

---

34. One exception to this is the fact that Merton discerns an inchoate apprehension of the Trinity in Hui Neng's understanding of the Unconscious, which confirms that he believes *fides qua* to be gifted generously even to non-Christians.

In other words, Merton accepts that many religious beliefs are objectifications of the human search for wisdom and spirit, and accepts that the revelation of Christ meets and fulfills that searching but he will not assume that the grace of faith belongs exclusively to explicitly professed Christians. The revolutionizing event and encounter is often operative in persons without them knowing that Christ is the very One with whom they are in love. He acknowledges, along with the church, the *possibility* of truly mystical and supernatural contemplation beyond the visible church "since God is the master of His gifts and wherever there is sincerity and an earnest desire for truth, He will not deny the gift of His grace" (*IE*, 26). But through his dialogue with Suzuki, and his continued foray into *dzogchen*, he discerns, with always tentative judgment, the *actuality* of grace operating effectively among non-Christian contemplatives who are cooperating with it.

Secondly *DI* cautions that "the theory of the limited, incomplete, or imperfect character of the revelation of Jesus Christ, which would be complementary to that found in other religions, is contrary to the Church's faith" (*DI* 6.1). It should be clear by now that Merton's understanding of the complementary quality of other contemplative traditions is not the sort that assumes an incompleteness or imperfection on the part of Christian revelation. However, he continued to affirm and to emphasize that "even when God reveals Himself He remains a mystery beyond words, if you understood Him it would not be God" (*CCC*, 230) and that "we *should not* allow ourselves to be satisfied" with our limited understandings of God (*SSM*, 191). In other words, because he honored the distinction between what is revealed in Christ and our *understanding* of that revelation, which continues to grow, not only in unique persons, but also in the church as a pilgrim community, he was open to learning from others in ways that would help him as a Christian to understand the transcendent mystery of God more fully.

He wrote:

> Zen is not Kerygma but realization, not revelation but consciousness, not news from the Father who sends his Son into this world, but awareness of the ontological ground of our own being here and now, right in the midst of the world . . . the supernatural Kerygma and [this awareness] are far from being incompatible . . . they well complement each other, and for this reason Zen is perfectly compatible with Christian belief. (*ZBA*, 47)

And to Pallis he wrote: "I think that I am as much a Chinese Buddhist in temperament and spirit as I am a Christian.... A Buddhist outlook... is by no means incompatible with Christian belief" (*HGL*, 465).

The kerygmatic *revelation* supersedes what unaided intentional consciousness can conceive, and what graced consciousness can fully grasp. But the awareness or apprehension *right here and now* of the creating and loving *ground* of our own being can be deepened through the study and practice of Zen, which for Merton in no way diminished his love for Christ, Who reveals and is that ground of love. Rather, he found Zen to be very effective for awakening this "awareness."

Because he not only endorsed the third meaning of "God" but also understood it as successively related to the prior two, he did not hold his commitment to Christ as a stumbling block to dialogue. He did not consider that his Christocentric world view impeded his ability to learn from other contemplatives and their traditions, which could teach him not only "techniques" but also, as Lawrence Cunningham noted, could deepen his "Christian understanding [of] that self-emptying which is incumbent on every believer who wishes to follow 'Christ in his kenosis.'"[35] He wasn't interested in simply subsuming non-Christian contemplative traditions in a way that would nullify their differences; rather he often found what was different to be spiritually helpful to him as a Christian. They helped him be more fully catholic, with a "unified vision and experience of the one truth shining out in all its various manifestations" (*CWA*, 207).

Thirdly, *DI* asserts that "it would be contrary to the faith to consider the Church as *one way* of salvation alongside those constituted by the other religions, seen as complementary to the Church or substantially equivalent to her, even if these are said to be converging with the Church toward the eschatological kingdom of God" (*DI* 21). This assertion proved to be the most contentious after the promulgation of *DI* because it appeared to ignore the enormous ecclesiological advances achieved by Vatican II.[36] At face value there is no distinction between the visible and the invisible church; and while the distinction between the Catholic Church and the Church of Christ is recognized, it is brought up for the sole purpose of emphasizing that "the single Church of Christ continues to exist fully only in the Catholic Church" (*DI* 16.3).[37] The term "Catholic Church" here

---

35. Cunningham, *Spiritual Master*, 46.
36. See for example McBrien, "*Dominus Iesus*."
37. This is why the same principle of "canonical exegesis" applies to magisterial

does not seem to refer to those of us who "are the church," with all of our moral failures, selfishness, pettiness, and sometimes cruelty. Rather the term seems to refer to a purely theological reality unsoiled by our sin and scandal, obviously much greater than the pilgrim people of God who plod along toward an eschatological fullness of which we are already somehow mystriously a part.

Even before the Council would effectively employ such distinctions in ways that would advance both the Christian and the wider ecumenical movements, Merton wrote to his non-Christian friend, Dona Luisa Coomaraswamy:

> You must understand by now that I do not entertain formally conventional notions of the Church. I certainly believe with all my heart in the Church, none more so. But I absolutely refuse to take the rigid, stereotyped, bourgeois notions that are acceptable to most Catholics and which manage in the long run to veil the true mystery of Christ and make it utterly unattainable to some people. You can pull my leg all you want, it stretches indefinitely, and we both understand quite well the way in which you belong to Christ. We both belong to Him in His mercy which . . . reaches into the inmost depths of every being, but especially of all who, with all their deficiencies and limitations, seek only truth and love, as best they can. I do not understand too much of any kind of Church which is made up entirely of people whose external conformity has made them comfortable and . . . has given them the privilege of looking down on everybody else who is automatically "wrong" because not conformed to them. This does not seem to me to have a great deal to do with the message of Christ. (*HGL*, 133)

After guiltily confessing in a letter to Rosemary Radford Ruether that he often felt more in common with Zen Buddhists than with many confessing Catholics, he asked: "is the Church a community of people who love each other or a big dog fight where you do your religious business seeking, meanwhile, your friends somehere else?" (*AHTW*, 17). Writing in response to his friend Czeslaw Milosz, who had criticized the church and confessed to Merton that he was on the "outside" of it, Merton wrote: "You can say absolutely nothing about the Church that will shock me. . . . In effect, my 'happiness' does not depend on any institution or any establishment. As

---

teaching and conciliar and curial documents. If *DI* is interpreted in isolation from the documents of Vatican II it can read like a throwback to a pre-conciliar ecclesiological paradigm that is institutionalist.

for you, you are part of my 'Church' of friends who are in many ways more important to me than the institution" (*CT*, 85–86).

Without explicitly utilizing the distiction between the Church of Christ and the Catholic Church, or the Church of Christ and its visible structure and boundaries, he implcitly employed the distinction regularly. He knew himself as a sinner in need of mercy and had little patience for uncareful words about the church that uncritically conflated the Church of Christ with the quarrelsome lot of his earth-dwelling siblings who make the Catholic Church visible to most people. That is to say, the all too visible depravity and dereliction of Catholics and of those who are sometimes meant to serve as the visible face of the church compound the problem of the one true Church of Christ being made truly visible. For Merton, the *true* church is visible in the sacraments and in the saints. He wrote, "The Church is indeed visible, yes, but it depends on what you mean by "visible." Not Cadillacs, surely" (*HGL*, 133). As Ratzinger asserted, holiness is the essense and *raison d'etre* of the Church's identity and mission.[38] The seeds of such holiness can be found sown in the rites and customs of non-Christian religious traditions (*LG* 17), and saints can be found beyond the "visible structure" of the Catholic Church.[39]

In its "Responses to Some Questions Regarding Certain Aspects of the Doctrine of the Church" (2007) the Congregation for the Doctrine of the Faith stated: "It is possible, according to Catholic doctrine, to affirm correctly that the Church of Christ is present and operative in the churches and ecclesial communities not yet fully in communion with the Catholic Church, on account of the elements of sanctification and truth that are present in them." This statement is fascinatingly careful. Asserting that it is "possible to affirm correctly" suggests that even though it is true Catholics

---

38. In his lecture "The Ecclesiology of Vatican II," Ratzinger said: "To understand the ecclesiology of Vatican II one cannot ignore chapters 4 to 7 of the Constitution *Lumen Gentium*. These chapters discuss the laity, the universal call to holiness, the religious and eschatological orientation of the Church. In these chapters the inner goal of the Church, the most essential part of its being, comes once again to the fore: holiness, conformity to God."

39. When the non-Catholic Brother Roger Schutz of Taizé passed away in 2005, Cardinal Tarzisio Bertone said "now that he has entered into eternal joy, he continues to speak to us." Cardinal Walter Kasper said of him: "Few persons of our generation have incarnated with such transparency the gentle and humble face of Jesus Christ." Such accolades from official prelates of the Catholic Church read as an implicit canonization of someone "outside the visible structure" of the church. See Allen, "Another Tribute for Taizé from the Vatican."

are not *required* to affirm this, and that it is also possible to affirm it *incorrectly* (on the basis of a misunderstanding). However, since it does say it's possible "on account of the elements of sanctification and truth that are present in them" it would follow that it is possible, according to Catholic doctrine, to affirm correctly that the Church of Christ is present and operative in *other religions* on account of the elements of sanctification and truth that are present in them.

Granted, the Church of Christ can be distinguished from the Spirit of Christ, which is undoubtedly present and operative universally. But the "elements of sanctification and truth" belong to the Church of Christ, so where those are present and operative so too the Church of Christ. "Church of Christ" includes both the Spirit of Christ and the human *community* formed by the Spirit of Christ, the *koinonia* characterized by those exhibiting the fruits of the Spirit (Gal 5:22), a community that extends beyond the visible boundaries of the church and the numerical boundary of those explicitly affirming the Christian faith (*Fides quae*). In my judgment, Merton would argue that not only other *Christian* traditions play a positive role in God's universal plan for humanity, but also other non-Christian contemplative traditions *because of* the elements of sanctification and truth present in them.

Finally, it should be noted that Merton would strongly affirm the way *DI* approaches interreligious dialogue within the context of evangelization. *DI* states:

> The Church's proclamation of Jesus Christ, "the way, the truth, and the life" (John 14:6), today also makes use of the practice of inter-religious dialogue. Such dialogue certainly does not replace, but rather accompanies the *missio ad gentes*, directed toward that "mystery of unity," from which "it follows that all men and women who are saved share, though differently, in the same mystery of salvation in Jesus Christ through his Spirit" (*DP* 29). (*DI* 2.2)

He was ever an evangelist, not aiming to be himself the cause of another's conversion, for grace alone does that, but because his joy burst forth in an apostolic spirit desiring to proclaim God's infinite love (*HGL*, 129). If that joy were to prove contagious he did not pretend to know whether it would lead another into juridical communion with Rome but he believed it did lead to interior communion in Christ, one that might remain hidden, perhaps indefinitely. The document *Dialogue and Proclamation* (*DP*), issued by the Pontifical Council for Interreligious Dialogue acknowledged that genuine conversion can be unfolding in the lives of persons who do not explicitly confess Christian faith, just as it does in the lives of those that do. Such conversion is a matter of the heart's desire for increasing union with and conformity to God (*DP* 11). Such a position makes room for a positive appraisal of religious pluralism all the while conceding that such elements "impel toward catholic unity"—a "mysterious unity" that values difference.

All people, Christians and non-Christians, believers, agnostics and atheists are directed toward that "mystery of unity." But the word "mystery" would be every bit as important to Merton as the word "unity" in this instance. A mysterious unity is neither measured nor determined by quantifiable marks of external conformity. Indeed if all who will share in that same mystery will do so *differently*, then an apophatic humility that is joyously open to diversity must constantly accompany the kataphatic proclamation of the Christ in whom and through whom all are made one.

Seeds of a Contemplative Theology of Religious Pluralism: A Conclusion

Elizabeth Johnson indicated that theologians today are trying to answer the question of how Christians are to understand the meaning of the positive role played by non-Christian religions in God's plan for creation. Merton does not answer the question definitively; his contemplative theology always suggests more than it explicitly says, but his example indicates that whatever or how much of that meaning can be understood involves a hermeneutical process, and an ongoing one, open to correction and evolution. Merton was an attentive and intelligent reader/listener who engaged in a dialogical process seeking to understand the meaning of that positive role. Moreover, dialogue for him accorded with the church's understanding of dialogue as "all positive and constructive interreligious relations with individuals and communities of other faiths which are directed at mutual understanding and enrichment" (*DM* 3). Such "mutual enrichment" aptly describes his appreciation of non-Christian contemplative traditions as complementary to his own.[40]

---

40. As Merton noted in his Journal on November 2, 1968: "*A fortiori*, we should not try to set up a pseudocommunity of people from different traditions, Asian and Western. . . . But I had wondered about some different approach . . . re-exploring . . . Christian monasticism in relation to the Eastern traditions, i.e., in the light thrown on them by the East" (*OSM*, 240).

Seeds in the Garden of New Growth

His own approach to the question came out of and expressed his commitment to Christ and to scripture. However, just as an historical interpretive process of rereading was necessary, as Ratzinger pointed out, for "the words of the Bible to *become* Scripture," Merton engaged in an *interpretive* process of other contemplative traditions, and of his own dogma, whereby he discovered that the *one truth* "gradually unfolds its inner potentialities, already somehow present like seeds, but needing the challenge of new situations, new experiences and new sufferings, in order to open up."[41] He focused on the seeds found sown in other contemplative traditions, reading them anew, "in continuity with their original sense" ready to offer tacit correction and give added depth and breadth of meaning. As a humble iconoclast, however, he was open to the fact that his own *understanding* sometimes needed tacit correction, added depth and breadth, and would continue to open up through a mutually beneficial dialogical process. He discovered through that process that "we are already one"[42] in the "mystery of unity" but believed that continuing the process could create a more robust community of *explicitly* shared meanings and values, a catholic unity in which "all men and women share, though differently, in that same mystery of salvation through Jesus Christ in the Spirit" (*DP* 29; *DI* 2.2).

The seeds Merton sows for a theology of religious pluralism suggest four interrelated features. As an autobiographical and contemplative theologian, his work cannot be properly understood or appreciated apart from the fact that he belonged to and embodied a *living contemplative Christian tradition*. These four words are italicized since each is an important marker. A *contemplative* is one who explores interior consciousness, its ground and goal, and responds affirmatively to the experienced inchoate fulfillment of human consciousness. A *Christian* contemplative is one who "contemplates the Trinity," meaning that person understands and affirms human fulfillment always in explicit *relation* to Christ and to what has been revealed in and through Christ. It means that he reads not just the Bible, but all of life

---

41. Ratzinger, *Jesus of Nazareth*, xviii–xix.

42. In a talk given in Calcutta in October of 1968 Merton said that through dialogue "we discover an older unity . . . we are already one . . . what we have to be is what we are" (*AJ*, 308). In his impromptu prayer at the First Spiritual Summit Conference in Calcutta he said: "Oh God, we are one with You. You have taught us that if we are open to one another, You dwell in us. Help us to realize that there can be no understanding where there is mutual rejection. Oh God, in accepting one another wholeheartedly, fully, completely, we accept You, and we thank You, and we adore You, and we love You with our whole being, because our being is in Your being" (*AJ*, 318–19).

and of history through the lens of a Christological hermeneutic. A *tradition* has a treasured past behind it, and a *living* tradition has an as-yet-to-be-fully-known future. An important implication of these four features is that a contemplative theology embraces the dynamism of a moving viewpoint. It will not be content to settle for the repetition of formulas whose meanings can become obscured and misunderstood; rather it will critically engage those formulas so that their intended meanings can be continuously rediscovered, re-appropriated, and freshly applied in ever-changing contexts.

Dogmas as formulated have a past; the formulations are contextual and emerged from the historical particularities of dialectical processes— histories we continue to learn from in each dawning age. The *meaning* of dogma is permanent but theology is ever seeking a coherent understanding of that meaning, or seeking to recover a sufficient grasp of the originally intended meaning in each new situation. But for Merton the meaning of a dogma is not something contained *in* the propositional statements *about* God, and certainly not reducible to them, but can be mediated through those words and be revealed through a knowledge *of* God whose meaning is inexhaustibly infinite and existentially consequential. While *affirming* the truth of dogma he would *deny* that its meaning is exhaustively explicable through propositions and arguments, but whose truth can be *realized* in a way that bears out its meaning existentially through a holy life in loving communion with God and every other creature. Being an instrument of the lion's roar, he would silence any idolatrous assertion *about* the church that would veil the mystery of Christ and make it utterly unattainable for some people. The Church of Christ, while subsisting fully in the Catholic Church, remains a mystery beyond visible boundaries which can in no way limit a limitless God.

On the basis of interiority Merton could affirm common meanings of God and person, which he also affirmed to be *true*, across religious borders. On that basis he recognized that Suzuki knew not only of God's ineffable transcendence, but God's gracefully transformative immanence, bestowing *prajna* disposed as liberty and compassion. He sought these common meanings because he believed in the universal and operative presence of the Trinity. But he also *learned from* Suzuki that Christian contemplation was not superior in terms of it anticipating some eschatological fullness unanticipated by the Zen practitioner. He came to believe that both he and Suzuki anticipated and inchoately realized something of that same fullness/emptiness. He also came to more fully appreciate, through his studies of Zen, how distinctions can become unexamined presuppositions that turn into dualistic divisions and hinder rather than help communication and clearer understanding. Properly conceived and affirmed distinctions are actually commensurate with coherence and clarity, but forgetting or ignoring their origin and function can be disastrous, causing distinctions to become divisions. Suzuki was adamant about getting back down to the unity of consciousness so that subsequent distinctions could be properly grasped in a "penetrating insight" and never harden into reified binaries that bifurcate reality.

The fact that Merton risked recognizing "supernatural" mysticism in non-Christian contexts meant he was prepared to admit not only that the Spirit of Christ was present in such contemplatives, and mediated through their contemplative traditions, but also *known by* them, even if by other names.[43] Having been formed by thinkers like Gregory of Nazianzus, Maximus the Confessor, and St. Bernard of Clairvaux, all of whom expounded on the mystery of perichoresis or circumincession, he was exuberant over the possibility of discovering the Three, and knowledge of the Three, in the concrete particular contemplative traditions he was exploring. He knew that the mystery of the Trinity itself would be known in various degrees and by other names. Such a conclusion merits the affirmation that non-Christian contemplative traditions, and to some extent the broader religions to which they belong "can be affirmed correctly" as serving a positive role in God's universal plan for humanity.

Ever cautious of a "facile syncretism," he would reject the conclusion that the *religions* are all the same, or all equally true. This conclusion is false not only from the particular point of view of his own tradition, but is the reasonable conclusion to be drawn by any serious student, coming out of any other tradition, who inevitably runs across genuinely dialectical oppositions between truth-claims where the doctrines of one tradition cannot be reconciled, with their intended meaning still preserved, with the opposing claims of others. As he wrote to Marco Pallis, "The differences must be respected, not brushed aside, even and especially where they are irreconcilable with one's own view" (*HGL*, 469). In such cases some claims

---

43. By suggesting that Christ can be known by different names, I do not mean that Christ is more than Jesus, or that the Jesus of history can in any sense be separated from the Christ of faith, or that there would or could be other *Incarnations*. The New Testament as well as liturgical tradition references Jesus by many names and titles—e.g., Word, Wisdom, Lion of Judah, Immanuel, etc. A Buddhist may know Holy Wisdom and name that wisdom, and not yet recognize that Jesus *is* that Wisdom.

will turn out to be true and others to be false. But because he was a contemplative attuned to the interior life, he believed that the same *fides qua* could lead people to a more expansive and more explicit unity. As a "promoter of peace between peoples and religions" he discovered that when contemplatives speak to each other, heart to heart, the seeds "found sown" among them begin to blossom and reveal an "already" mysterious unity organically emerging toward a not yet fully realized community, centered on the Person of Christ.

Bibliography

Abe, Masao. "Buddhism." In *Our Religions: The Seven World Religions Introduced by Preeminent Scholars from Each Tradition*, edited by Arvind Sharma, 69–138. San Francisco: HarperCollins, 1993.
———. "Editor's Introduction." In *A Zen Life: D. T. Suzuki Remembered*, edited by Masao Abe, xv–xix. New York: Weatherhill, 1986.
———. "Kenotic God and Dynamic Sunyata." In *The Emptying God: A Buddhist–Jewish–Christian Conversation*, edited by John B. Cobb and Christopher Ives, 3–55. Maryknoll, NY: Orbis, 1991.
———, ed. *A Zen Life: D. T. Suzuki Remembered*. New York: Weatherhill, 1986.
"Ahern, Barnabas Mary." *New Catholic Encyclopedia*, October 18, 2020. Online. https://www.encyclopedia.com/religion/encyclopedias-almanacs-transcripts-and-maps/ahern-barnabas-mary.
Allen, John. "Another Tribute for Taize from the Vatican." *National Catholic Reporter*, August 11, 2010.
Anatolios, Khaled, ed. *Athanasius*. New York: Routledge, 2004.
Anselm of Canterbury. *Proslogian: With the Replies of Gaunilo and Anselm*. Translated and edited by Thomas Williams. Indianapolis: Hackett, 1995.
Apel, William. "How to Disagree: Peacebuilding in the Interfaith Letters of Thomas Merton and Doña Luisa Coomaraswamy." *The Merton Seasonal* 44.3 (2019) 18–22.
———. *Signs of Peace: The Interfaith Letters of Thomas Merton*. Maryknoll, NY: Orbis, 2006.
Balthasar, Hans Urs von. *First Glance at Adrienne von Speyr*. Translated by Antje Lawry and Sr. Sergia Englund. San Francisco: Ignatius, 1981.
Barron, Robert. *Catholicism: A Journey to the Heart of the Faith*. New York: Image, 2011.
Bracken, Joseph. *Subjectivity, Objectivity, and Intersubjectivity: A New Paradigm for Religion and Science*. West Conshohocken, PA: Templeton Foundation, 2009. Online. https://www.metanexus.net/subjectivity-objectivity-and-intersubjectivity-toward-post-post-modern-metaphysics.
Brahmachari, Mahanambrata. *The Philosophy of Sri Jiva Goswami (Vaisnava Vedanta of the Bengal School)*. Chicago: University of Chicago Press, 1937
Brown, Raymond E. *An Introduction to New Testament Christology*. Mahwah, NJ: Paulist, 1993.
Burrows, William R., ed. *Redemption and Dialogue: Reading "Redemptoris Missio" and "Dialogue and Proclamation."* Maryknoll, NY: Orbis, 1993.

Bibliography

Carr, Anne E. *A Search for Wisdom and Spirit: Thomas Merton's Theology of the Self.* Notre Dame, IN: University of Notre Dame Press, 1988.

Catholic Church. *Catechism of the Catholic Church: Revised in Accordance with the Official Latin Text Promulgated by Pope John Paul II.* Vatican City: Libreria Editrice Vaticana, 1997.

Clooney, Francis X. "Thomas Merton's Deep Christian Learning across Religious Borders." *Buddhist-Christian Studies* 37 (2017) 50–64.

Coady, Mary Francis. "A Fire That Burns: Thomas Merton, Catherine De Hueck Doherty and the Story of the Secular Journal." *The Merton Annual* 30 (2017) 41–54.

Cobb, John B., Jr. *Beyond Dialogue: Toward the Mutual Transformation of Christianity and Buddhism.* 1982. Reprint, Eugene, OR: Wipf & Stock, 1998.

Collins, John. "A Passionist Friendship: Barnabas Ahern and Thomas Merton." *The Merton Seasonal* 34.2 (2009) 17–29.

Congregation for the Doctrine of the Faith. *Dominus Iesus: Declaration on the Unicity and Salvific Universality of Jesus Christ and the Church.* August 6, 2000. Online. http://www.vatican.va/roman_curia/congregations/cfaith/documents/rc_con_cfaith_doc_20000806_dominus-iesus_en.html.

Conn, Walter E. "Bernard Lonergan's Analysis of Conversion." *Angelicum* 53 (1976) 362–404.

———. *The Desiring Self: Rooting Pastoral Counseling in Self Transcendence.* Mahwah, NJ: Paulist, 1999.

———. "Merton's 'True Self': Moral Autonomy and Religious Conversion." *Journal of Religion* 65 (1985) 513–29.

Corless, Roger "In Search of a Context for the Merton–Suzuki Dialogue." *The Merton Annual* 6 (1993) 76–91.

———. *The Vision of Buddhism: The Space under the Tree.* St. Paul, MN: Paragon, 1989.

Cracknell, Kenneth. *In Good and Generous Faith: Christian Responses to Religious Pluralism.* Cleveland: Pilgrim, 2006.

Crowe, Frederick. "Son of God, Holy Spirit and World Religions." In *Appropriating the Lonergan Idea*, edited by Michael Vertin, 324–44. Washington, DC: Catholic University of America Press, 1989.

Cunningham, Lawrence. "Introduction." In *Thomas Merton: Spiritual Master. The Essential Writings*, edited by Lawrence S. Cunningham, 15–55. Mahwah, NJ: Paulist, 1992.

Dadosky, John. "The Church and the Other: Mediation and Friendship in Post-Vatican II Roman Catholic Ecclesiology." *Pacifica* 18 (2005) 302–22.

———. "Merton's Dialogue with Zen: Pioneering or Passé?" *Fu Jen International Religious Studies* 2.1 (2008) 53–75.

Dalai Lama XIV. *Dzogchen: The Heart Essence of the Great Perfection.* Edited by Patrick Gaffney. Translated by Geshe Thupten Jinpa and Richard Barron. Ithaca, NY: Snow Lion, 2000.

Dennett, Daniel C. *Consciousness Explained.* New York: Little, Brown, 1991.

Dulles, Avery. *Models of the Church.* Expanded ed. New York: Image Classics, 1991.

Dumoulin, Heinrich. *A History of Zen Buddhism.* Translated by Paul Peachey. New York: Pantheon, 1963.

Dunne, John S. *The Way of All the Earth: Experiments in Truth and Religion.* Notre Dame, IN: University of Notre Dame Press, 1978.

Dupuis, Jacques, ed. *The Christian Faith in the Doctrinal Documents of the Catholic Church.* 7th ed. New York: Alba, 2001.

Bibliography

———. *Jesus Christ at the Encounter of World Religions*. Maryknoll, NY: Orbis, 1991.
———. *Toward a Christian Theology of Religious Pluralism*. Maryknoll, NY: Orbis, 2001.
Evans-Wentz, W. Y. *Tibetan Yoga and Secret Doctrines: Seven Books of Wisdom of the Great Path*. Foreword by Donald S. Lopez Jr. London: Oxford University Press, 2000.
Flannery, Austin, ed. *Vatican Council II: The Basic Sixteen Documents*. Northport, NY: Costello, 1996.
Forest, Jim. *The Root of War is Fear: Thomas Merton's Advice to Peacemakers*. Maryknoll, NY: Orbis, 2016.
Francis. "Address of the Holy Father: Visit to the Joint Session of the United States Congress." *The Merton Annual* 28 (2015) 16–24. Online. https://w2.vatican.va/content/francesco/en/speeches/2015/september/documents/papa-francesco_20150924_usa-us-congress.html.
Frye, Northrop. *The Great Code: The Bible and Literature*. New York: Harcourt, 1982.
Galvin, John. "Salvation Outside the Church." In *The Gift of the Church*, edited by Peter Phan, 249–67. Collegeville, MN: Liturgical, 2000.
Gilson, Etienne *The Spirit of Medieval Philosophy*. Notre Dame, IN: University of Notre Dame Press, 1991.
Gordon, Mary. *On Thomas Merton*. Boston: Shambhala, 2019.
Grayston, Donald. *Thomas Merton and the Noonday Demon: The Camaldoli Correspondence*. Eugene, OR: Cascade Books, 2015.
Hartshorne, Charles, and William L. Reese. *Philosophers Speak of God*. Chicago: University of Chicago Press, 1963.
Heft, James L., ed. *Beyond Violence: Religious Sources of Social Transformation in Judaism, Christianity, and Islam*. New York: Fordham University Press, 2004.
———, ed. *Catholicism and Interreligious Dialogue*. New York: Oxford University Press, 2012.
Heschel, Abraham. *I Asked for Wonder*. Edited by Samuel H. Dresner. New York: Crossroad, 1983.
Hick, John. *The Metaphor of God Incarnate: Christology in a Pluralistic Age*. Louisville: John Knox, 1993.
Higgins, Michael W. *Heretic Blood: The Spiritual Geography of Thomas Merton*. Toronto: Stoddart, 1998.
———. *Thomas Merton: Faithful Visionary*. Collegeville, MN: Liturgical, 2014
———. *The Unquiet Monk: Thomas Merton's Questing Faith*. Maryknoll, NY: Orbis, 2015.
Higgins, Michael W., and Kevin Burns. *Genius Born of Anguish: The Life and Legacy of Henri Nouwen*. Mahwah, NJ: Paulist, 2012.
Horan, Daniel. *The Franciscan Heart of Thomas Merton: A New Look at the Spiritual Inspiration of His Life, Thought, and Writing*. Notre Dame, IN: Ave Maria, 2014.
International Theological Commission. *The Interpretation of Dogma*. October 1989. Online. http://www.vatican.va/roman_curia/congregations/cfaith/cti_documents/rc_cti_1989_interpretazione-dogmi_en.html.
John Paul II. *Fides et Ratio: Encyclical Letter of the Supreme Pontiff to the Bishops of the Catholic Church on the Relationship between Faith and Reason*. September 14, 1998. Online. http://www.vatican.va/content/john-paul-ii/en/encyclicals/documents/hf_jp-ii_enc_14091998_fides-et-ratio.html.
Johnson, Elizabeth. *Consider Jesus: Waves of Renewal in Christology*. New York: Crossroad, 1990.

Bibliography

———. *Quest for the Living God: Mapping Frontiers in the Theology of God*. New York: Bloomsbury, 2007.
Johnston, William. *The Inner Eye of Love: Mysticism and Religion*. San Francisco: Harper & Row, 1982.
———. *Mystical Theology: The Science of Love*. Maryknoll, NY: Orbis, 1995.
———. *Silent Music: The Science of Meditation*. San Francisco: Harper Collins, 1979.
Katz, Steven T. "Language, Epistemology, and Mysticism." In *Mysticism and Philosophical Analysis*, edited by Steven Katz, 22–73. New York: Oxford University Press, 1978.
Keating, Thomas. *The Human Condition: Contemplation and Transformation*. Mahwah, NJ: Paulist, 1999.
Keenan, John P. "The Limits of Thomas Merton's Understanding of Buddhism." In *Merton & Buddhism: Wisdom, Emptiness & Everyday Mind*, edited by Bonnie Bowman Thurston, 118–37. Louisville: Fons Vitae, 2007.
Kilcourse, George. *Ace of Freedom: Thomas Merton's Christ*. Notre Dame, IN: University of Notre Dame Press, 1993.
Knitter, Paul. *Introducing Theologies of Religions*. Maryknoll, NY: Orbis, 2002.
———. *No Other Name? A Critical Survey of Christian Attitudes toward the World Religions*. American Society of Missiology Series 7. Maryknoll, NY: Orbis, 1990.
LaCugna, Catherine Mowry. *God for Us: The Trinity and Christian Life*. San Francisco: HarperSanFrancisco, 1991.
———. "God in Communion with Us: The Trinity." In *Freeing Theology: The Essentials of Theology in Feminist Perspective*, edited by Catherine Mowry LaCugna, 83–114. San Francisco: HarperSanFrancisco, 1993.
Lentfoehr, Theresa. *Words and Silence: On the Poetry of Thomas Merton*. New York: New Directions, 1979.
Levada, William. "Responses to Some Questions Regarding Certain Aspects of the Doctrine on the Church." June 29, 2007. Online. http://www.vatican.va/roman_curia/congregations/cfaith/documents/rc_con_cfaith_doc_20070629_responsa-quaestiones_en.html.
Lipsey, Roger. *Make Peace before the Sun Goes Down: The Long Encounter of Thomas Merton and His Abbot, James Fox*. Boston: Shambhala, 2015.
———. "Merton, Suzuki, Zen, Ink: Thomas Merton's Calligraphic Drawings in Context." In *Merton & Buddhism: Wisdom, Emptiness, and Everyday Mind*, edited by Bonnie Bowman Thurston, 137–75. Louisville: Fons Vitae, 2007.
Lonergan, Bernard. "Exegesis and Dogma." In *Philosophical and Theological Papers 1958–1964*, edited by Robert C. Croken et al., 142–54. Collected Works of Bernard Lonergan 6. Toronto: University of Toronto Press, 1996.
———. *Insight: A Study of Human Understanding*. 2nd ed. Toronto: University of Toronto Press, 1992.
———. *Method in Theology*. Vol. 14 of *Collected Works of Bernard Lonergan*. Edited by Robert M. Doran and John D. Dadosky. Toronto: University of Toronto Press, 2017.
———. *Philosophy of God and Theology*. Philadelphia, PA: Westminster, 1973.
———. "Prolegomena to the Study of the Emerging Religious Consciousness of Our Time." In *A Third Collection*, edited by Robert M. Doran and John D. Dadosky, 55–74. Vol. 16 of *Collected Works of Bernard Lonergan*. Toronto: University of Toronto Press, 2017.
———. "Theology in Its New Context." In vol. 1 of *Theology of Renewal*, edited by L. K. Shook, 34–46. New York: Herder & Herder, 1968.

Bibliography

———. *The Way to Nicea: The Dialectical Development of Trinitarian Theology*. Louisville: Westminster, 1976.

Maréchal, Joseph. *Le point de départ de la métaphysique: leçons sur le développement historique et théorique du problème de la connaissance*. 5 vols. Bruges: Leuven University Press, 1922–1947.

Marion, Jean-Luc. *God Without Being*. Translated by Thomas A. Carlson. Foreword by David Tracy. Chicago: University of Chicago Press, 1991.

Martin, David, and Hugh Turley. *The Martyrdom of Thomas Merton: An Investigation*. Hyattsville, MD: McCabe, 2018.

McBrien, Richard P. "Dominus Iesus: An Ecclesiological Critique." Lecture given at the Centro Pro Unione, Rome, January 11, 2001. Online. http://columbanird.org/systems/wp-content/uploads/2015/04/McBrien-Richard-2001-Dominus-Iesus.pdf.

McFague, Sallie. *Metaphorical Theology: Models of God in Religious Language*. Philadelphia: Fortress, 1982.

McGinn, Bernard. *The Flowering of Mysticism: Men and Women in the New Mysticism 1200–1350*. New York: 1998.

———. *The Foundations of Mysticism: Origins to the Fifth Century*. New York: Crossroad, 1995.

———. *The Growth of Mysticism: Gregory the Great through the Twelfth Century*. New York: Crossroad, 1996.

McGregor, Michael N. "The Persistence of Harlem in the Life and Legacy of Thomas Merton." *The Merton Annual* 29 (2016) 90–98.

———. *Pure Act: The Uncommon Life of Robert Lax*. New York: Fordham University Press, 2017.

Merton, Thomas. *The Ascent to Truth*. New York: Harcourt Brace Jovanovich, 1951.

———. *The Asian Journal of Thomas Merton*. Edited by James Laughlin et al. New York: New Directions, 1973.

———. *The Behavior of Titans*. New York: New Directions, 1961.

———. *Bread in the Wilderness*. Collegeville, MN: Liturgical, 1953.

———. *Cassian and the Fathers*. Vol. 1 of *Initiation into the Monastic Tradition*. Edited by Patrick F. O'Connell. Kalamazoo, MI: Cistercian, 2005.

———. *Cistercian Fathers and Forefathers: Essays and Conferences*. Edited by Patrick F. O'Connell. Hyde Park, NY: New City, 2018.

———. *The Cistercian Fathers and Their Monastic Theology*. Vol. 8 of *Initiation into the Monastic Tradition*. Edited by Patrick F. O'Connell. Kalamazoo, MI: Cistercian, 2016.

———. *The Collected Poems of Thomas Merton*. New York: New Directions, 1977.

———. *Conjectures of a Guilty Bystander*. Garden City, NY: Doubleday, 1966.

———. *Contemplation in a World of Action*. Foreword by Robert Coles. 1971. Notre Dame: University of Notre Dame Press, 1998.

———. *Contemplative Prayer*. Garden City, NY: Doubleday, 1971.

———. *The Courage for Truth: Letters to Writers*. Edited by Christine M. Bochen. New York: Farrar, Straus & Giroux, 1993.

———. *Dancing in the Water of Life, 1963–1965*. Edited by Robert E. Daggy. The Journals of Thomas Merton 5. San Francisco: HarperCollins, 1997.

———. *Disputed Questions*. New York: Farrar, Straus & Cudahy, 1960.

———. *Entering the Silence: Becoming a Monk & Writer, 1941–1952*. Edited by Jonathan Montaldo. The Journals of Thomas Merton 2. San Francisco: HarperSanFrancisco, 1996.

Bibliography

———. *Exile Ends in Glory: The Life of a Trappistine, Mother M. Berchmans OCSO.* Milwaukee: Bruce, 1948.

———. *Faith and Violence: Christian Teaching and Christian Practice.* Notre Dame, IN: University of Notre Dame Press, 1968.

———. *The Hidden Ground of Love: The Letters of Thomas Merton on Religious Experience and Social Concerns.* Edited by William H. Shannon. New York: Farrar, Straus & Giroux, 1985.

———. *Honorable Reader: Reflections on My Work.* Edited by Robert E. Daggy. New York: Crossroad, 1989.

———. "The Inner Experience." *Cistercian Studies* 18.1 (1983) 3–15; 18.2 (1983) 121–34; 18.3 (1983) 201–16; 18.4 (1983) 289–300; 19.1 (1984) 62–78; 19.2 (1984) 139–50; 19.3 (1984) 267–82; 19.4 (1984) 336–45.

———. *An Introduction to Christian Mysticism.* Vol. 3 of *Initiation into the Monastic Tradition.* Edited by Patrick F. O'Connell. Kalamazoo, MI: Cistercian, 2008.

———. *Ishi Means Man: Essays on Native Americans.* Greensboro, NC: Unicorn, 1976.

———. *Learning to Love: Exploring Solitude and Freedom, 1966–1967.* Edited by Christine M. Bochen. The Journals of Thomas Merton 6. San Francisco: Harper Collins, 1997.

———. *The Literary Essays of Thomas Merton.* Edited by Patrick Hart. New York: New Directions, 1981.

———. *Love and Living.* Edited by Naomi Burton Stone and Patrick Hart. New York: Harcourt Brace Jovanovich, 1985.

———. *A Monastic Introduction to Sacred Scripture: Novitiate Conferences on Scripture and Liturgy 1.* Edited by Patrick F. O'Connell. Eugene, OR: Cascade Books, 2020.

———. *The Monastic Journey.* Edited by Patrick Hart. Garden City, NY: Image, 1978.

———. *Mystics and Zen Masters.* New York: Farrar, Straus & Giroux, 1967.

———. *The New Man.* New York: Farrar, Straus & Cudahy, 1961.

———. *New Seeds of Contemplation.* Norfolk: New Directions, 1961.

———. *No Man Is an Island.* New York: Harcourt, Brace, 1955.

———. *The Non-Violent Alternative.* New York: Farrar, Straus & Giroux, 1980.

———. *The Other Side of the Mountain: The End of the Journey, 1967–1968.* Edited by Patrick Hart. The Journals of Thomas Merton 7. San Francisco: Harper Collins, 1998.

———. *Pre-Benedictine Monasticism.* Vol. 2 of *Initiation into the Monastic Tradition.* Edited by Patrick F. O'Connell. Kalamazoo, MI: Cistercian, 2006.

———. *Raids on the Unspeakable.* New York: New Directions, 1964.

———. *The Road to Joy: Letters to New and Old Friends.* Edited by Robert E. Daggy. New York: Farrar, Straus & Giroux, 1989.

———. *Run to the Mountain: The Story of a Vocation, 1939–1941.* Edited by Patrick Hart. Vol. 1 of *The Journals of Thomas Merton.* San Francisco: HarperSanFrancisco, 1995.

———. *A Search for Solitude: Pursuing the Monk's True Life, 1952–1960.* Edited by Lawrence Cunningham. The Journals of Thomas Merton 3. San Francisco: HarperSanFrancisco, 1996.

———. *Seeds of Contemplation.* Norfolk: New Directions, 1949.

———. *Selected Essays.* Edited with an Introduction by Patrick F. O'Connell. Maryknoll, NY: Orbis, 2013.

———. *The Seven Storey Mountain.* New York: Harcourt, Brace, 1948.

———. *The Sign of Jonas.* New York: Harcourt Brace, 1953.

———. *A Thomas Merton Reader.* Edited by Thomas P. McDonnell. New York: Doubleday, 1974.

Bibliography

———. *Thoughts on the East*. Edited with an introduction by George Woodcock. New York: New Directions, 1995.

———. *Turning toward the World: The Pivotal Years, 1960–1963*. Edited by Victor A. Kramer. The Journals of Thomas Merton 4. San Francisco: HarperSanFrancisco, 1996.

———. *The Way of Chuang-tzŭ*. New York: New Directions, 1965.

———. *What Are These Wounds? The Life of a Cistercian Mystic: Saint Lutgarde of Aywières*. Milwaukee: Bruce, 1950.

———. *The Wisdom of the Desert: Sayings from the Desert Fathers of the Fourth Century*. New York: New Directions, 1960.

———. *Witness to Freedom: Letters in Times of Crisis*. Edited by William Shannon. New York: Farrar, Straus & Giroux, 1994.

———. *Zen and the Birds of Appetite*. New York: New Directions, 1968.

———. "The Zen Revival." *Continuum* 1 (1964) 523–38.

———. *The Zen Revival*. London: Buddhist Society, 1971.

Mott, Michael. *The Seven Mountains of Thomas Merton*. Boston: Houghton Mifflin, 1984.

Murti, T. R. V. *The Central Philosophy of Buddhism: A Study of Madhyamika System*. 2nd ed. London: Allen & Unwin, 1960.

Nasr, Seyyed Hossein. "Islam." In *Our Religions: The Seven World Religions Introduced by Preeminent Scholars from Each Tradition*, edited by Arvind Sharma, 425–533. San Francisco: HarperSanFrancisco, 1993.

Newman, John Henry. *Essay on the Development of Christian Doctrine*. London: Longmans, Green, 1909.

———. *The Idea of a University*. 1891. Reprint, Washington, DC: Regnery, 1999.

———. "On the Inspiration of Scripture." *The Nineteenth Century* 15.84 (1884) 185–99.

Nhat Hanh, Thich. *Being Peace*. Edited by Arnold Kotler. Berkeley: Parallax, 1987.

———. *Living Buddha, Living Christ*. New York: Riverhead, 1995.

———. *Thundering Silence: Sutra on Knowing the Better Way to Catch a Snake*. Translated by Annabel Laity. Berkeley: Parallax, 2005.

Nichols, Aiden. *The Shape of Catholic Theology*. Collegeville, MN: Liturgical, 1991.

Nishitani, Keiji, *Religion and Nothingness*. Translated by Jan van Bragt. Foreword by Winston L. King. Berkeley: University of California Press, 1982.

O'Collins, Gerald. *The Second Vatican Council: Meaning and Message*. Collegeville, MN: Liturgical, 2014.

———. *The Tripersonal God: Understanding and Interpreting the Trinity*. 2nd ed. Mahwah, NJ: Paulist, 2014.

O'Connell, Patrick F. "Islands in the Stream: Thomas Merton's Poetry of the Early 1950s." *The Merton Annual* 22 (2009) 61–105.

———. "Mending Walls: The Changing Forms of Thomas Merton's Poetic Imagination." *The Merton Journal* 13.1 (2006) 24–37.

———. "Merton on the Eve of the Third Millennium—ITMS Presidential Address." *The Merton Seasonal* 22.3 (1997) 3–9.

———. "Nurture by Nature: Emblems of Stillness in a Season of Fury." *The Merton Annual* 21 (2008) 117–49.

O'Connor, Flannery. *Collected Works*. New York: Library of America, 1988.

———. *Mystery and Manners*. New York: Noonday, 1969.

Okamura, Mihoko. "Wondrous Activity." In *A Zen Life: D. T. Suzuki Remembered*, edited by Masao Abe, 160–73. New York: Weatherhill, 1986.

Bibliography

Origen of Alexandria. *De Principiis.* In vol. 4 of *The Ante-Nicene Fathers,* edited by Alexander Roberts et al., 239–382. Translated by Frederick Crombie. Buffalo, NY: Christian Literature, 1985.

Oyer, Gordon. *Pursuing the Spiritual Roots of Protest: Merton, Berrigan, Yoder, and Muste at the Gethsemani Abbey Peacemakers Retreat.* Eugene, OR: Cascade Books, 2014.

Panikkar, Raimundo. "The Jordan, the Tiber, and the Ganges: Three Kairological Moments of Christic Self-Consciousness." In *The Myth of Christian Uniqueness: Toward a Pluralistic Theology of Religions,* edited by John Hick and Paul Knitter, 89–117. Maryknoll, NY: Orbis, 1989.

———. *The Unknown Christ of Hinduism.* Maryknoll, NY: Orbis, 1981.

Park, Jaechan Anselmo. *Thomas Merton's Encounter with Buddhism and Beyond: His Interreligious Dialogue, Inter-Monastic Exchanges, and Their Legacy.* Collegeville, MN: Liturgical, 2019.

Pennington, Basil. *Thomas Merton: Brother Monk.* New York: New City, 1987.

Pontifical Council for Interreligious Dialogue. *Dialogue and Proclamation: Reflection and Orientations on Interreligious Dialogue and the Proclamation of the Gospel of Jesus Christ.* May 19, 1991. Online. http://www.vatican.va/roman_curia/pontifical_councils/interelg/documents/rc_pc_interelg_doc_19051991_dialogue-and-proclamatio_en.html.

Pontifical Secretariat for Non-Christians (PSNC). "Reflection and Directives on Dialogue and Mission." *Acta Apostolicae Sedis* (1984) 816–28.

Pramuk, Christopher. *Sophia: The Hidden Christ of Thomas Merton.* Collegeville, MN: Liturgical, 2009.

Raab, Joseph Q. "Insights from the Inter-Contemplative Dialogue: Merton's Three Meanings of 'God' and Religious Pluralism." *The Merton Annual* 23 (2010) 90–106.

———. "Introduction: Celebrating the Questions (and Answers)." *The Merton Annual* 28 (2015) 7–15.

———. "Madhyamika and Dharmakaya: Some Notes on Thomas Merton's Epiphany at Polonnaruwa." *The Merton Annual* 17 (2004) 195–206.

———. "Openness and Fidelity: Thomas Merton's Dialogue with D. T. Suzuki and Self-Transcendence." PhD diss., Toronto School of Theology, 2000.

Rahner, Karl. *Foundations of Christian Faith.* Translated by William V. Dych. London: Dartman, Longman & Todd, 1978.

Ratzinger, Joseph. "The Ecclesiology of Vatican II." January 23, 2002. Online. https://www.ewtn.com/catholicism/library/ecclesiology-of-vatican-ii-2069.

———. *Jesus of Nazareth: From the Baptism in the Jordan to the Transfiguration.* Translated by Adrian J. Walker. New York: Doubleday, 2007.

———. *Truth and Tolerance: Christian Belief and World Religions.* San Francisco: Ignatius, 2003.

Ricoeur, Paul. *Freud and Philosophy: An Essay on Interpretation.* New Haven: Yale University Press, 1970.

Ruysbroeck, John. *John Ruusbroec: The Spiritual Espousals, the Sparkling Stones, and Other Works.* Translated by James A. Wiseman. Mahwah, NJ: Paulist, 1986.

Samartha, Stanley. "The Cross and the Rainbow: Christ in a Multireligious Culture." In *The Myth of Christian Uniqueness: Toward a Pluralistic Theology of Religions,* edited by John Hick and Paul Knitter, 69–88. 1989. Reprint, Eugene, OR: Wipf & Stock, 2005.

Bibliography

Schmidt-Leukel, Perry. *Religious Pluralism and Interreligious Theology*. Maryknoll, NY: Orbis, 2017.

Scruggs, Ryan. "Contemplation and the *Cogito*: Thomas Merton on the Philosophical Roots of Modern Alienation." *The Merton Annual* 28 (2015) 159–80.

———. "Faith Seeking Understanding: Theological Method in Thomas Merton's Interreligious Dialogue." *Journal of Ecumenical Studies* 46.3 (2011) 1–16.

Second Vatican Council. "*Ad Gentes*: Decree on the Church's Missionary Activity. Promulgated by Pope Paul VI, December 7, 1965." In *Vatican Council II: The Basic Documents*, edited by Austin Flannery, 443–97. Northport, NY: Costello, 1996.

———. "*Dei Verbum*: Dogmatic Constitution on Divine Revelation. Promulgated by Pope Paul VI, November 18, 1965." In *Vatican Council II: The Basic Sixteen Documents*, edited by Austin Flannery, 97–118. Northport, NY: Costello, 1996.

———. "*Gaudium et Spes*: Pastoral Constitution on the Church in the Modern World. Promulgated by Pope Paul VI, December 7, 1965." In *Vatican Council II: The Basic Sixteen Documents*, edited by Austin Flannery, 163–282. Northport, NY: Costello, 1996.

———. "*Lumen Gentium*: Dogmatic Constitution on the Church. Promulgated by Pope Paul VI, November 21, 1964." In *Vatican Council II: The Basic Sixteen Documents*, edited by Austin Flannery, 1–95. Northport, NY: Costello, 1996.

———. "*Unitatis Redintegratio*: Decree on Ecumenism. Promulgated by Pope Paul VI, November 21, 1965." In *Vatican Council II: The Basic Sixteen Documents*, edited by Austin Flannery, 499–523. Northport, NY: Costello, 1996.

Secretariat for Non-Christians. "The Attitudes of the Church Towards the Followers of Other Religions: Reflections and Orientations on Dialogue and Mission." *Bulliten Secretariatus pro non Christianis* 56 (1984) 13.

Sells, Michael. *Mystical Languages of Unsaying*. Chicago: University of Chicago Press, 1994.

Sevant, John. "Follow that Metaphor: What Faith, Jazz & Poetry Have in Common." *Commonweal* 11.18 (2005). Online. https://www.commonwealmagazine.org/follow-metaphor.

Shannon, William H., et al. *The Thomas Merton Encyclopedia*. Maryknoll, NY: Orbis, 2002

———. *Silent Lamp: The Thomas Merton Story*. New York: Crossroad, 1992.

Sharf, Robert. "The Zen of Japanese Nationalism." *History of Religions* 33 (1993) 1–43.

Shields, Christopher. "Aristotle's Psychology." *Stanford Encyclopedia of Philosophy*, October 12, 2020. Edited by Edward N. Zalta. Online. https://plato.stanford.edu/archives/win2020/entries/aristotle-psychology.

Suchocki, Majorie Hewitt. *Divinity and Diversity: A Christian Affirmation of Religious Pluralism*. Nashville: Abingdon, 2003.

Suzuki, Daisetz Teitaro. *Essays in Zen Buddhism, First Series*. London: Rider, 1949.

———. *Essays in Zen Buddhism, Second Series*. London: Rider, 1950.

———. *Essays in Zen Buddhism, Third Series*. London: Rider, 1953.

———. *An Introduction to Zen Buddhism*. New York: Grove, 1964.

———. *Manual of Zen Buddhism*. New York: Grove, 1960.

———. *Studies in Zen*. London: Rider, 1955.

———. *The Training of the Zen Buddhist Monk*. New York: University Books, 1959.

———. *The Zen Doctrine of No-Mind*. London: Rider, 1949.

———. *Zen Buddhism: Selected Writings of D. T. Suzuki*. Edited by William Barrett. Garden City, NY: Doubleday, 1956.

Bibliography

———. *Zen and Japanese Buddhism*. Tokyo: Japan Travel Bureau, 1958.

———. *Zen and Japanese Culture*. New York: Pantheon, 1959.

Talbott, Harold. *Tendrel: A Memoire of New York and the Buddhist Himalayas*. Marion, MA: Buddhayana Foundation, 2019.

Tardiff, Mary, ed. *At Home in the World: The Letters of Thomas Merton and Rosemary Radford Ruether*. Maryknoll, NY: Orbis, 1995.

Thomas Aquinas. *Summa Theologiae: A Concise Translation*. Translated by Timothy McDermott. Westminster, MD: Christian Classics, 1989.

The Thomas Merton Center at Bellarmine University. "Books Cited by Merton." Online. http://www.merton.org/Research/Quotations/default.aspx.

———. "Thomas Merton's Marginalia." Online. http://merton.org/research/marginalia.

Thurston, Bonnie Bowman, ed. "The Light Strikes Home: Notes on the Zen Influence in Merton's Poetry." In *Merton & Buddhism: Wisdom, Emptiness, and Everyday Mind*, edited by Bonnie Bowman Thurston, 199–213. Louisville: Fons Vitae, 2007.

———. *Merton & Buddhism: Wisdom, Emptiness, and Everyday Mind*. Louisville: Fons Vitae, 2007.

Tracy, David. *The Analogical Imagination: Christian Theology and the Culture of Pluralism*. New York: Crossroad, 1981.

Vorgrimler, Herbert, ed. *Commentary on the Documents of Vatican II*. New York: Crossroad, 1989.

Weil, Simone. *Waiting for God*. Translated by Emma Craufurd. 1951. Reprint, New York: Harper & Row, 1973.

Weis, Monica. *The Environmental Vision of Thomas Merton*. Lexington: University of Kentucky Press, 2011.

Whitson, Robley Edward. *The Coming Convergence of World Religions*. New York: Newman, 1971.

Wilkins, Jeremy. *Before Truth: Lonergan, Aquinas, and the Problem of Wisdom*. Washington, DC: Catholic University of America Press, 2018.

Zyniewicz, Matthew C. "The Interreligious Dialogue between Thomas Merton and D. T. Suzuki." PhD diss., University of Notre Dame, 2000.

Index

Abe, Masao, 52, 95, 102
Ahern, Barnabas, 40
Apel, William, 8, 48
anatta/anatman, 9, 84, 109, 116, 117
anicca, 84, 109
Aquinas, St. Thomas, 17, 21, 38, 91, 110, 112–17, 121, 135, 139
Aristotle, 112, 113, 159
Arius, 113, 114
The Asian Journal, 128, 129, 132
Athanasius, St., 111, 120, 121
Augustine, St., 17, 22, 23, 40, 58, 77, 98, 114, 116, 126, 135

Balthazar, Hans Urs von, 39, 79
Barron, Robert, 14
Barth, Karl, 6, 22, 46, 49
Basil St., 114
Benedict XVI, Pope, *see* Ratzinger, Joseph
Bernard of Clairvaux, St., 23, 58, 104, 149
Blake, William, 2, 3, 32
Bodhidharma, 85, 88, 113
Boethius, 115
Bonhoeffer, Dietrich, 22, 46
Brahmachari, Mahanambrata, 16, 17, 25, 26
Burrows, William R., 10

Carr, Anne, 2, 3, 4, 80, 88, 110, 111
Camus, Albert, 2, 49
Cardenal, Ernesto, 30
Carson, Rachel, 13
Carus, Paul, 9
Cassian, John, 65–66, 70, 78–79, 80–81

Ch'an, 85, 87, 138
"Christian Culture Needs Oriental Wisdom," 94, 112, 119, 125
Chenu, M. D., 39
Goswami, Sri Jiva, 17
Clooney, Francis X., 137, 138, 152
Coady, Mary Frances, 2
Congar, Yves, 39
Conjectures of a Guilty Bystander, 29, 99, 126
Conn, Walter E., 25
Contemplation in a World of Action, 103
Coomaraswamy, Dona Luisa, 56, 143
Corless, Roger, 9, 127, 129
Crowe, Frederick, 104
Cracknell, Kenneth, 43
Cunningham, Lawrence, 37–38, 142

Dadosky, John, 12
Daggy, Robert, 53, 69
Dante, 64
Darwin, Charles, 48
Day, Dorothy, 1, 2
Dennett, Daniel C., 116
dogma, 7–8, 18–24
dogmatic theology, 29, 38
Dostoyevsky, Fyodor, 64
D'Souza, Henry, 6
Dulles, Avery, 124
Dumoulin, Heinrich, 85, 87
Dunne, John S., 128
Dupuis, Jacques, 5, 6, 8, 43
Dzogchen, 128, 130, 134, 135, 136, 138, 141

Index

Eckhart, Meister, 17, 59, 60, 61, 62, 64, 65, 70, 71, 131
Enlightenment and second meaning of "God," 95–97
Eunomius, 114
Evans-Wentz, W. Y., 83, 132, 133, 134
Evagrius Ponticus, 106

fides qua vs. *fides quae*, 22, 45, 140
Forest, Jim, 3
Fox, James, 30
Francis, Pope, 1
Freedgood, Seymour and Helen, 17
Fromm, Erich, 49
Frye, Northrop, 19

Gilson, Etienne, 14–23
Ginsberg, Allen, 63
Gordon, Mary, 28
Graham, Aelred, 3
Grayston, Donald, 27
Gregory of Nazianzus, 114, 149
Gregory of Nyssa, 114, 115, 126
Griffiths, Bede, 3

Haight, Roger, 6
Heft, James L., 23–24
Heidegger, Martin, 52
Heschel, Abraham, 8, 94
Hick, John, 5, 8, 20, 23
Higgins, Michael W., xiii, 1, 3, 32, 153
Hopkins, Gerard Manley, 17, 47, 133
Horan, Daniel, 25
Hui Neng, 44, 87, 88, 89, 106, 107, 109, 114, 140
Humphreys, Christmas, 76, 84
Hung-Jen, 87

Interbeing, 116–19

John, Gospel of, 43–44
John of the Cross, St., 2, 65, 131
John Paul II, Pope, 41
Johnson, Elizabeth, 4, 6, 146
Johnston, William, 3, 11, 56

Kazi, Sonam, 128
Keenan, John, 11, 54, 154
Kerouac, Jack, 63
King, Jr., Martin Luther, 1
Knitter, Paul, 5, 6, 8
Kolvenbach, Peter-Hans, 6
LaCugna, Catherine Mowry, 114, 122
Lama, Dalai, 8, 117, 128, 131, 136, 138
LaSalle, Enomiya, 3
Lax, Robert, 17, 21, 24–26, 155
Lentfoehr, Theresa, Sr., 32–33, 66
Leo XIII, Pope, 38
Lincoln, Abraham, 1
Lipsey, Roger, 53, 72, 83
Loisy, Alfred, 46
Lonergan, Bernard, 9, 11–12, 18, 37–38, 44, 80, 83, 92–111, 114, 116
Lopez, David S., 132–34
Lubac, Henri de, 39

Mahamudra, 132, 134
Mahakaruna, 128, 134
Maréchal, Joseph, 38
Maritain, Jacques, 17, 110, 112
Martin, David, 3
McBrien, Richard, 142
McDermott, Timothy, 113
McFague, Sallie, 20
metaphors, poetic and doctrinal, 19–20
Mott, Michael, 17
Murti, T. R. V., 129–32
Mystics and Zen Masters, 76, 103, 106, 125

Nagarjuna, 95, 129
Nasr, Seyyed Hossein, 94
Newman, John Henry, St., 38, 47–48
Ninshitsu, 113
Nishitani, Keiji, 93
Nhat Hanh, Thich, 8, 13, 116–17, 120, 122, 138
Nichols, Aidan, 22, 40
No Man is an Island, 13, 29

O'Collins, Gerald, 108, 125
O'Connell, Patrick F., 28, 32, 40, 42, 45, 62, 72, 133, 136

Index

O'Connor, Flannery, 23, 47, 135–36
Okamura, Mihoko, 70, 72, 117
Origen of Alexandria, 113–14
Oyer, Gordon, 3

Pallis, Marco, 137, 140, 142
Panikkar, Raimundo, 3, 5, 11
Park, Jaechan Anselmo, 3, 53, 56
Paz, Octavio, 71
Pennington, Basil, 31
Pessoa, Fernando, 71
Phan, Peter, 153
Pius XII, Pope, 39
Plato (Platonist), 70
Polonnaruwa, 14, 127–28, 132, 134
Pramuk, Christopher, 3, 7, 39, 84, 107
Price, James, 94

Question of God, and first meaning of "God," 92–94

Raab, Joseph Q., 1, 3, 91, 127
Rahner, Karl, 16, 23, 38, 39, 75, 92, 138–39
Raids on the Unspeakable, 13
Ratzinger, Joseph, 39, 41–42, 44, 124, 144, 147
Revelation, and the third meaning of "God," 101–2
Ricoeur, Paul, 20
Rinpoche, Chatral, 127, 128, 134, 138
Ruether, Rosemary Radford, 45, 78, 143
Ruysbroeck, John, (also Ruusbroec), 68–69

Samartha, Stanley, 5
Schmidt-Leukel, Perry, 49
Schuon, Fritjof, 11
Scruggs, Ryan, 32, 49, 137
Shaku, Soyen, 9

Shannon, William H., 29, 30, 37
Shen-hsiu, 87
Stone, Naomi Burton, 30
"subsistent relation, as *person*" 109, 115, 116
Suchocki, Marjorie Hewitt, 122

Talbott, Harold, 14, 117, 128, 136
Tao te Ching, 9, 34, 63, 94, 112
Tardiff, Mary, 45
Tendrel, 117
Thurston, Bonnie Bowman, 11, 32, 53, 127
Tracy, David, 2
Traherne, Thomas, 17
Turley, Hugh, 3
Tworkov, Helen, 136

Ummon, 69
The Upanishads, 94

Von Speyr, Adrienne, 79

Weil, Simone, 34
Weis, Monica, 13
Wilkins, Jeremy, 120

Xavier, St. Francis, 113

Yandell, Lunsford, 85
Yungblut, June, 46

Zaehner, R. C., 110
Zen poems, 32–36
"The Zen Revival" 76, 84–89, 103, 106, 109
Zenji, Bunan, 61
Zilboorg, Gregory, 14, 29–31, 34
Zyniewicz, Matthew C., 53, 79

www.ingramcontent.com/pod-product-compliance
Lightning Source LLC
Chambersburg PA
CBHW071456150426
43191CB00008B/1369